Nature, Neo-Colonialism, and the Spanish American Regional Writers

❧ REENCOUNTERS WITH COLONIALISM: NEW PERSPECTIVES ON THE AMERICAS

DARTMOUTH COLLEGE SERIES EDITORS
Marysa Navarro
Donald E. Pease
Ivy Schweitzer
Silvia Spitta

For a complete list of titles in the series, please see
WWW.UPNE.COM

❧ Nature, Neo-Colonialism, and the Spanish American Regional Writers ❧

JENNIFER L. FRENCH

DARTMOUTH COLLEGE PRESS
Hanover, New Hampshire

Published by University Press of New England
Hanover and London

DARTMOUTH COLLEGE PRESS
Published by University Press of New England,
One Court Street, Lebanon, NH 03766
www.upne.com
© 2005 by Jennifer L. French
Printed in the United States of America
5 4 3 2 1

All rights reserved. No part of this book may be reproduced in any form or by any electronic or mechanical means, including storage and retrieval systems, without permission in writing from the publisher, except by a reviewer, who may quote brief passages in a review. Members of educational institutions and organizations wishing to photocopy any of the work for classroom use, or authors and publishers who would like to obtain permission for any of the material in the work, should contact Permissions, University Press of New England, One Court Street, Lebanon, NH 03766.

Library of Congress Cataloging-in-Publication Data

French, Jennifer.
  Nature, neo-colonialism and the Spanish American regional writers / Jennifer L. French.—1. ed.
      p. cm.—(Reencounters with colonialism—new perspectives on the Americas)
  Includes bibliographical references and index.
  ISBN 1-58465-479-1 (cloth : alk, paper) — ISBN 1-58465-480-5 (pbk.: alk. paper)
  1. Latine American fiction—20th century. 2. Great Britain—Relations—Latin America.
  3. Quiroga, Horacio, 1878–1937. 4. Lynch, Benito, 1880–1951. Inglés de los güessos.
  5. Rivera, José Eustasio, 1888–1928. Vorágine. I. Title. II. Series.
PQ7082.N7F64 2005
863'.60998—dc22   2005000910

*En la memoria de Susana Rotker,
que me enseñó el camino*

Contents

	Acknowledgments	ix
	Introduction: The Invisible Empire	1
1.	"The Freedom in the Field": Empire and Ecology in the Misiones Stories of Horacio Quiroga	39
2.	The Geography of Resistance in Benito Lynch's *El inglés de los güesos*	71
3.	*La vorágine:* Dialectics of the Rubber Boom	112
	Afterword: Fertile Ground	155
	Notes	159
	Bibliography	179
	Index	189

Acknowledgments

This book was begun under the guidance of the late Susana Rotker; its every page bears the imprint of her intelligence, commitment, and seemingly boundless faith. In the days and weeks after her tragic passing, her colleagues Jorge Marcone, John McClure, and especially Tomás Eloy Martínez dealt with their own grief while encouraging me to carry the project forward. To all three of them, I am endlessly grateful. Many thanks to Ben. Sifuentes Jáuregui, for his guidance and professional know-how. I thank the Faculty of Arts and Sciences at Rutgers, the State University of New Jersey, for the Bevier Fellowship that allowed me to dedicate myself full-time to research and writing and for the Excellence Fellowship that supported me during the years of planning and preparation. I also thank Josephine Diamond and the Graduate Program in Comparative Literature for encouragement, flexibility, and a generous grant to pursue research in South America. For their valuable feedback I thank the graduate students of Professor Marcone's seminar on the *novela de la selva,* who heard many of the ideas in the chapters on Quiroga and Rivera in their early stages.

I thank the trustees and Dean of Faculty Office at Williams College for generously supporting the publication of this book. Since moving from Rutgers to Williams College my book and I have been nurtured by friends and colleagues in the Department of Romance Languages and the Center for Environmental Studies. I am particularly grateful to Gene Bell-Villada for his careful reading of draft chapters and to Leyla Rouhi for indulging my vociferous enthusiasm for *La vorágine*. I thank Kashia Pieprzak and Soledad Fox for their solidarity. The manuscript has also benefited immensely from the comments of Carlos J. Alonso and a second, anonymous reader at University Press of New England; both of them have my profound gratitude. For wise advice on researching the history of British colonialism in Latin America, I am grateful to Robert Aguirre and Ross Forman. I thank Erna von der Walde for direction on José Eustasio Rivera and Latin American cultural history; I also thank Francine Masiello, Mary Louise Pratt, and Jean Franco for their suggestions and enthusiasm.

My parents, Barbara and George French, often sustained me body and soul through the years of intense and exciting work that have gone into this book. I thank also my dear friends, Jennifer Russo and Rebecca Malberg, for their encouragement and cheer. And finally, I thank Paul Fischer for renewing me every day with his patience, humor, and warmth.

Nature, Neo-Colonialism, and the Spanish American Regional Writers

Introduction

The Invisible Empire

IN 1806, WHILE MUCH OF EUROPE was engulfed in the Napoleonic Wars, an exiled Spaniard named Juan María Maury y Benítez published a poem that urgently warned his compatriots of the danger their nation faced. The focus of his concern was not the Iberian Peninsula, even though at the time occupied by France; Maury was an ardent Francophile and unconcerned with Napoleon's occupation of Spain. Instead, Maury's poem, entitled *La agresión británica,* decries the danger that the Royal Navy posed to Spain's American empire. The poem begins by comparing the violence in Europe to a bucolic and peaceful American scene: *Here,* the poet writes, the gods Sylvan and Bacchus throw off their ordinary accoutrements to prepare for the coming war, while *there* the sheep continues to yield "the innocent treasure of its wool" to the shepherd's gentle hand, while indigenous plants are made into beautiful dyes to color the wool "like modest blush on a modest face."[1] Drawing images inspired by Virgil's *Georgics,* informed by accounts of tropical flora and fauna such as are found in the work of Bernardin de Saint Pierre and Alexander von Humboldt, Maury offers a lengthy tribute to the continent's natural beauty and abundance, which he repeatedly compares to the lesser wonders of Europe.

But the idyllic scene is interrupted by the threat of Britannic aggression:

Deja el rico metal su cuna estrecha
Para bogar por los inmensos mares.
¡Ay! que ya astuta y ávida le acecha
La vil codicia! Altivos insulares,
No os infaméis; sin dolo ni sospecha
Juró España la paz; en sus altares
Ardiendo está la antorcha todavía,
De esperanza y contento aurora y guía.
¡Esperanza falaz! ¡Triste contento!

[The rich metal leaves its narrow crib
To wander the immense seas.
Ay! Astute and avid,

Vile greed lies in wait. Arrogant islanders,
Do not make yourselves infamous; without deceit or suspicion
Spain swore to uphold the peace; in its altars
The torch still burns,
Of hope, happy dawn and guide.
Deceitful hope! Sad happiness!]

Addressing the "arrogant islanders" directly, Maury pinpoints Spanish America's gold and silver deposits as the most immediate target of British greed. Classical mythology overlaps with Christian iconography in the figure of the creole as a kind of Good Shepherd caring for his flock, so as to intensify the contrast between the Spaniards' nobility and the crass capitalism of the British, who are likened to so many cradle robbers intent on carrying off American metals. The speaker goes on to imagine the violence and destruction that will result from Britain's desire to plunder the natural wealth of Spanish America: Hell unleashes the demons of war, innocent women are raped, towns pillaged, and "Antes abiertos / Los abismos del mar naves y gentes / Hundan" [Once opened / The abysses of the sea drag down / ships and people]. Admiral Nelson's recent devastation of the French and Spanish fleets at Trafalgar was clearly on Maury's mind.

Today *La agresión británica* is all but forgotten, found only in the most copious anthologies of nineteenth-century Spanish verse. But as Marcelino Menéndez y Pelayo demonstrated decades ago, Maury's poem was a major influence on one of the most significant texts of the Spanish American independence era, Andrés Bello's famous ode, *La agricultura de la zona tórrida*, first published in 1826. In his introduction to the Real Academia Española's *Antología de poetas hispano-americanos,* Menéndez y Pelayo writes:

> And is there not basis enough to say, although it has not been noted before now, that certain octaves of Maury's *La agresión británica,* published in 1806, already contain the program of *La agricultura en la zona tórrida,* and could and did influence Bello, who so much admired the technical skill of the Malagan poet, and considered him one of the best artists of meter in our language?[2]

Beginning with the famous words, "*Salve, fecunda zona!,*" Bello's twelve-page poem, written like Maury's in the elevated and intricate style of Neo-classical Spanish, also celebrates the Spanish American landscape with a lengthy list of its natural wonders; in line after line Bello praises the natural fecundity and beauty of America, cataloguing the continent's abundance in a concatenation of geographical features, fauna, and agricultural products, many of which are explained in footnotes added by the author himself.[3] Though Bello is often credited, along with the Cuban José María

Heredia, with inaugurating the Americanist tradition of landscape poetry, as Menénedez y Pelayo writes, "the art of American description, or at least description by great masses, was already discovered" in *La agresión británica,* and Bello borrowed heavily from it.[4] Maury's wool-dyeing scene praises a tropical insect called a "cochineal" and the indigo plant, both of which yield brilliant dyes: "Mientras purpúreo el insectillo indiano / Ya del sidonio múrice desdoro, / Los albos copos á teñir se apresta / Cual púdico rubor frente modesta / Se apresta el polvo que en pureza tanta / Copia el zafiro del cerúleo cielo" [While America's purple insect / By violet Sidonian already tinged, / Is prepared to dye the white tufts, / Like a modest blush on a modest face. / A powder is prepared so pure that / It emulates the sapphire of the cerulean sky]. The same images, altered only slightly, reappear in *La zona tórrida:*

> Bulle carmín viviente en tus nopales
> Que afrenta fuera al múrice de Tiro,
> Y de tu añil la tinta generosa
> Emula es de la lumbre del zafiro.[5]
>
> [Vivid carmine glows in your nopals
> That bear the violet hues of Tiro,
> And from your cochineal the generous tint
> Emulates the luster of the sapphire.]

It is extraordinary that this long-forgotten poem should be considered, along with Virgil's *Georgics* and Humboldt's *Personal Narrative of Travels to the Equinoctial Regions of the New Continent,* one of the key influences on Bello's poetics. Like Domingo F. Sarmiento, who based his famous depiction of Argentina's gauchos in *Facundo: Civilización y barbarie* (1845) on the narratives of European travelers like Charles Darwin and Francis Bond Head,[6] *La zona tórrida* offers another example of a foundational creole text that is heavily mediated by European discourse. In this case the irony is even richer: while Bello was self-consciously engaged in formulating aesthetic principles upon which to base the new republics' ideological emancipation, Maury was writing in support of Spain's continued control of the colonies. This overlapping of colonial and postcolonial discourses is part of the genealogy of one of the most influential texts of the nineteenth century: Bello is often credited with founding the new republics' cultural independence from Spain on the pleasures and virtues to be derived from living in close contact with the natural abundance of the New World, eschewing the materialism of the metropolis in exchange for the bucolic paradise of the American countryside.[7] "You seek perdurable pleasures?" he asks his readers, then advises:

Id a gozar la suerte campesina;
La regalada paz, que ni rencores
Al labrador, ni envidias acibaran;
La cama que mullida le preparan
El contento, el trabajo, el aire puro;
Y el sabor de los fáciles manjares,
Que dispendiosa gula no le aceda

[Go to find your fortune in the country;
The laborer's gift of peace,
That neither rancor no envy can mitigate;
The bed prepared for him
By happiness, toil, the pure air;
and the taste of simple delicacies
Unsoured by costly gluttony]

What I find most intriguing in Bello's response to Maury's *La agresión británica,* however, is not so much the style and imagery that the Venezuelan incorporated into his own poem as the material he preferred to leave aside: *La zona tórrida* makes no mention of the British threat so urgently described by Maury. And as it turns out, Maury's prediction was not at all incorrect. In 1806, the very year his poem was published, British forces attacked Buenos Aires and Montevideo in what was to be the first stage of a large-scale assault on Spain's Latin American possessions. The assault was the spontaneous initiative of Commander Home Riggs Popham, who had taken the Dutch colony of Cape Town just months before, but London enthusiastically supported his efforts, sending thousands of soldiers and sailors to besiege the Atlantic coast of South America and making plans for subsequent attacks on Caracas and the Mexican port of Veracruz. Although definitively defeated in 1807, the British invasion of the Río de la Plata contributed to the Spanish American independence movement in two important ways. On the one hand, the success of the local militias who defended the two cities against British troops gave confidence and fighting experience to the creoles who would soon become revolutionary armies; on the other, the defeat at Montevideo marked a change only in Britain's tactics, not its purpose with regard to Latin America. Thereafter the British Foreign Office, led by Lord George Canning, worked aggressively to supplant Spain's economic monopoly by informal means that included ensuring the colonies' independence from Spain. After the Independence Wars broke out in 1816, some six thousand British officers and enlisted men again embarked for South America, this time to join the patriot armies in their struggle, while the Royal Navy effectively prevented French ships from crossing the Atlantic in Spain's aid. In 1824, as the republics were beginning to achieve their independence, Canning famously declared that "Spanish America is free and if we do not mismanage our affairs sadly she is *English*!"[8]

Of course this story is not told in Bello's *La zona tórrida;* the canonical text makes no reference to the 1806 invasion, to Britain's involvement in the independence movement, or to the legions of British entrepreneurs who went to Latin America during and immediately after the war to set up merchant houses or take over mines that had fallen into abandon during the last decades of Spanish rule. This omission is striking enough given the degree to which Bello appropriates Maury's subject matter and diction, and all the more so when we consider that his prophecies had at least partially been fulfilled by the time *La zona tórrida* was written. Mary Louise Pratt, who takes up Bello's poem in her groundbreaking book *Imperial Eyes: Travel Writing and Transculturation,* argues that *La zona tórrida* may in fact be read as an emphatic, if discreet, challenge to the capitalist invasion in its depiction of Latin America as a noncapitalist and agrarian utopia: "The non-industrial, pastoral outlook of his 'Silva,'" she writes, "should probably be understood not simply as nostalgic or reactionary, but as a dialogic response to the commodifying, greed-glazed gaze of the English engineers."[9] Bello, as Pratt explains, was anything but insensitive to Spanish America's precarious relationship with Great Britain. In 1810 he had traveled to London with Simón Bolívar and Luis López Méndez as a delegation seeking British support against the Spanish, and he stayed on until 1829, writing poems and essays, publishing his magazine *Repertorio Americano,* researching Castillian philology at the British Library, earning a meager living as a tutor and scribe and eventually serving as secretary of the Colombian legation.[10]

If Bello, situated as he was in the center of the European metropolis, was geographically located so as to perceive clearly the neo-colonial invasion of the 1820s, and if he was apprehensive enough about the outcome of that event to articulate a kind of poetic resistance in the verses of *La zona tórrida,* then the contrast between his response and Maury's is all the more intriguing: it underscores the Venezuelan's reluctance to commit to writing the threat that Britain represented. For the Francophile Spaniard Juan María Maury y Benítez, it must have seemed natural enough to combine the various components of his cosmopolitan background—classical pastorals, Spanish narratives of discovery and exploration, French romanticism—to formulate a nostalgic protest against Britain's gradual usurpation of Spain's position as the leading colonial power. For Bello, on the other hand, self-consciously establishing the cultural discourse of the newly independent republics, Latin America's historical negotiation with Britain had to be dealt with more carefully. He may have felt that the important rhetorical gesture of that "Salve, fecunda zona" depended upon a celebratory mode of discourse that did not admit fears of economic vulnerability. At the same time, the survival of the nascent republics depended in very real ways on Britain's continued support (a fact that Canning used to advantage by extending diplomatic recognition to Buenos Aires, Mexico, and Colombia only in exchange for trade agreements highly advantageous to the British), and Bello must have been reluctant to alienate London from the cause of independence.[11]

I begin my discussion of the Spanish American regionalist writers of the 1920s with a look back to this foundational text because I see *La agricultura en la zona tórrida* establishing two interrelated patterns that have continued, through various manifestations, to this day. The first is the almost complete occlusion of neo-colonialism in Spanish American cultural discourse of the nineteeth century. By the term *neo-colonialism* I refer to the region's forcible economic subordination to Great Britain from the immediate post-independence period till the 1920s, when the United States became the dominant power in the Americas. While maintaining the appearance of autonomy, the Latin American republics, particularly but not exclusively in South America, performed the same economic functions as Britain's official colonies elsewhere. And they suffered many of the same deplorable results: growing debt and dependency on foreign manufactures, and devastating exploitation of workers and the natural environment.[12] The relationship between Britain and Latin America, according to historians and economists, was one of the singlemost important factors in the region's development, and a very real cause of its economic subordination to the metropoles of the United States and northwestern Europe today. Yet it is all but absent from the literature and even the political writings of the nineteenth century.[13] Likewise, contemporary literary scholars continue to neglect the subject, even after Pratt's groundbreaking work. Scholarship in our field tends to follow the official discourse of a given historical period, and in the case of the nineteenth century questions of neo-colonialism are almost entirely absent. Bello's poem, in other words, initiates a rhetorical tradition of omitting from cultural discourse the danger that Britain's aggressive economic and demographic expansion posed for Spanish America throughout the nineteenth and early twentieth centuries.

A few texts from the early national period bear witness to the obtrusive presence of Britishers in the Independence era by including scheming Englishmen among their characters: Enrique Otway's very name gives away his intention to enrich or *enriquecerse* at the creoles' expense in Gertrudis Gómez de Avellaneda's *Sab* (1841), and the Argentinean José Marmol's *Amalia* (1851) includes a Machiavellian minister from London. With these few exceptions, the problem all but disappears from Spanish American cultural discourse as Britain's policy of aggressive economic "development" becomes increasingly assimilated into the liberal political discourse of the republics. Another of the national romances of the nineteenth century, Jorge Isaacs' *María* (1867), is much more typical of discourse on neo-colonialism in its representation of Britain as a place of wealth, power, and technological knowledge that subtly contributes to the decline of the creole family: while his beloved cousin languishes at home in Colombia's Cauca valley, the young narrator is sent off to England to study medicine.[14] Discourse on the informal imperialism of the British is almost always equally oblique: unlike the more overt aggression of the United States, whose military invasion and appropriation of Spanish American territory provoked widespread public outcry, Britain pursued and maintained what I call an "invisible" empire in Latin America, a hegemonic formation that was effective enough to dominate economic (and, consequently, social and cultural) life in Latin America, and yet almost imperceptible there.[15]

The second pattern established by *La zona tórrida* is that in Spanish American cultural discourse the tensions created by neo-colonialism are consistently displaced onto a discourse on nature. In this regard the comparison between Bello and Maury is especially significant; *La agresión británica* establishes a tripartite structure that is repeated in Bello's work and well beyond. The conflict between Britain and Spain, extended to the Americas, takes shape as a figure of three: Britain menaces Spain by threatening to usurp its colonies, which are implicitly identified with nature. If we read Bello's poem through Maury's, interpreting *La zona tórrida* as a palimpsestic text, we see that Bello maintained the triangulated structure of the original and altered the terms only slightly. The primary conflict, ostensibly, is now between Spain and an independent Spanish America, which Bello negotiates through the republics' relationship to nature. If Bello does not address the British directly, however he implicitly argues for a specific kind of relationship with Britain (nonexploitative) through the relationship with nature he envisions for Spanish America (bucolic, noncapitalist). In contrast to the stark Manichean oppositions that, as Abdul R. JanMohamed and others have noted, dominate the discourse of formal imperialism, we will see that the discourse of informal imperialism is consistently structured by figures of three, a more open and flexible form that allows for a creative reordering of elements and exploration of the dialectical and shifting relationships between human societies and the environment.[16]

Neo-colonialism does not become visible in Spanish-American cultural discourse until decades later: only when Britain's international hegemonic formation begins to break down in the post–World War I era do the cracks in the economic and social order bring the Invisible Empire into relief for Latin Americans. The discussion of three regionalist writers—Uruguayan Horacio Quiroga (1878-1937), Argentinean Benito Lynch (1885-1951), and Colombian José Eustasio Rivera (1889-1928)—that constitute the chapters to follow are based on the belief that these authors' representations of rural life are informed and even motivated by changes in the international economic order that were most violently felt in the agricultural productive sector of the Spanish American economies. They, uniquely in Spanish American literature, make the problem of specifically British imperialism explicit by describing those changes while engaging in a dialogue with European authors like Joseph Conrad, William Henry Hudson, and Rudyard Kipling, whose narratives also show the growing fissures in Britain's overseas empire. I shall have a good deal more to say about the articulation and disintegration of the Invisible Empire in the pages to follow, but first it is necessary to look more closely at the discourse of nature as it descends from the statesmen-poets of the independence era to the regionalist writers of the 1920s.

Reconstructing the "Nature" of the Regional Novel

The work of the regionalist writers of the early twentieth century represents one of the most neglected bodies of texts in the Spanish American canon. Key examples of the *novelas de la tierra* (literally, novels of the earth) or *novelas telúricas* (telluric novels), as their fictions are collectively known—José Eustasio Rivera's *La vorágine* (1924), for example, or Ricardo Güiraldes's *Don Segundo Sombra* (1926)—are familiar enough among students of Spanish American fiction. Yet in terms of scholarship they lie lost or disregarded between the great literary achievements of the twentieth century: *modernismo* and *vanguardismo* in poetry and the *nueva novela* that made Latin American fiction an object of international admiration in the 1960s. Scholarship tends to define the regionalist writers, as the rubric itself implies, by their attention to local or regional themes and their rejection of European literary forms. Early criticism of the regionalist writers celebrated the nativism of their work as a mark of authenticity and a significant step toward cultural liberation. During the "Boom" years, however, the regionalist writers were sharply devalued as writers formulated their own aesthetic principles in opposition to previous generations, representing the regional novels as a literary precondition, hopelessly backward in their representational simplicity, their isolation from international literary developments, and their naive political formulas. In his important reevaluation of the genre, *The Spanish American Regional*

Novel: Modernity and Autochthony, Carlos Alonso suggests that the phrase *novela de la tierra* has come to be taken literally in its various overlapping meanings: regionalism is characterized by its geographical specificity, its thematic focus on the earth and the natural environment, and the "position these works are deemed to occupy in the edifice of contemporary Spanish American letters: they are considered to be the coarse, unfinished foundation of the structure, whose principal function is to give support to the building erected on them."[17]

Both Alonso's book and Roberto González Echevarría's *The Voice of the Masters: Writing and Authority in Modern Spanish American Literature,* with which it has a good deal in common, reassess the regionalist novels by liberating them from decades of critical material, positive and negative, that has attributed to the texts its own understanding of the relationship between environment and culture in Spanish America, limiting thereby the novels' significance to a transparent and frequently simplistic representation of life in a particular natural environment.[18] Alonso and González Echevarría begin by tracing the long tradition of representing Spanish American national and regional identity through metaphors drawn from nature, in order to show the historical roots of this seemingly unproblematic tendency. "The vigor of the nature metaphor," González Echevarría writes, "has been so great in Spanish American literature and criticism that it is difficult to find an important work that does not invoke it, from the beginnings of romanticism to *Piedra de sol*—nature and, more specifically, the metaphoric system that makes up the concept, have been the surface on which Spanish American literature has inscribed the myth of its legitimacy."[19] What they find is that the apparently simple notions of "nature" and "autochthony" are themselves highly tendentious and ideologically informed categories invoked for the express purpose of legitimating a particular group's claim to authority: for González Echevarría, the "myth of nature" represents primarily a normalization or substantiation of the discourse of state power; for Alonso the notion of autochthony is a response to the crisis faced by Spanish American intellectuals when the European discourse of modernity threatens to disqualify their cultural discourse. Although their interests ultimately diverge, both scholars begin their discussions of regionalist novels by demonstrating that these texts themselves subtly subvert and deconstruct the myths of nature and autochthony that critics—as well as the novelists themselves—have long posited as their "purpose" and defining characteristic.

Both *The Voice of the Masters and The Regional Novel* are highly regarded among Spanish Americanists. Nonetheless, scholarship on the regional novels has remained relatively unchanged in the years since their publications: little revisionary criticism of these novels has been written in response. For dramatically different reasons, *La vorágine* and *Don Segundo Sombra* constitute the two main exceptions to this rule. With its unreliable narrator and fractured, heteroglot discourse, *La vorágine* has become a favorite of poststructuralists; Güiraldes's ability to fuse the poetics of the *vanguardia* with centrist national ideology, on the other hand, has secured *Don Segundo Sombra*'s interest for critics of Argentinean culture. With few exceptions, however, these novels remain relatively undervalued in contemporary criticism. Here I shall continue the work of Alonso and González Echevarría in calling for a revaluation of the *novelas de la tierra*, while proposing a somewhat different path by which they may be reconsidered.

It is my intention to re-pose the invaluable insights of these two scholars in order to consider the discursive problematic they describe in terms of material and economic conditions as well as its cultural and political context. The opportunity for revisionist scholarship on the regionalist writers coincides, remarkably, with a period of intense rejuvenation in Marxist literary criticism in general and in Spanish American studies in particular. As critics ranging from Roberto Fernández Retamar to Fernando Coronil have commented, the rapid pace of globalization in the 1980s and 1990s signals a historical moment in which materialist and dialectical criticism needs to be reconsidered if it is to be used productively to interpret Spanish American literary and cultural production. Much of Marx's writing, and the subsequent writing of Marxist theorists, is based upon European models of industrial development and urbanization; while the work of writers like Walter Benjamin has been indispensable for understanding the problems of urbanization and rationalization or commodification in the nineteenth and twentieth centuries, for example, it is insufficient for understanding aspects of Spanish American reality that are neither similar nor analogous to European models. On the other hand, the paradigms suggested by dependency theory in the 1970s and 1980s, which have proven useful in understanding economic and sociological aspects of the contemporary neo-colonial world order, have ultimately had debilitating effects on theories of culture: they ascribe to Spanish America a sense of "lack" or belatedness that is inadequate for explaining the region's rich literary and artistic production. As Fernández Retamar suggests, the alternative is not to fetishize Spanish America's essential cultural "difference," but rather to incorporate study of the region's historical particularities into a framework describing the international spread and intensification of economic, cultural, and political relations and the imbalances of power and wealth they have promoted since the time of the Industrial Revolution: "In our case, it will not do simply to apply criteria based on other realities (criteria that, at best, were born of the analysis of *different* conditions) or to turn our backs on history, cut ourselves off from other realities, and enumerate our own real or imagined characteristics with an eye toward proclaiming an absurd segregationist difference from everyone else. We must make plain our 'concrete conditions.'"[20]

We need a materially oriented theory of literature that is fully dialectical in its understanding of the relationship between economics and cultural production and that is based upon the principle of locating the specificities of Spanish American literature and history within the context of global change. It is my hope that this book will form part of that project. In setting this goal I am inspired and instructed by Fernando Coronil's *The Magical State: Nature, Money and Modernity in Venezuela*, an exploration of the relationships between Venezuela's petroleum-based economy and the discourse of the state in the twentieth century.[21] As Coronil explains, the project involves reorienting Marxist theories in order to account for the international division of labor, as Marx's own writing was frequently based on the model of a relatively autonomous national economy, a perspective that "has been useful for the analysis of nations at the center of the international capitalist system, [but] has profoundly obscured the understanding of societies at its periphery" (32). A more appropriate model, Coronil argues, would take as its starting point the greatly increased role that the natural environment plays in the economic production of peripheral nations, since until very recently the international division of labor ascribed almost exclusively the production of raw materials, minerals, and agricultural products to the periphery while the metropolis in turn has supplied large quantities of technology and manufactured goods (35). This theory, therefore, must account for the economic and cultural impact of the dependence upon imported manufactures and consumer goods, as well as the centrality of agricultural and extractive activities at the center of national production. He writes:

> Commodities express hierarchies among cultures, not just magnitudes of value. In the quest for foreign exchange, domestic productive powers are channeled into the production of one or a few commodities, such as sugar, bananas, coffee, rubber, gold, copper, and oil. These commodities mark the place of primary exporters in the international division of labor and to a significant extent define their national identity, specifically labeling them as oil nations, banana republics, or plantation societies, for example, or broadly as underdeveloped or backward nations. (37)

Any new or reformulated theory of the relationship between literature and economics in Spanish America must therefore deal with the region's role on the periphery of international economic structures and the local economic and social structures that have developed over time in relation to predominantly mono-crop agricultural or extractive industries.

Coronil's recommendations for Latin American studies correspond to the "greening" of Marxist scholarship in general that has occurred in recent years. In the early and mid-twentieth century, conventional Marxist thought perpetuated an artificial and unsustainable opposition between the needs of human beings and the environments they inhabit. Walter Benjamin explains the problem with characteristic conciseness: "The new conception of labor amounts to the exploitation of nature, which with naive complacency is contrasted with the exploitation of the proletariat."[22] Adorno and Horkheimer develop the same line of thinking much further in *Dialectic of Enlightenment,* in which they argue that the domination of nature that has become increasingly pervasive in the modern, industrialized (and industrializing) world is inextricably tied to the domination of some social groups and classes by others. "The history of man's efforts to subjugate nature," writes Horkheimer, "is also the history of man's subjugation by man."[23] Today, with rising concern about nonrenewable resources and environmental destruction, the Left has become increasingly aware that the well-being of human societies, and especially their most marginal members, depends upon the protection of their environment. Contemporary scholars such as David Harvey, Fernando Mires, Richard Peet, and Michael Watts have developed this innovation in dialectical thinking even further, indicating new intersections between cultural studies and fields like geography, environmental history and environmental science.[24] In some cases this means returning to founding texts by Marx and Engels—*Grundrisse, Capital, Dialectics of Nature*—the "green" or ecological aspects of which have generally been overshadowed by the environmental disasters of the Soviet era.

This growing insistence on the centrality of nature to Spanish American economic (and correspondingly, political and cultural) structures leads me to reconsider the propositions of Alonso and González Echevarría. As these two argue, the importance of the "discourse of autochthony" and "the nature myth" in Spanish American literature and cultural discourse dates as far back as the independence movement's roots in romantic philosophy and the manifestos of aesthetic and cultural independence (themselves weighted in the particularly romantic science of philology) that flourished during the early republican years. González Echevarría, for instance, writes, "Literature as a concept and Spanish America as an entity are both creations of modernity. . . . [B]oth were conceived in Spanish America as a metaphoric field whose ground is nature, if I may avail myself of the same kinds of metaphors. Nature, the landscape, created through its own uniqueness and originality a new and original being who expressed himself or herself in the form of a new and different literature."[25] What González Echevarría refers to as "modernity" is in fact the epistemic shift brought on by the Industrial Revolution: the discursive identification of nature with cultural authenticity and political legitimacy is just one aspect in the changing relationships among humans and the environment brought on by the industrialization of northwestern Europe. As Raymond Williams shows in *The Country and the City* and the essay "Ideas of Nature," industrialization, romanticism, and colonialism are all inextricably linked. Born out of the same process that sent them off to the Americas, Asia, and Africa in search of raw materials and markets for their manufactures, romanticism, for the bourgeoisie of northwestern Europe, acquired a new sense of nature as the antithesis to industry, a place of refuge from the anxiety and alienation associated with urbanization and industrialization. "Nature was where industry was not," writes Williams, "and then in that real but limited sense had very little to say about the operations on nature that were proceeding elsewhere. . . . But in another sense it had a great deal to say."[26]

Romanticism, as critics have often pointed out, was central to the discursive formulations of Spanish America's cultural independence: civic-minded writers of the nineteenth century freely appropriated romantic discourses by the likes of Bernardin de Saint Pierre, Chateaubriand, Lord Byron, and Shelley and adapted them to their own purposes, which were in many cases less iconoclastic than those of the Europeans they claimed to emulate. But in Spanish America the relationship between nature and industry was almost antithetical to the European situation Williams describes: in the tropical republics of the economic periphery, nature was the source of potential wealth and the site of economic growth and development. Rather than the "escape" from the realities of industrial capitalism that romanticism offered to European readers, Spanish American nature writing much more directly represents the continent's predominant economic forms and, as a result, its gradual incorporation into the international capitalist system. The human forms inscribed in the landscape, therefore, occupy distinct and dynamic socioeconomic positions. We have already seen the negotiations among Spain, Britain, and Spanish American creoles that inform Bello's "Silva"; as Pratt has shown, his vision of nature also includes a rigidly structured national society: the plantations of his agrarian utopia continue to be run on slave labor.[27]

The foundational discourses of Spanish America are for good reason dominated by a rhetoric of nature: nature was to be the economic basis of the new republics, in the eyes of both European capitalists and the creole elites who shaped their post-independence development. But in the post-revolutionary period the sense of conflict between Britain and Spanish America so clearly and urgently represented by Maury all but disappears from Spanish American cultural discourse. What remains to be perpetuated by landscape poets in the era of the Invisible Empire is the lordly, celebratory perspective on nature codified by Bello's *La agricultura*. Once the neo-colonial order is established, the local elites' colonial relationship to the land and its indigenous inhabitants supports rather than contradicts the British goal of maximizing the continent's output of precious metals and agricultural products. As Gwen Kirkpatrick has explained, the evocation of landscape in the poetry that occupies such a conspicuous position in Spanish American cultural discourse of the nineteenth century participates in a literary exchange with other parts of the world that is inseparable from economic trade relations.[28] This discourse, I believe, was successful and enduring because it assimilated the discursive tradition of Spanish America into the new hegemonic formation dominated by British capital.

To choose just one of many possible examples, Gregorio Gutiérrez González's twenty-five-page poem *Memoria: Sobre el cultivo de maíz en Antioquia* [Memoir: On the cultivation of maize in Antioquia] clearly continues the tradition established in *Agricultura* with its praise of the tropics' natural abundance and lavish descriptions of exotic plants and animals:

El azuceno, el floro azul, el caunce
Y el yarumo, en el monte se dibujan
Como piedras preciosas que recaman
El manto azul que con la brisa ondula.[29]

[The lily, the flowering *azul*, the *caunce*
And the *yarumo*, on the mountain are drawn
Like precious stones that embellish
The blue mantel undulating in the breeze.]

With the pride of a successful plantation owner, the speaker describes the activity of "treinta peones y un patrón por jefe" [thirty peons and a landowner for boss] as they clear the land, prepare the fields by burning the vegetation, plant seeds, scare off animals, and harvest the ripe ears. His agricultural seriousness combines with an aesthetic attention to picturesque folkways that anticipates the *costumbrista* movement in prose narrative; like the *costumbristas*, Gutiérrez's narrator describes the rustic pleasures of the scene while maintaining a genteel distance from the working men he observes. The workers are heavily idealized: handsome, robust, and cheerful, they laugh, chatter, and sing a *guavina* as they work. The speaker's final warning to readers echoes Bello's urging to savor the simple pleasures of the rural aristocracy: "En fin . . . vuestra vejez será horrorosa / Pues no habéis asistido á una cogienda" [In conclusion . . . your old age will be horrific / If you haven't attended a harvest] (146).

The prevalence of the nature myth that descends from Maury and Bello to Gutiérrez, the *costumbristas*, and the regionalist writers may be compared to a similar discourse in the literature of the United States. The

United States was also born in the romantic era and used that literary mode to articulate its national identity in metaphors borrowed from nature: one need look no farther than the authors of the American Renaissance—Cooper, Emerson, Thoreau, and Whitman—to see that North Americans also imagined their country's spirit to lie in frontier values and its economic potential in natural resources. This literature is of course also "colonial" in its efforts to legitimize the usurpation of Indian lands and its self-conscious formulation of a new hegemonic state and culture. On the other hand, in the United States this discourse relatively quickly was supplemented if not altogether replaced by other metaphors signifying change, incorporation, and invention—the fundamental values of industrialization. When nature reappears after the mid-nineteenth century it is in increasingly nostalgic tones, as in the novels of Cather, Steinbeck, and even Faulkner. In Spanish America, on the other hand, the central metaphor of nature as national identity and source of productivity persists well beyond the early national period, often standing side by side with the more urban poetics that began developing in the late nineteenth century, as in the case of the regionalist novels and even the "Boom" of the 1960s. It is this persistence of nature as central cultural metaphor, transcending periods, literary movements and styles, changing with changes in industries and products (silver, coffee, bananas, oil, beef, coca) that reflects the relatively unchanging economic circumstances or "concrete conditions" in which it was produced.

I believe that in the repeated but varying articulation of the nature myth can be read a sort of economic and political history of the region, but only if we accept literary texts as what Adorno calls "dialectical images": "crystallizations of the historical process" or "objective constellations in which the social condition represents itself."[30] In a predominantly agricultural or extractive society, the domination of nature in its productive capacity signifies access to wealth and power, and the various and dynamic relations to nature of different individuals and social classes within that society are themselves—though mediated in extremely complex ways—articulations of economic and political power that should be registered within international patterns and structures.

Adumbrating the Invisible Empire

The conventional interpretation of the nineteenth-century empire continues to rest upon study of the formal empire alone, which is rather like judging the size and character of icebergs solely from the parts above the water-line.

—John Gallagher and Ronald Robinson,
"The Imperialism of Free Trade"

Few scholars working in Latin American literary and cultural studies today would argue that Latin America has not become a target of neo-colonialism. Yet most would describe that neo-colonialism as a largely twentieth-century phenomenon, one that began around the time of the Spanish-American War and the Panama Canal controversy of 1902–3. Great Britain's impact on the republics has been all but overlooked by scholarship on early twentieth-century Latin America, of which Alonso's work may be considered representative if only in its distinction of the Spanish-American War as the defining circumstance of the period. As Alonso explains, the United States' military action, coupled with the alarming decree of "Pan-Americanism," created a real crisis among Spanish American intellectuals and renewed the old urge to define Spanish America's regional identity, this time in order to avoid being subsumed by the menacing northern neighbor. Writers such as Manuel Ugarte, Rufino Blanco, José Martí, José Vasconcelos, and José Enrique Rodó produced "the affirmation of a cultural unanimity among the Spanish American nations that must be tapped in order to confront the United States," projecting "the belief that Spanish American countries share a cultural essence and project that is incompatible with the conception of culture represented by the United States."[31] The immediate and long-term effects of the Spanish-American War, including the construction of the Panama Canal, on articulations of Spanish American identity are absolutely indisputable. Nonetheless, if critical focus on this event is justified in particular by the subsequent century of hemispheric relations, it has tended to obscure Great Britain's influence on Spanish America's economic (and cultural, political) development, an influence that was felt, if not always identified, from the Independence Era through the Second World War.

My study of the regional novels in based on the belief that the crisis of 1898 was preceded (and in very real ways, precipitated) by a long era of British neo-colonialism, and that the protracted experience of British neo-colonialism had profound implications for the cultural discourse Latin Americans produced in the 1920s. From the time of independence to the First World War (and even later in the case of Argentina), Britain maintained an empire that was scarcely perceptible in contrast to the blatant jingoism of U.S. imperialism—or, for that matter, the formal empire that Britain was simultaneously pursuing in other parts of the world. British neo-colonialism was invisible because it was almost entirely economic in nature: although Latin America suffered many of the same economic, political, and cultural changes as the official colonies of India, Africa, and the Middle East, Britain rarely deployed military power or overt political means to influence local events. Thus while British discourse on Latin America repeats many of the tropes and assumptions of other colonial discourses,[32] it provides a crucial counterpoint to the culture of imperialism that Edward Said has identified as "a commitment . . . over and above profit" to the idea that "distant territories and their native peoples *should* be subjugated" and to the "*imperium* as a protracted, almost metaphysical obligation to rule subordinate, inferior, or less advanced peoples."[33] At home in the metropolis, there was no particular need to inspire heroism and self-sacrifice with the kind of mobilizing narratives that Martin Green, Andrea White, and Patrick Brantlinger have identified in the English adventure tradition; nor was there much need to legitimate a colonial administration in Latin America with recourse to the civilizing mission that sent thousands of would-be reformers into India and Africa.[34] In most cases spreading the values and assumptions of consumer capitalism was effective enough.

In Latin America the relative discretion of British entrepreneurs kept their influence on local politics and decision-making from drawing much public attention. Historian Tulio Halperín Donghi writes:

> British imperialism was content to operate through local private interest kept firmly in its economic orbit. The great virtue of this policy was its quiet prudence, and it worked marvelously most of the time. Britain's hesitancy to engage in direct political manipulations also saved it from potentially damaging blunders. . . . The subtle qualities of British hegemony prevented it from becoming a matter of public debate in Latin American countries. Occasionally, a disgruntled politician might attempt to make an issue of British domination, but the public tended to remain indifferent, attributing the complaints to private resentment. Only after the international financial collapse of 1929, when the neocolonial order disintegrated, did most Argentines or Brazilians discover that they had been victims of British imperialism.[35]

The effects of British imperialism were insidious rather than dramatic. By the time of the Spanish-American War, Latin America had functioned as an economic colony of Great Britain for more than five decades. The results of neo-colonialism were clear in the preponderance of mono-crop agriculture and extractive industries (characterized by cycles of boom and bust as demand fluctuated on the world market) and enormous national debts caused by overspending on imported manufactures and costly "development" projects like the construction of docks and railroads.

As Halperín's remarks suggest, British neo-colonialism depended less upon brute force and political maneuvering than upon the dissemination of the ideology of consumer capitalism. In that regard his reference to British "hegemony" in Latin America is much closer to the concept developed by Antonio Gramsci than to more traditional usage of the term. In Gramsci's *Prison Notebooks,* "hegemony" refers to a highly attenuated network of political, social, and cultural forces that operate to establish and maintain the power of the ruling class over subordinate groups.[36] Gramscian hegemony is based upon the idea that direct domination or coercion is used only when necessary to establish the predominance of a given class or secure it in moments of crisis: the threat of forcible discipline is constant, but the social, political, and economic status quo is generally maintained by heterogeneous and highly refined articulations of power—among them the cultural and discursive work carried out by the intellectuals who ensure the "spontaneous" compliance of the people.

In Latin America, as Robinson and Gallagher signaled in their landmark essay "The Imperialism of Free Trade" (1953), the British deployed direct force during the first three decades of the nineteenth century, when London concentrated upon reestablishing its power in the hemisphere after the loss of its North American colonies. After Commander Popham's short-lived invasion of the Río de la Plata, the Foreign Office more successfully orchestrated the Royal Navy's mission of escorting the Portuguese royal family out of war-torn Europe to its new home in Rio de Janeiro (1807), after which the monarchs were convinced to sign treaties awarding British merchant ships lower tariffs than even the Portuguese paid. Britain's contribution to the Spanish-American independence struggle, as mentioned earlier, secured similar privileges in much of Spanish America. From the time of independence on, Latin America's "ruling class" was the British entrepreneurial class that exercised its economic and political superiority to influence political, economic, and cultural decision-making in the region as a whole, but maintained the support of the elites by distributing power and privilege to those who mediated between foreign capitalists and local sources of labor and environmental resources.

After "a few false starts" in the 1830s and 1840s—Argentinean dictator Juan Manuel de Rosas' opposition to foreign trade and the suspension of diplomatic ties with Brazil after the imposition of a stop-and-search policy for suspected slave ships—rights of access and tariff privileges were secured, allowing British merchants and traders to develop successful businesses in Latin America. This commerce radically altered consumption and production patterns in the new republics, created discord between the countryside and the modernizing cities, and solidified the independence era alliance between Britain and Latin America's governing elites. When the economies of northern Europe began their rapid expansion after 1850, the Latin American republics had become stable enough to support a large-scale increase in British trade and investment. Although some individuals warned about growing debt and dependence on foreign capital, elite-controlled governments frequently welcomed the foreign firms that sponsored railways and other development projects, as integration into international economic structures meant increased profits for export-directed agriculture and extractive industries. After 1870 Latin American economies became increasingly focused on the production of specific crops for export on the international market, and increasingly dependent upon foreign loans and manufactures.[37]

In Latin America, where political and discursive power long remained in the hands of a relatively small elite, the national states were more often than not partners in the hegemonic formation dominated by British capital. The result was the establishment of apparently independent countries whose economies were increasingly subjugated to metropolitan needs, and who—like the formal empire—supplied the metropolis with raw materials for industry and consumers for British manufactures. Because political autonomy was at least nominally respected, and because the elites frequently stood to benefit from commercial ventures, the issue of neo-colonialism is all but absent from official discourse of the time. Where resistance to that hegemonic formation occurs, it is generally represented as opposition to the state itself, the modern, democratic nation the elites were establishing. Indeed, a map of the Invisible Empire would suggest unseen connections between seemingly unrelated events: the civil wars and class conflicts that occurred during the era of positivism and "progress" and, internationally, the rise of the neo-colonial order.

These connections are in fact the articulations of a particularly pernicious and destructive form of "double" colonialism, in which internal and external dynamics of domination and exploitation support and reproduce each other. Rather than prompting a sense of national or regional unity among Spanish Americans as U.S. imperialism did, the British style of informal or business imperialism had the opposite effect, perpetuating and aggravating the preexistent divisions in Spanish America's social structure. Thus while the relationship between Spanish America and Great Britain became "neo-colonial," the countries' internal dynamic closely repeated the situation of the old Spanish colonies in the European-identified elites' domination of a predominantly indigenous and mestizo laboring class. This combination of internal and external colonialism was characteristic of much large-scale agriculture and mining in the nineteenth and early twentieth centuries and continues today as oil drilling threatens the environment and the welfare of the Amazon jungle's indigenous peoples. To understand it we turn again to Marxist theories of capitalist expansion and imperialism.

Marx's writings on China and India are justifiably disparaged among postcolonial scholars because of their essentialist criticism of traditional Asian societies and what he frequently referred to as "Asiatic despotism," as well as Marx's belief that British colonialism was a relative gain for

India, as it was a "necessary" step in the progress toward socialist revolution. However, if we look beyond the texts dedicated explicitly to colonial issues, we find in Marx the seeds of a more nuanced analysis of the situation, seeds that theorists like Rosa Luxemburg and Pierre Philippe Rey have used to develop a dialectical account of imperialism and its effects on the societies of the economic periphery. The relevant material from Marx is chapter 20 of the third volume of *Capital*, "Historical Data Concerning Merchants' Capital," in which Marx describes the role of merchants as mediators between capitalist and precapitalist societies during periods of capitalist expansion. The establishment of trade relations with the capitalist metropolis inevitably initiates economic changes in the peripheral society; as Marx suggests here, however, the development of capitalism in a precapitalist society may be protracted and highly complex:

> The development of commerce and merchants' capital brings forth everywhere the tendency toward production of exchange values, increases its volume, multiplies and monopolizes it, develops money into world money. Commerce therefore has everywhere more or less of a dissolving influence on the producing organizations, which it finds at hand and whose different forms are mainly carried on with a view to immediate use. To what extent it brings about a dissolution of the old mode of production, depends on its solidity and internal articulation. And to what this process of dissolution will lead, in other words, what new mode of production will take the place of the old, does not depend on commerce, but on the character of the old mode of production itself.[38]

A few pages later he reiterates and clarifies the last idea, affirming that the intervention of merchant capital "cannot by itself do much for the overthrow of the old mode of production, but rather preserves it and uses it as its premise" (393). As Marx makes clear, contact and trade with capitalist merchants rapidly accelerates production in the peripheral, precapitalist society; rather than imposing an immediate change to capitalist modes of production, however, it exploits the modes of production already in place in the region.

Marx's analysis is remarkably consistent with what we know of the expansion of agricultural production and the exploitation of rural laborers in Spanish America during the decades after independence. According to historian Arnold Bauer, life in the agricultural regions of the continent's interior was relatively unchanged from the seventeenth century to the 1870s: indigenous communities coexisted with haciendas worked by laborers who lived on the premises or nearby. After 1870, however, the situation changed: with the development of infrastructure locally and a population surge globally, the international market demanded a rapid increase in agricultural production. Local elites, many of whom had complained of labor shortages from the time of abolition, were generally unable or unwilling to offer cash wages high enough to maintain the desired workforce. So, although the interior became integrated into the international capitalist system, Bauer writes,

> The years between 1870 and 1930 do not reveal a linear transition to wage-labour and the triumph of a full capitalist mode of production, but rather a discontinuous, pragmatic advance and retreat, compulsion and resistance, that depended ultimately upon the strength of the new forces of production, the political power of individual *hacendados* or the landowning class, and peasant resistance.[39]

Various forms of forced labor were in use throughout the period, many of them carryovers from the Spanish Colony. Debt peonage was among the most widespread; it frequently resulted in the laborer's perpetual obligation to a landowner or mining company or, in the most infamous cases, to the rubber traders of the Amazon region. Elsewhere anti-vagrancy laws provided a convenient excuse to round up the underemployed, who were forced to choose between incarceration and labor on the mines or haciendas. Perhaps the most insidious measure was the appropriation of communally held Indian lands in Mexico, Bolivia, Colombia, Guatemala, and Peru: while the territory itself was partitioned and sold to local landholders, the real purpose of the measure may have been to force the Indians onto such small and infertile parcels of land that they were obliged to sell their labor under exploitative conditions and for minimal wages on the haciendas. Inherited privilege, combined with pragmatic legislation by the governments of the time and augmented by the unofficial power of landholders resulted, according to Halperín, Donghi in "an effective system of labor discipline *that advanced hand in hand with the expansion of export agriculture.*"[40]

Subsequent Marxist theories of imperialism neglected this valuable line of thought, which remained relatively obscure until Rey developed it further in the 1970s. Rey, like Ernesto Laclau, differs significantly from other "dependency theorists" of the era in stressing the development of social formations (or "economic systems," for Laclau) that combine heterogeneous modes of production. For Rey, the sustained coexistence of two contradictory modes of production typifies colonial and neo-colonial social formations: "we know that in every country where capitalism is still in the first stages of its process of domination, that is, in every 'underdeveloped' country, the development of capitalist relations of exploitation is necessarily accompanied by the development of relations of exploitation typical of the pre-existing modes of production."[41] His work is particularly original in grasping the importance of the dynamic between the two modes and in suggesting that these two modes, albeit contradictory in that one will eventually replace the other, are also complementary in the sense that during the period of transition their workings will reproduce one another.[42]

Rey developed these theories while studying the effects of colonialism on the Congo-Kinshasa region of Africa, but they offer insights that can be applied to Spanish America as well. In Congo, the European capitalist exploiters of the nineteenth century met and collaborated with what Rey terms "ancestral traditions," in the form of the lineage system that structured traditional African society, and augmented the relative privilege of the old tribal elite. In Spanish America the situation is even more complex, because the period of violent or "extra-economic" methods used to force cooperation with international traders began at a much earlier time, during the period of initial contact and conquest by the Spanish. Thus a colonial system with its own competing and mutually reinforcing modes of production was already well established when a new form of colonialism began to develop in the early nineteenth century. Neo-colonialism, with its increased flow of capital and demand for increased agricultural production, began to interact with the older colonial mode still in place, and with indigenous modes of production where they remained. The result was a pattern of exploitation and capitalist expansion that varied widely among Spanish America's countries and regions as historical preconditions and the specificities of the trade at hand produced heterogeneous systems and practices.

The situation was intensified by the highly volatile international market of the late nineteenth century, which even more radically destabilized the long-standing conditions of agricultural production in Spanish America by offering extremely high profits for the sale of goods to be drawn from previously isolated areas. As technologies and tastes changed in the metropolis, one tropical crop or product after another came into demand. A sudden boom meant a frenzy to increase supply and, in consequence, to claim and conquer the land and people capable of producing it. As a result new territories were constantly being conquered and exploited: increased demand for Argentinean beef (a land-intensive but low-labor industry) resulted in the *Conquista del Desierto* and the extermination of the pampas Indians during 1879–80; high coffee prices led to the white settlement of São Paulo, Brazil, and Colombia's Cauca Valley; and the demand for natural rubber after the invention of vulcanization led to the horrors of the Amazonian *cauchería*. In each case indigenous peoples previously living in isolation from the region's Spanish-speaking society were subject to tactics made all the more brutal by distance from the regulating norms of "civilized" society and the alienating effects of racial and ethnic difference. In real as well as imaginary ways the conquest of new territories in the nineteenth and early twentieth centuries uncannily reproduced the Spanish conquest of centuries before.

Although more slowly and subtly than did economic structures, cultural forms also began to reflect the neo-colonial relationship between Britain and Latin America. It would be an exaggeration to suggest that British culture was ever "dominant" in Latin America in a conventional sense; Latin American artists and intellectuals have always been more closely affiliated with the Spanish and French traditions. Nevertheless, the large numbers of Britishers who migrated to Latin America in the nineteenth century, the economic opportunities they represented for some Latin Americans, and the vast quantities of imported goods they made available had a significant impact on Latin American cultures. As Coronil points out, "commodities express hierarchies among cultures, not just assignments of value."[43] The popularity of British goods like textiles, hygiene products, medicines, and firearms contributed to an overall sense of British efficiency and competence; what is more, the same qualities were available to those Latin Americans who could afford to purchase imported goods. As Anne McClintock describes in her insightful discussion of "commodity racism," British manufactures of the late nineteenth century were often marketed as indicators of economic divisions and even racial categories: thus items like Pears soap came to be seen as crucial to one's identity as a "civilized" and "modern" person.[44] In Spanish America—where the categories of civilization and barbarism pervaded political and social thinking—the phenomenon of commodity racism reproduced ideologically the economic and geographic divisions brought on by the continent's uneven entry into the international capitalist economy.

Literature must also be counted among the many goods that enterprising Englishmen made available to Spanish Americans at the height of the Invisible Empire. Indeed, that literature (thoroughly permeated, as Said writes, by the ideology of imperialism)[45] had a significant impact on Spanish American writers of the early twentieth century, whose privileged position in their internally divided countries contrasted with their location on—or even beyond—the margins of the British Empire. Among the first literary texts to register the peripheral elites' ambivalence toward the British Empire is the Chilean Pedro Prado's *La reina de Rapa Nui* (The queen of Rapa Nui, 1913).[46] The fanciful story of a young man's journey to Easter Island (Rapa Nui) comes closer to the genre of romance than to the realism of the regionalist writers, but it is remarkably explicit in describing the reception of Victorian England's colonialist cultural values in Spanish America. The anonymous narrator's first sentences are strongly reminiscent of Marlow's famous encounter with the map of Africa in *Heart of Darkness,* announcing that his childhood has planted in him a love of the sea and desire for maritime adventure. At the same time, the speaker implicitly compares his native Chile to England: "Se ha dicho que Chile es una isla, y yo creo que hay pocas islas tan islas como nuestro territorio" [It has been said that Chile is an island, and I think there are few islands so isolated as our territory] (17). Continuing, the narrator describes the childhood fascination with the sea that has left him obsessed with the idea of making a voyage of adventure and exploration. His plan to have the trip financed by the newspaper he works for, *El Heraldo,* invokes classic scenes from colonial literature: Henry Morton Stanley's famous exploits in Africa were supported (not to mention publicized) by his employers at the *New York Herald,* and the young protagonist of Arthur Conan Doyle's *Lost World* (1911) is financed by the London *Gazette.*

The scene's repetition in *La reina de Rapa Nui* hardly seems coincidental, given the narrator's explicit, even boastful comparison of Chile and Britain. Imagining the possibility of visiting Easter Island, he remarks:

¡La Isla de Pascua! ¡Rapa Nui! Cuando estudié geografía, mi ramo predilecto, me llenaba de orgullo el párrafo aquel que dice: "Chile posee en la Oceanía la Isla de Pascua, la única colonia que puede ostentar la América del Sur." ¡La única colonia era nuestra! Encontré natural que se nos comparara a los ingleses. (18)

[Easter Island! Rapa Nui! When I studied geography, my favorite subject, I was filled with pride by the paragraph that says, "Chile possesses, in Oceania, Easter Island, the only colony of which South America can boast." The only colony was ours! I found it natural that we should be compared to the English.]

When the enterprising journalist approaches his editor, however, his hopes are rudely disappointed. "Amiguito," the editor replies,

es usted el fantástico al pensar que *El Heraldo* pueda facilitar dinero para una empresa semejante. Aquella isla es completamente inútil; todas otras naciones la han despreciado, y a ello debemos que sea colonia nuestra. ¡Mire usted que hacer tamaño viaje, y todo para venir después y contarnos crudezas de unos salvajes aficionados a los placeres de Venus! No, amigo; no. (18)

[you must be mad to think that *El Heraldo* can support an enterprise like that. That island is completely useless; all the other nations have scorned it, and that's the only reason why it is our colony. To make such a journey, and all to return telling us the vulgarities of savages addicted to the pleasures of Venus! No, my friend; no.]

This first encounter, drawing on similar scenes described by Stanley, Doyle, and Conrad, disparages the young Chilean's pretensions to imperial grandeur by pointing out the inferiority of their only colony. Being the major maritime power in South America, Prado seems to suggest, does not make Chile the equal of the European nations, but only a laughable imitator.

The story that follows, however, gradually revises the young narrator's admiration for Europe, and voices an emergent resistance to the spread of neo-colonialism. He eventually does reach Rapa Nui, having paid his own way on a ship bound for Tahiti, and once there falls in love with the islanders' beautiful queen, Coemata Etu, a graceful and amorous, even-tempered child-woman. He soon learns that Rapa Nui is plagued by two Europeans, a Dane named Adams and the Frenchman Bornier. Adams merely complains to Coemata Etu that her subjects, whose ethical system eschews capitalist notions of personal property, repeatedly steal his whisky and sheep, but Bornier has managed to infiltrate the community, seduce Coemata Etu, and have himself declared prince consort. So that his power over the natives will be unchallenged, Bornier writes a letter to the Catholic priests who have established missions nearby, hypocritically ordering them to leave the islanders in peace (48). Eventually Adams and Bornier both leave the indigenous community, and the narrator stays behind.[47] Now the only "civilized" person among the natives, he learns the tribe's customs and history, and suffers with the others when a prolonged drought threatens to destroy the community.

This strange story, oscillating between romance and ethnography, demonstrates the historical transition that I will investigate more thoroughly in the regionalist writers. The narrator's childhood and education in Chile have interpellated him into a national culture apparently modeled on Victorian England, with its close association of the sea and adventure and pride in its one colonial possession. The experience on Easter Island, however, reveals to him both the realities of neo-colonialism—exploitation, manipulation, greed—and the existence of a worldview that is neither based on capitalist values nor in a "pre-capitalist" and "primitive" state. As a result he recoils from that earlier identification with northwestern Europe: what follows is not the exploitation of the exotic he had originally intended, but a valorization of the indigenous culture and a desire to meld or unify it with his own Hispanic heritage.

Regionalism as Colonial Literature

As *La reina de Rapa Nui* suggests, the hegemonic formation of the Invisible Empire entered a period of crisis in the first decades of the twentieth century, even before the international economic collapse of 1929. In Quiroga's native Uruguay, the government of José Batlle y Ordóñez (1905–1911) was among the region's first to challenge the neo-colonial order with protectionist tariffs, trade regulation, and social reform. Around the same time, reports of an Anglo-Peruvian rubber company's exploitative labor practices in the Amazon jungle brought informal imperialism into relief for many Colombians. Elsewhere in Latin America, World War I marked the turning point in relations with Britain. In Argentina, Chile, Peru, Brazil, and Mexico trade and investment links had soared during the twenty years prior to the war. (As a major supplier of wheat and the chief producer of beef for Britain, Argentina was by far the most favored of these countries.) Historian Rory Miller writes that the outbreak of the war ended this period of prosperity and lay bare the economic control exercised by Britain, accelerating "the growth of nationalist ideologies and labour protest, with potentially serious implications for the many British firms operating there." The flow of British capital all but stopped when the war began, bringing "a temporary but almost total collapse of the financial and commercial infrastructures of Spanish America."[48] Shipping and insurance became extremely expensive, while loans evaporated almost completely. Trade was an equally serious problem; many European imports were simply unavailable during the war. With the publication of the blacklists prohibiting trade with many German firms, the British gained an effective monopoly on trade with Spanish America, and as early as 1915 the British used the board of trade to purchase all essential supplies for the Allies, keeping prices of sugar, wheat, meat, and nitrates well below their normal levels. Products considered unessential, like Peruvian cotton and Brazilian coffee, were suddenly without a market.

With the war's end, Britain struggled to rebuild its economy but lacked the capital needed to resume its former role in Spanish American finance. Spanish American export producers, expecting a return to the boom of the prewar years, were disappointed to find that British demand for beef and agricultural products remained low. The particularly anti-English nationalism that began during the war years was increasingly targeted at British-owned utilities companies, which were notoriously poor in responding to the demands of their local customers. In Peru, Venezuela, and Mexico, conflict arose over oil resources exploited by British corporations that were infamous for earning high profits while paying little to Spanish American employees who labored in conditions that were often extremely dangerous, and paying little tax to the local government. In Mexico, in fact, Porfirio Díaz's inability to nationalize the oil industry was one of the major causes of the 1910 revolution. While dissatisfaction with British control of particular industries grew, the United States was rapidly outstripping Great Britain in the critical areas of manufacturing and investment capital: by the crash of 1929, Miller writes, the United States was dominant in Mexico, Central America, and the west coast of South America, with only Chile, Argentina, and Brazil remaining under predominantly British influence.[49]

The internal constitution of Latin American societies had also changed dramatically enough to allow anticolonial discourse to emerge in the continent's literature. Latin America's political and intellectual cultures changed radically with urbanization and the turn-of-the-century rise in literacy, challenging the elite monopoly on literature and other forms of official or public discourse that had effectively concealed the neo-colonial order during the nineteenth century. As Angel Rama writes in his influential book *La ciudad letrada* (The lettered city), the surplus wealth generated during the late nineteenth century, unevenly distributed though it was, actually supported the careers of writers who would eventually criticize the neo-colonial order:

> The economic liberalism dominant among the modernizers allowed a certain diffuseness of social development and expanded the service sector enough to permit a small flow of economic surplus to be absorbed by intellectuals involved in political dissent. . . . In the twentieth century, the cities of letters would be populated not only by the children of the "best" families, as had previously been the norm.[50]

The Mexican Revolution (1910–22), the Russian Revolution (1917), and the overt aggression of the United States in Mexico and the Caribbean brought both imperialism and the national class conflicts it exacerbates to the forefront of political debate in many parts of Latin America. By the end of the First World War, socialist and anti-imperialist ideas were circulating throughout Latin America, adapted to the region's historical particularities and disseminated by theorists like the Peruvians José Carlos Mariátegui and Victor Raúl Haya de la Torre, founders of APRA, the Popular Revolutionary Alliance of the Americas. Labor unions formed in most cities, and workers, consumers, and intellectuals alike began to perceive the impact informal imperialism had had on their countries' economic development and social structures.

The major regional narratives or *novelas de la tierra* were all written during this period of economic complexity and change: Quiroga's *Cuentos de amor de locura y de muerte* (1917) and *Los desterrados* (1926), José Eustasio Rivera's *La vorágine* (1924), Ricardo Güiraldes's *Don Segundo Sombra* (1926), Rómulo Gallegos's *Doña Bárbara* (1929), and *Canaima* (1934). Their authors, though born into relatively privileged families, reflect the expansion and growing diversification among the members of the lettered city. In contrast to previous generations of writers whose work depicts Latin America's countryside, the regionalists of the 1920s display the benefits of new forms of mobility in their sharp awareness of the disparate effects of modernization on urban and rural areas. At the same time, the various forms of economic activity their protagonists pursue frequently end in frustration, suggesting a profound disillusionment with modern narratives of upward social mobility. Occasionally, as in the encounter with English slaughter-house workers in *Don Segundo Sombra,* that frustration is explicitly targeted at their Anglo-Saxon competitors. Even when foreign encroachers are not explicitly mentioned, the financial failure of protagonists like *La vorágine*'s Arturo Cova or Williams Fernández of Lynch's *Plata dorada* resigns them to a position that is closely aligned with the uneducated workers of the rubber groves or the pampa. In other words, the lordly and colonial perspective on nature and laborers that dominated Spanish American rural literature from the time of Bello to Gutiérrez and the *costumbristas* was finally replaced by a voice that identifies, albeit through layers of complex mediation, with working men and women. Antonio Cândido's assessment of the regionalist literature of the 1930s and 1940s can just as easily be applied to the *novelas de la tierra* produced in the 1920s:

> This fiction abandons its agreeableness and its *curiosity,* foreseeing or perceiving what there was of masking over in the picturesque enchantment or in the ornamental gentlemanliness with which the rustic man had been treated before. It is not false to say that the novel acquired, from this point of view, a demythifying force which anticipates the awakening of consciousness of the economists and politicians.[51]

As Cândido suggests, it is in the specific form of the textualization of nature that the "consciousness of underdevelopment" begins to emerge in Spanish American fiction. The innovation of the regionalist writers is to problematize the relationship between people and the land that previous generations of writers had preferred to idealize or "naturalize" in bucolic representations of rural life according to the tradition inaugurated by Bello.

For decades, readers of Spanish American regionalism have complained that the writers' attention to the all-powerful forces of nature dominates the texts to the detriment of their characters and plot. Perhaps Peruvian writer Ciro Alegría best summarized this feeling when he wrote, "[R]esulta que nuestra novela tiene más de sociología, de geografía, de folklore, de tesis, de reportage, de tratado de materias primas, que de novela misma" [It turns out that our novel consists more of sociology, geography, folklore, theory, reportage, treatise on raw materials, than of novel itself].[52] Gallegos unwittingly contributed to the same perception by declaring that his famous novel *Doña Bárbara* was conceived around a scrap of gossip about a legendary woman who ruled the llano with her beauty, cruelty, and shrewdness: "habiendo mujer simbolizadora de aquella naturaleza bravía, ya había una novela" [as there was a woman who symbolized that wild nature, there was already a novel].[53] If the *novelas de la tierra* are primarily about the relationship between people, on an individual and collective (national and international) scale, and nature in its productive capacity—or sociology, geography, folklore, and raw materials, in Alegría's words—then it seems appropriate to locate them within an international body of literature produced from approximately 1870 to 1930, a corpus that reflects the global struggle for access to land and control of natural resources. The place of the regionalist novels in the canons of Spanish American and Hispanic literature is incontrovertible; I propose that they also belong to the international literature on colonialism. They register Spanish America's experience in the globalization (or metropolitan monopolization) of the world's natural resources and the establishment of a global economy dominated by the production of manufactured goods in the northern metropoles; they also register a profound sense of anxiety about the future development of those structures. Set on Latin America's internal frontiers, the *novelas de la tierra* represent the rapid expansion of capitalist agriculture and extractive industries into the forests and plains of the continent's interior, where new lands were settled and their inhabitants either displaced or coerced into working for the newcomers.

This process, as Edward Said writes, is the essential experience of colonialism:

> Everything about human history is rooted in the earth, which has meant that we must think about habitation, but it has also meant that people have planned to *have* more territory and therefore must do something about its indigenous residents. At some very basic level, imperialism means thinking about, settling on, controlling land you do not possess, that is distant, that is lived on and owned by others.[54]

If Spanish American nature writing is, as I have argued, continuously inflected and reinflected with economic and political significations, the regionalist writers' tireless focus on the interactions between human beings and nature on the frontier of capitalist expansion makes their work colonial discourse, in the sense of writing that engages with the experience and effects of colonization. Prioritizing the changing relationships among human groups and the territories they inhabit in both sets of texts, I read the *novelas de la tierra* in dialogue with the international and particularly British literature on imperialism, with which they have a surprising amount in common.

Significantly, British literature only became a noticeable factor in Latin America during the historical moment I have just described, when the hegemonic formation of the Invisible Empire was breaking down under internal and external pressures. It may be true that unstated economic and political risks inhibited nineteenth-century intellectuals who might otherwise have expressed an interest in English literature. The more conventional theory is that natural affinities link Spanish Americans to the Catholic and Latinate culture of France, making the comparatively utilitarian cultures of Britain and the United States all but irrelevant. Certainly this was true in the cases of *modernismo,* a predominantly poetic movement that began in the 1880s under the influence of French symbolism, and the fin de siècle urban planners who modeled Latin America's capitals from Mexico City to Buenos Aires on the broad, tree-lined avenues of Paris.

For the regionalists, however, taking part in the Oedipal struggles among literary generations meant self-consciously differentiating themselves from the Francophile *modernistas,* and invocations of British culture became a way to signal their distance from a movement they frequently represented as "decadent" and "effeminate."[55] Literary movements and styles, as they are produced and reproduced by writers and critics alike, are often decidedly gendered, and the regionalist writers invented their own masculinity by invoking the more aggressive, competitive culture that was widely promoted in British literature (Kipling, Rider Haggard, Doyle) and institutions like the Boy Scouts.[56] Thus while the conventionally "feminine" sphere of the domestic was still dominated by French fashion and design (one thinks immediately of the young heroine of Teresa de la Parra's *Ifigenia,* who returns from Paris with the latest modes in fashion and manners) the social circles in which the male regionalist writers moved distinguished themselves with prestige objects imported from Britain. Like Arturo Cova's dogs, Martel and Dólar, signs of Anglo-Saxon material culture trail everywhere behind them. Arturo's creator, José Eustasio Rivera, often joined his literary friends at the Bogotá "Gun Club" and the nearby "Café Windsor." Lynch, for his part, became an enthusiastic boxer while still an adolescent, and spent most of his adult life as a patron of the elite Jockey Club of the city of La Plata. Güiraldes, similarly, was known to dress up occasionally in gaucho attire, but he more commonly entertained guests at his cattle ranch in well-tailored English tweeds.[57]

But there is a more profound explanation for the regionalists' attraction to British culture than a simple desire to differentiate themselves from the *modernistas.* As Sommer shows in her influential book *Foundational Fictions,* the national novels of the nineteenth century—sentimental love stories like Gómez de Avellaneda's *Sab* or Jorge Isaacs' *María*—used the narrative structure of the marriage plot adapted from French models like

Bernardin de St. Pierre, Chateaubriand, and Sand to "domesticate" the new republics' unruly populations after the close of the independence struggle. For the regionalist writers of the early twentieth century, on the other hand, the British-style adventure narrative was the preferred genre to express their dissatisfaction with the economic and social order that had since been established. Fredric Jameson's *The Political Unconscious* develops a theory of the geopolitical economy of colonial adventure that is relevant to its appropriation by the Spanish American regionalists. According to Jameson, the colonial adventure tale is a recent manifestation of the enduring genre of quest romance, a narrative almost antithetical to the romance plots Sommer discusses in that the protagonist of a quest romance *leaves* his home to undertake a journey to distant lands toward a specific, predetermined, and enunciated goal.[58] According to Jameson, the social function of the adventure tale as descended from its origins in medieval chivalric literature is to satisfy society's "collective longing for magic and providential mystery," a need that for Western societies was exacerbated during the nineteenth century by industrialization and the process Max Weber termed "rationalization." Writers located in the modern metropolitan centers sent their would-be heroes into the uncodified, "uncivilized" regions still beyond the grasp of modernity's progress in search of "authentic" values, spiritual and physical energies that had been deadened at home.

The heroes of Victorian and Edwardian adventure fiction are thus paradoxical and ambiguous figures, unconventional individuals who enter the service of the Royal Navy, foreign office or other government agency as a way of escaping from "stultifying civilization" at home and become "agents of progress" working on behalf of the very forces they have fled. Latin America was a frequent destination for Britons—real and fictitious alike—seeking wealth and relief from the ennui of the European metropolis for the better part of a century: Francis Bond Head's *Rough Notes* (1826), Charles Kingsley's *Westward, Ho!* (1855), Conrad's *Nostromo* (1904), Arthur Conan Doyle's *Lost World* (1912), and Virginia Woolf's *The Voyage Out* (1915) all feature Europeans seeking adventure, riches, and romance in the jungles, waterways, mountains, and plains of the South American interior. Like the rebellious youths who populate British adventure tales, the protagonists of Spanish American regionalism also suffer the dispiriting effects of rationalization in the rapidly expanding urban centers of Latin America. And they too, like the young boy who leaves his aunts' Buenos Aires residence to join the gauchos in Güiraldes' *Don Segundo Sombra,* break out of their bourgeois urban homes in search of adventure, challenge, physical and spiritual renewal.

The structure of the colonial quest romance that Jameson describes often informs the work of Jorge Luis Borges, whose consistent identification with

European civilization and nostalgia for the romantic Victorian Age offer a striking counterexample to the radical political engagement of the regionalists. Among the Spanish American authors who have expressed an admiration for Britain's colonial literature, Borges is undoubtedly the most enthusiastic. And although he remained a prolific writer until his death in 1986, Borges is relevant to our discussion because he was only slightly younger than the regionalist writers: his "Manuscrito hallado en un libro de Joseph Conrad" [Manuscript found in a book by Joseph Conrad], for example, was published in 1925, between the appearance of *La vorágine* and Quiroga's *Los desterrados*. The brief, melancholy poem conveys an image of the young Borges inscribing his own existential inquisitions into the margins of *Heart of Darkness*. The son of Jorge Guillermo Borges, who taught classes—in English—on the psychological theories of William James, Argentina's greatest writer learned to read in the private library supplied by his father and maternal grandmother, a Staffordshire native named Fanny Haslam.[59] According to Borges' memoirs, the best-loved books of his childhood included *Huckleberry Finn*, Captain Marryat's novels of high seas adventure, H. G. Wells's *The First Men on the Moon; Treasure Island, Alice in Wonderland,* Richard Burton's translation of *Arabian Nights,* and *Don Quijote*. "Todos estos libros los leí en inglés," Borges declares. "Cuando más tarde leí *Don Quijote* en español me pareció una pobre traducción" [I read all of these books in English. When I later read *Don Quijote* in Spanish I thought it a poor translation].[60]

As his playful jab at *Don Quijote* suggests, Borges delighted in representing his English education as a personal eccentricity. In the memoirs, however, it is also unmistakably used to indicate his membership in both a privileged social class and a distinguished literary tradition—which he would formally present to Latin American readers with his *Introducción a la literatura inglesa* in 1965.[61] For Borges, whose identity as a writer was inextricably tied to his place in the Western tradition, British colonial literature corresponded to the sense of history and personal destiny he inherited from both sides of the family, his English paternal grandmother and the creole forebears who had fought in the Indian Wars of the pampa.[62] It is not coincidental that in "El sur" [the south], "Historia del guerrero y la cautiva" [Story of the warrior and the captive, 1949], and "El cautivo" [The captive, 1960], Borges represents the pampa of the late nineteenth century as a frontier and a wilderness on which the forces of civilization and barbarism are diametrically opposed. In the empire of his imagination, the pampa—by that time already the site of modernized agribusiness—remained a setting on which colonial contests between European civilization and native savagery were still played out.[63]

Introduction   33

The story "El sur," which most clearly bears the imprint of Borges' enthusiasm for Conrad, illustrates the Spanish American appropriation of the British adventure genre to structure fictions that rebel against the economic and social order of the early twentieth century. The story's central character is Juan Dahlmann, who works (as Borges did) in the municipal library of Buenos Aires. Descended from a Protestant missionary and a hero of the Indian wars, Dahlmann becomes obsessed with escaping the tedium of his urban existence, wishing for a more active life and some kind of proof that he, like his ancestors, is a man of courage. Dahlmann's opportunity arises, ironically, only in the last instants of his life. After falling down a flight of stairs in his home, Dahlmann is hospitalized. As he lies in his room, he imagines or hallucinates that he is walking out of the hospital and toward a station, where he boards a train headed south. In Dahlmann's fantasy (which the narrator continues to present as if it were real) he disembarks at a station in provincial Buenos Aires of the 1870s or 1880s. Clutching a copy of Victorian England's favorite piece of colonial exotica, *The Arabian Nights,* Dahlmann enters a bar where an old gaucho challenges him to the knife fight that will end his life. For Dahlmann, as for Conrad's Kurtz, to die in the colonial wilderness is to have escaped from the banal hypocrisies of civilized society into a realm where moral absolutes like good and evil, courage and cowardice are still possible; he dies thinking that "ésta es la muerte que hubiera elegido o soñado" [this is the death he would have chosen or dreamed]. Borges' version of the colonial quest romance moves beyond the economy described by Jameson into more abstract and philosophical forms: in "El sur" the narrative journey is a nostalgic projection into the past undertaken entirely within the mind of the main character.

In the work of the regionalist writers, in contrast to Borges', the adventure narrative remains aggressively engaged in the realities of capitalist expansion and addresses Latin America's contradictory position in the geopolitical structures of neo-colonialism. The hero is almost always a young, creole male who wishes to escape the ennui of the capital; rather than traveling to Asia or Africa he embarks on a journey to the dark heart of the South American interior, a trajectory that often represents, as in the discourse of the civilizing mission, a descent from the safety and security of the metropolis into barbarism and even the depths of hell. But the reality the protagonist encounters in the wilderness is far more complex than he anticipated, and his initial sense of moral and intellectual clarity begins to break down during the journey. As we have seen in *La reina de Rapa Nui,* the crucial distinction between civilization and barbarism—a nineteenth-century thought-structure that was exceptionally strong and pervasive in Spanish America—becomes threatened as the hero recognizes admirable aspects of "primitive" cultures as well as the savagery and violence of the colonists. As in much European-authored colonial narrative, and *Heart of Darkness* in particular, there is a period of crisis in which the protagonist or narrating subject becomes identified, for better or worse, with the forces of nature and savagery to which he was ostensibly opposed.

This is the trajectory that structures Gallegos's *Doña Bárbara*, considered by many to be the quintessential *novela de la tierra*, or Rider Haggard's *She* (1887), with which it has a surprising amount in common. In both texts a well-educated young man sets off from his urban home to the wilderness of the south armed with documents that prove his legal right to inherit properties his forefathers have neglected; in both cases he must confront a beautiful and powerful woman who uses her sexuality and her knowledge of the occult to dominate the region and its inhabitants. In *She*, of course, the hero's quest takes him to darkest Africa, where he meets the white witch Ayesha; in *Doña Bárbara* Santos Luzardo travels to the Venezuelan plains, where Doña Bárbara and an American called Mr. Danger have encroached on the family cattle ranch. As Gallegos's story unfolds it modulates from the colonial adventure mode back into the discourse of domesticity that Sommer has identified in Latin America's "foundational fictions": the hero proves the legitimacy of his claim to the land, banishes Mr. Danger and Doña Bárbara from the territory, then educates and marries her abandoned daughter Marisela. This resurgence of the marriage plot is not coincidental, since of all the regionalists, Gallegos, who served briefly as Venezuela's president in 1948, most resembled the nineteenth-century authors in his commitment to the ideology of the normative liberal state. Like Sarmiento's *Facundo*, *Doña Bárbara* stages a political allegory in the contest between civilization and barbarism, figuring the ousting of dictator Juan Vicente Gómez—himself a native of the plains—in Luzardo's triumph over Doña Bárbara.[64]

In contrast to Borges and Sarmiento, the regionalist writers—including Gallegos—are sensitive to their own ambivalent positioning between the discourses of internal and external colonialism, self-conscious about the fact that in safeguarding against further incursions of neo-colonialism, their best rhetorical defense is to legitimate the claims of previous colonizers. González Echevarría's analysis of the problematics of writing in *Doña Bárbara* shows that the hero's claim to legitimate authority is itself based on conquest and the rule of force; the genealogy Santos Luzardo traces to establish his legitimate ownership of the land goes back to his ancestor Evaristo Luzardo, who was a brutal usurper and wreaker of genocide.[65] The narrator, describing the history of the Altamira ranch, remarks, "Hombre de presa, *El Cunavichero* les arrebató a los indígenas aquella propiedad de derecho natural, y como ellos trataron de defenderla, los exterminó a sangre y fuego" [A man of prey, el Cunavichero stole from the aboriginal settlers the property that was their natural right, and when they tried to defend it, exterminated them with blood and fire] (93).[66] As in Faulkner's novels of Yoknapatawpha County, the violence of conquest hangs over Gallegos' llano with the implacable weight of original sin. It is embodied, moreover, in Doña Bárbara herself, who is twice over the product of colonial violence. "Fruto engendrado por la violencia del blanco averturero en la sombría sensualidad de la india" [A fruit engendered by the violence of the white adventurer on the dark sensuality of the Indian](35), while still a teenager Bárbara was raped by the men she saw kill her lover Asdrúbal, and it was this early, violent, and traumatic experience—not some inherent depravity—that inclined her toward sorcery and domination. The suggestion that Doña Bárbara, "la devoradora de hombres," [the devourer of men] is the product of colonial violence sits uncomfortably with her elimination at the novel's end—especially as she has by then been "recuperated" (civilized and feminized, according to the patriarchal value system that orders the text) by her love for Santos Luzardo—and undermines the optimism of the new national romance that emerges in his relationship with Marisela. These unresolved issues that threaten to unravel the allegorical meaning of the narrative suggest that *Doña Bárbara* implicitly recognizes the double bind of neo-colonialism and the political and rhetorical contradictions of at once resisting the neo-colonial order and constructing a modern democratic state out of the colonial past.

The kind of ambivalence encapsulated in Santos Luzardo's confrontation with his own colonial heritage arises repeatedly in the regional novels, which with the exception of *Don Segundo Sombra* follow a fairly consistent trajectory from a state of relatively unproblematic identification with the hegemonic metropolitan authority through a growing realization of their own ambiguous positioning between the two contradictory and symbiotic systems of internal and external colonialism I identified earlier.[67] On the other hand, two factors distinguish *Doña Bárbara* from the texts I examine in the chapters to follow. The first is that Santos Luzardo's legitimation as owner of the Altamira ranch and his ousting of Mr. Danger in particular are symbolic of Gallegos's opposition to the imperialism of the United States, which since the Spanish-American War had pursued a policy of open intervention in the Caribbean basin. The second, less obvious reason is that in contrast to the other novels I am considering, the reconquered territory in *Doña Bárbara* is only symbolically relevant to the issue of neo-colonialism. By the time the novel was written in the late 1920s, cattle ranching was of marginal importance in Venezuela's economy, which was dominated instead by petroleum: it was on the oil fields of Maracaibo rather than the distant llanos that Venezuelans were subject to neo-colonial exploitation by companies such as Royal Dutch Shell and Standard Oil. His liberal policies toward foreign drilling companies were a major complaint against Gómez, but *Doña Bárbara* leaves the issue of how to develop Venezuela's oil resources unaddressed, perhaps in order to pursue a more controllable political narrative on the solid ground of the plains.[68]

This distinction is highly relevant to my reading of the *novelas de la tierra*, since I explore the relationships among human beings and the natural environment that evolve as a result of neo-colonial pressures on the production of agricultural and extractive goods. In the novels I discuss more extensively, nature is represented in its productive capacity, specifically as the locus of a political contest among local workers, the national elite, and foreign capitalists. When neo-colonial industries exploit the inhabitants of the economic periphery, it is invariably through a deformation of their established relationship to the land: they are displaced, like the Brazilian peons of Quiroga's *Los desterrados,* confined to tiny parcels of land like the tenant farmers in *El inglés de los güesos,* exposed to insufferable conditions and forced to destroy their own habitat like the Indians enslaved by rubber traders in *La vorágine.* Unlike Gallegos's *Doña Bárbara,* which modulates from colonial adventure to the marriage plot, these texts resist domestication, remaining outdoors to interrogate aggressively the colonialist ideology they initially supported. Their revisions of colonial discourses include rethinking fundamental Western notions about the ownership and use of land, such as the Doctrine of Dominion, which established the Judeo-Christian subject's authority over nature. The regionalists' engagement with the colonial adventure tradition and its ethical and epistemological underpinnings occurs both on the levels of plot and characterization and on a much deeper semantic register; as my readings will demonstrate, the regionalist texts of Quiroga, Lynch, and Rivera formulate a new, ecological poetics through their radical and dialectical representations of place.

The chapters to follow will continue to trace out the Invisible Empire as it is presented and contested in the work of the Spanish American regionalist writers. In the first chapter I look more specifically at the issue of literary affiliation in the contact zone, considering Quiroga's pattern of self-conscious identification with and distancing from the colonial adventure tradition as represented by Conrad and Kipling. Quiroga, personally committed to pioneering in Argentina's tropical forest, argues for nonexploitative and ecologically responsible forms of colonization. Chapter 2 discusses a novel set in the plains of Argentina, Benito Lynch's *El inglés de los güesos.* This text, which has all but fallen out of the Spanish American canon, deserves reconsideration for its eccentric version of the traditional *novela gauchesca* and its sharp critique of the system of land tenure that left the traditional working classes of the pampa impoverished during a time of great national prosperity. It unfolds as a lighthearted romance set in the "picturesque" Argentine countryside, but ultimately develops into a bleak, incriminating picture of a scholarly English adventurer and the terrible repercussions of his casual conquest. Chapter 3 turns to the most enigmatic of the regionalist novels, *La vorágine*, which at once exposes and almost entirely conceals the role of British neo-colonialism in the genocide of Amazonian Indians during the rubber boom of the early twentieth century. Rivera shares modes of representing the colonized jungle with both *Heart of Darkness* and Roger Casement's *Amazon Journal;* he disavows, however, the liberal European anticolonial discourses in order to formulate a new, nativist, and distinctly Colombian critique.

It is my hope and expectation that the theoretical ground that has been broken in this introductory chapter—with its joint emphasis on Britain's informal imperialism in Latin America and the particularly environmental effects of colonial economic structures in general—will enable the reader to interpret these and other texts, canonical or obscure, in productive new ways. The period of 1910–1930 is unique in Latin American history, in its convergence of economic, political and cultural events, including both the apex of British investment in Latin America and many Latin Americans' rude awakening to the deleterious effects that investment was having on their human and natural landscapes. In the sense that *Nature, Neo-Colonialism, and the Spanish American Regional Writers* endeavors to examine these conditions of production with all possible rigor, it is very much a historical study. On the other hand, this book was also written with the sense of urgency that can only come from an awareness that the issues at stake—including the most fundamental questions of economic and environmental justice—are far from resolved today. I believe that awareness will also resonate through the studies of Quiroga, Lynch, and Rivera that follow.

1

"The Freedom in the Field"

Empire and Ecology in the Misiones Stories of Horacio Quiroga

He de morir regando mis plantas, y plantando el mismo día de morir.
No hago más que integrarme en la naturaleza, con sus leyes
y armonías oscurísimas aún para nosostros, pero existentes.
                                              —Horacio Quiroga

IN HIS FAMOUS BIOGRAPHY OF Horacio Quiroga (1878–1937), *El desterrado*, Emir Rodríguez Monegal remarks on the difficulty of identifying Robert Hilton Scott, an Englishman whom Quiroga had encountered in Paraguay in 1907, as the source for the protagonist of the story "La insolación," published one year later. "Perhaps," writes Rodríguez Monegal, "the image of the drunken Englishman who disintegrates in the tropical jungle is too generic (it is magnificently developed in Hudson, in Conrad, and in Kipling, whom Quiroga was already avidly reading) to attempt a definitive identification."[1] The confusion Rodríguez Monegal points to, I believe, is hardly coincidental: Quiroga's stories resonate with British colonial fiction because the events he describes—the large-scale colonization of Argentina's Chaco and Misiones regions during the early twentieth century—were part of the same economic and cultural processes as Britain's establishment of formal colonies in India, Africa, and elsewhere. In fact, many of the pioneers and agricultural entrpreneurs Quiroga encountered in tropical Argentina—including many Europeans and, as we will see, Quiroga himself—actually understood their own efforts as a somewhat belated episode in the history of colonialism. Under these circumstances, it cannot be surprising that Rodríguez Monegal has such a hard time distinguishing between the fictive and the real in Quiroga's *cuentos del monte*": the intertextual relationship between Quiroga and British colonial literature is inseparable from the overarching economic relationship between Britain and Latin America.

In the introduction, I described informal imperialism in terms of two interrelated dynamics: the external motor of the international capitalist market, which dominates supply and demand at the local level while ultimately debilitating Latin American economies; and the localized colonization of the internal frontier, where new sources of land and labor are integrated, often by force, into the national economy. In Quiroga's Misiones stories these two forms of colonialism coincide and overlap, as thousands of European and particularly British colonists arrive to try their hand at farming or logging on Argentina's northeastern frontier. Historically, this situation developed because of the peculiar intensity of Britain's relationship with the Río de la Plata in the nineteenth and early twentieth centuries and the socioeconomic position of the northeastern frontier within the Argentinean nation. After the failed invasion led by Commander Home Riggs Popham in 1805–6, Britain was more successful in its efforts to ingratiate itself with creole leaders during the Independence Wars, when some five thousand British soldiers volunteered for service among the patriot armies.[2] Not by chance, traders like the famous Robertson brothers became established in the region soon after the war—despite the opposition of the dictator Juan Manuel de Rosas and an impolitic Anglo-French blockade of the Río de la Plata in the 1840s. Commercial ties between Britain and Argentina rapidly increased when Argentina came under the leadership of liberal politicians like Bartolomé Mitre and Domingo F. Sarmiento.

Under the modernizing agenda they helped to establish, Argentina became economically, socially, and to some extent even culturally integrated with Britain during the last decades of the nineteenth century. Spurred by government loans and private investment, much of which financed the construction of railroad networks by British workmen, by 1910 Argentina had become one of Britain's leading suppliers of beef and wool. At the same time Buenos Aires received some forty thousand British immigrants, making it the largest British settlement outside the official empire.[3] In Quiroga's native Uruguay the situation was much the same: in fact in 1890 the president of the republic described himself as "the manager of a great ranch, whose board of directors is in London."[4] Social and cultural historians generally minimize Britain's impact on the cultures of the Río de la Plata, emphasizing instead the overt Francophilia of Buenos Aires' writers, artists, and architects and the dynamism of great waves of immigrants from southern Europe. Nonetheless, writers including Victoria Ocampo and Jorge Luis Borges attest that by the early twentieth century the English language and English literature had acquired considerable prestige among the middle and upper classes due to the sheer number of British expatriates and travelers and the disproportionate wealth they controlled. Victorian literature, permeated as it was by the ideology of imperialism, was taught in public and private schools throughout the Río de la Plata.[5]

Discussions of modernization in turn-of-the-century Argentina generally focus on the growth of the railroads and the elimination of the Indians to the south, both of which made possible the vast pampa's conversion into the modern and technologically efficient agricultural zone Benito Lynch describes in *El inglés de los güesos*. But the tropical jungle of northern Argentina presented a different problem. A handbook for contemporary colonists, Robert Eidt's *Frontier Settlement in Northeast Argentina* (1971), explains the region's ongoing history: the potential wealth to be generated from growing cotton or yerba mate attracted Latin Americans (including Horacio Quiroga) to the region before and after the turn of the century, but few were successful enough to remain long. Therefore the government, seeing the region threatened by Brazilian squatters and smugglers, encouraged foreign settlement companies to foster colonization by Europeans.[6] For Europeans, Misiones offered an anachronistic revival of the promise of adventure and upward mobility that imperialism had offered previous generations: with economic opportunities dwindling in the official colonies, Argentina's tropical frontier suggested a viable alternative for Europeans driven by the romance of imperialism but lacking the money or connections to establish themselves elsewhere. Historian Oliver Marshall recounts the fascinating story of these colonists, which reached its anachronistic height in 1919 when Adolf J. Schwelm, a naturalized British citizen and fervent admirer of Cecil Rhodes, named his English-only settlement "'Victoria' . . . in homage to the era he wished to emulate."[7]

Quiroga's biography unfolds within the arc of Britain's informal imperialism in the Río de la Plata, from the so-called Golden Age of export-led development in the late nineteenth century to the public dissent against British hegemony that became sharpest, according to historian Rory Miller, during World War I. Miller cites economic hardships brought on by the British blacklists and other wartime trade restrictions as the principal cause of discontent in the cities, but Quiroga's recognition of informal imperialism occurred even earlier, and on the economic frontier rather than in the urban center.[8] After touring the Jesuit ruins of Misiones with the poet Leopoldo Lugones in 1903, Quiroga made his first attempt to establish himself on the frontier in the early months of 1904, this time in El Chaco. This first experience of colonization was a failed attempt to make his fortune as a cotton planter on six hundred acres of land purchased with almost the entirety of his inheritance. As so many of his protagonists would later, Quiroga naively underestimated the difficulty of the project: drought, illness, and—most significant—the resistance of his indigenous laborers put him out of business within two years. Rodríguez Monegal cites a letter of June 26, 1905, that describes first hand Quiroga's almost comical attempt at exploitation:

> Estos indios son de los más vil, ladrones y sin palabra que hay, y me hallo muy dispuesto a vengarme de todas las que me han hecho. Ahora bien,

como no entienden de números, nada más fácil que robarles cuatro o cinco kilos en un total de treinta. La primera pesada dio cuatro kilos y le dije tres. La otra dio cinco y le dije cuatro. Pero la cosa me dolía como el diablo, y en la tercera pesada—de ocho kilos—le quité sólo ½ kilo. En la cuarta—de nueve—no le quité nada. Pero cada vez estaba más rabioso conmigo mismo, y en el total le dije que era justo. Y para reconciliarme conmigo mismo le di diez centavos más de los que debía.[9]

[These Indians are the vilest thieves and liars in the world, and I'm inclined to take my revenge for everything they've done to me. Now, since they don't understand numbers, nothing could be easier than robbing them four or five kilos in a total of thirty. The first load weighed four kilos and I said three. The next was five and I said four. But it bothered me like the devil, and in the third load—weighing eight kilos—I only took off a half-kilo. In the fourth—nine kilos—I didn't take off anything. But I was getting more and more furious with myself, and in the total I said what was fair. And then in order to live with myself I gave him ten cents more than I owed.]

Two important points stand out in this passage. The first is Quiroga's apparent willingness to play the role of colonial oppressor, evident in the conventional racism of his description—"lo más vil, ladrones y sin palabra"—and his attempt to exploit the Indians' ignorance for material gain. While the frankness of the confession may be surprising, the underlying attitude is not: as I have argued, the Latin American elites' willingness to identify with Britain's colonial ambitions was part of the ideological support of informal imperialism. That identification combined the capitalist ideology of the nineteenth century—based on positivism, pseudoscientific racism, and commodity fetishism—with the Hispanic heritage of the Latin American creoles. As Quiroga would jocosely remind Ezequiel Martínez Estrada some twenty years later, they were themselves descended from a colonial class: "Piense en sus antepasados los conquistadores" [Think of your conquistador ancestors,] he wrote, urging Martínez Estrada to try the Misiones life for himself.[10] On the other hand, in practice, Quiroga is morally incapable of maintaining the role of conquistador or capitalist exploiter, even to complete a single dishonest transaction. Rodríguez Monegal no doubt correctly refers to Quiroga's ethical stance as a kind of "rebellion," as it requires him to break with centuries of tradition regarding white men's dealings with native laborers, in the Americas and elsewhere.

After his failed experiment in El Chaco, Quiroga renounces the dream of entering the planter aristocracy. When he returns to the frontier in 1910—this time with his wife Ana María, and outside the town of San Ignacio, in Misiones—he begins the more modest endeavor that will occupy his life and his literature for much of the next twenty-five years. He buys only a few rocky acres overlooking the Paraná River, out of which he will gradually, and almost entirely by his own labor, coax a tiny farm of orange trees, vegetables and *yerbales*. While they are rarely completely free of the ambiguites I have outlined above, the classic Misiones stories he writes from 1910 on will consistently contrast the exploitative practices of the region's large-scale logging and yerba mate industries with the more modest challenges of isolated pioneers and tract farmers like himself.

In the 1905 letter, it is Quiroga's conscience, his internal ethical sense—"cada vez estaba más rabioso conmigo mismo"—that prevents him from carrying out his exploitative plan; in the stories that morality develops into an outward expression of *solidarity* toward the Indians and other inhabitants of the jungle. A growing sense of solidarity, based on a shared knowledge and common dependence on the land, motivates Quiroga to open up the more limited structures of colonial literature in order to represent the impact of colonization according to the various perspectives of the region's heterogeneous population. One of the earliest examples of Quiroga's ecological experimentation with narrative perspective is precisely the story Monegal cited as a clear example of his interest in Britain's colonial literature, "La insolación," which I will discuss here as an illustration of Quiroga's expansion of the genre.[11] The story relates the last hours of an English colonist who dies of sunstroke in the Argentinean jungle; the event, witnessed by his team of fox terriers, is so typical of British attitudes toward the tropics that it could have prompted playwright Noel Coward's famous quip that only "mad dogs and Englishmen go out in the mid-day sun."[12] But the story radically alters the norms of colonial discourse: it is narrated almost entirely from the limited perspective of the fox terriers, who are able to foresee Mr. Jones's death in the personified form of *la Muerte,* and must explain to the youngest among them what the loss of the master will mean in their lives. Thus Quiroga introduces an alternative, ground-level narrative position that for this reader is one of the most innovative and individual characteristics of his style: "Luego la Muerte," he writes, "y con ella el cambio de dueño, las miserias, las patadas, estaba sobre ellos! Pasaron el resto de la tarde al lado de su patrón, sombríos y alertas" [Then Death, and with it the change of master, the misery, the kicks would come! They spent the rest of the afternoon by their master's side, somber and alert] (139). Jones dies of heatstroke the following day, knowing that he has brought about his own end by having "traspasado su límite de resistencia" [crossed the limit of his resistance] (142). In precise, condensed phrases the final paragraph communicates the effect of Jones' death on the human and animal community of the ranch:

Los peones, que lo vieron caer, lo llevaron a prisa al rancho, pero fue inútil todo el agua; murió sin volver en sí. Mister Moore, su hermano materno, fue de Buenos Aires, estuvo una hora en la chacra y en cuatro días liquidó todo, volviéndose enseguida al sur. Los indios se repartieron los perros que vivieron en adelante flacos y sarnosos, e iban todas las noches con hambriento sigilo a robar espigas de maíz en las chacras ajenas. (143)

[The peons who saw him fall hastily carried him to the ranch house, but all the water they threw on him was useless; he died without coming to. Mr. Moore, his stepbrother, came from Buenos Aires, spent an hour in the shed and in four days had liquidated everything. Then he immediately returned to the south. The Indians divided up the dogs, who from then on were thin and mangy, and went out each night with hungry stealth to steal ears of corn from neighboring sheds.]

The businesslike, efficient brother who travels north from Buenos Aires does not understand Jones's values and rapidly converts the land into cash. In his ironic portrayal of Mr. Moore, Quiroga initiates a theme that often reappears in his stories: the distinction between the rugged and independent colonists and the "lesser" men who prefer the comforts of the city. Then, with an extraordinary degree of compassion and insight, Quiroga describes the cruel fate that reduces the fox terriers to miserable foragers after their master's death, evincing what at the time must have been an usually strong sense of the interconnectedness of human and nonhuman species. In his attention to the dogs' biological needs Quiroga introduces an ecological perspective that also draws out the native peoples' changing relationship to the land: the sudden appearance of *indios* in the final sentences encapsulates the redistribution of natural resources that occurs after Jones's death and by implication also occurred upon his arrival in Misiones. There is no prior mention of indigenous persons in the text, and in these last sentences they emerge, phantomlike, as if from the margins of the social space, to inhabit once again the land as the wage-laboring peons leave the site of the ranch. The structure that appears in these final sentences is not a bipolar opposition between Jones and the dogs, on the one hand, and the hostile climate on the other; it is a more complex figure of the relationships among Jones, the environment, and the local people.

"La insolación" anticipates the aspects of Quiroga's work that form the principal concerns of this chapter: the affinity between Quiroga and British colonial writers that I read less in terms of shared technique than as a will to engage those writers in a dialogue about both the realities and the potential of colonization; the sense of environmental vulnerability common to late colonial literature, which in Quiroga develops into a radical ecological consciousness; and what I see as Quiroga's stylistic signature, the ground-level perspective through which he represents informal imperialism's effects on the bio-regional community of the jungle. As will be clear in the pages to follow, Quiroga's Misiones stories are exemplary of the regional writers' creative and active intervention in both the material practices and the discursive patterns of the Invisible Empire.

Quiroga's Colonial Fellowship

While my primary objective is to understand Quiroga's thematic and stylistic engagement with the literature of the British Empire, exploring those aspects of his work leads me to address the long-standing problem of establishing Quiroga's rightful place in literary history. The group of roughly one hundred stories known as Quiroga's *relatos de ambiente* or *cuentos del monte* have more conventionally been studied in relation to the Latin American *novela de la selva* than in the context of Victorian literature. Nevertheless, scholars of the *novelas de la selva*—which includes works like José Eustasio Rivera's *La vorágine* (Columbia, 1924), Rómulo Gallegos's *Canaima* (Venezuela, 1938), Alejo Carpentier's *Los pasos perdidos* (Cuba, 1953) and Mario Vargas Llosa's *La casa verde* (1966)— often remark upon its somewhat problematic origins. Novels like Jorge Isaacs' *María* (Colombia, 1867) and Juan León de Mera's *Cumandá* (Ecuador, 1879) are recognized starting points, but the dramatic contrast between the romantic landscapes of the nineteenth-century texts and the stark realism of Quiroga's make any notion of continuity problematic.[13] This inconsistency among the *novelas de la selva* coincides with a more general change in attitudes toward modernity and social conditions that critics have noted in Latin American writers of the 1930s.

In that regard, Quiroga is considered crucial to the transition between the idealizing gaze of the nineteenth-century *costumbrista* writers and the politicized literature of the "Boom" generation of the 1960s. In *La nueva novela hispanoamericana,* for example, Carlos Fuentes identified Quiroga as a pivotal figure in "el tránsito de la antigua literatura naturalista y documental a la nueva novela diversificada, crítica y ambigua" [the transition from the old naturalist and documentary literature to the new, diversified, critical and ambiguous novel].[14] Julio Cortázar had already come to a similar conclusion, naming Quiroga along with Ricardo Güiraldes and Benito Lynch as the three Río de la Plata writers who had most helped his own generation define their narrative practice.[15] Arguably, the emergence of a nativist poetics that Fuentes describes develops in Quiroga's representation of informal imperialism, his poetic articulation of the contradictory configurations of power characteristic of neo-colonialism. Noé Jitrik's

1957 study, *Horacio Quiroga: Una obra de experiencia y riesgo,* which remains one of the finest analyses of Quiroga's work, wrestles in its final chapter with precisely this problem of "locating" Quiroga within the Latin American tradition. In previous chapters Jitrik compares Quiroga to his contemporaries Ernest Hemingway and Franz Kafka, and finds that his mature work has more in common with those writers' than with that of either Lugones or Edgar Allan Poe.[16] As is well known, Quiroga turned, over the course of his career, from the influence of *modernistas* like Lugones and Rubén Darío that led him to pursue poetry as an adolescent and young adult, to a period of prose narrative inspired by Poe and Guy de Maupassant.[17] Under the influence of these last two, Quiroga wrote macabre stories like "El almodón de pluma," "La gallina degollada," and "La miel silvestre," all of which were published in *Cuentos de amor de locura y de muerte* in 1917. The immediate success and continued popularity of these stories, combined with the tragic and often violent events of Quiroga's life, have contributed to his reputation as a morbid and death-obsessed writer.[18]

As Jitrik demonstrates, however, Quiroga's most original stories are his unsentimental and realistic *relatos de ambiente*. Many of these also end in death, but as H. A. Murena writes, the "horror" in these texts is not imagined or fabricated, but carefully drawn from Quiroga's own experiences in the *selva:* "Droughts, venom, cruelty, an insane sun, carnivorous ants, jaguars, thirst and fear of an abysmal desperation were the presences that filled and besieged that era in his life."[19] Furthermore, with the exception of early stories like "La miel silvestre" (1911) the texts themselves are calibrated not to maximize the gruesome or macabre aspects of the situation, but to emphasize instead the poverty and isolation of the protagonists or the savagery of capitalist agriculture on the frontier. Jitrik ultimately concludes that the stimulus for change in Quiroga's style and thematics was less outside influence than the situations he encountered in Misiones: "His personality consolidates of its own accord, urged by a reality that in the end absorbs all his attention and his forces. While Quiroga becomes conscious of that reality, the process, metaphysical in nature, shapes his world accordingly, and has direct results in the clear, transcendent realism of *Los desterrados, Un peón, Yaguaí, La insolación* and other stories."[20] Given Jitrik's conclusion, it seems surprising that he does not explore more extensively the relationship between Quiroga and another of his preferred authors, Rudyard Kipling. Quiroga's enthusiasm for Kipling is especially significant, because the historical and material reality that according to Jitrik was so instrumental in shaping Quiroga's literary sensibility is the geographical experience of colonialism, the settler's necessary acculturation to a new environment, the often violent contest for territory, and the ensuing process of displacing or disciplining the region's earlier inhabitants. What is more, Quiroga's metaliterary writings show that he himself understood his narrative project within the international corpus of colonial fiction to which Kipling so clearly belongs.

By 1930 Quiroga was clearly feeling alienated from the literary scene of Buenos Aires, even though only a few years had passed since the publication of his best collection, *Los desterrados*. His frequently cited essay "Ante el tribunal" gives us ample evidence of Quiroga's very real concern that the rising generation of avant-garde writers—led by none other than the young Jorge Luis Borges—would definitively turn public opinion away from the realism and rustic themes of his stories.[21] Around the same time that "Ante el tribunal" was written, Quiroga published a number of other articles of literary theory and criticism that clearly show him shaping and directing an alternative orientation for his work, outside the Buenos Aires scene and within an international tradition of colonial adventure narrative. These texts convey an implicit sense of fellowship, particularly as Quiroga sets the special knowledge drawn from experience of frontier society and direct contact with nature against the hollow urbanity of the literary establishment. In 1922, for example, Quiroga published "Kipling en la pantalla," a review of the film version of Kipling's "The Unmade Nest," in which he defends the Anglo-Indian writer from the clumsy adaptation of two Parisian cinematographers who are "absolutely ignorant" of "the aspects of nature and the life of a country" represented in the fiction.[22] A few months later he criticized a translator of Hudson's *The Ombu*, a "stranger to the country" who failed to understand and thus to interpret the reality of the pampas and the language of its inhabitants. In October 1928, readers of *El Mundo Argentino* encountered "La novela trunca de un espíritu," a short, speculative and ironic report on news Quiroga claims to have heard via telegram from London: the ghost of Joseph Conrad had communicated with Arthur Conan Doyle (in fact a known spiritualist), pleading for assistance in completing a last, literally posthumous novel.[23] Quiroga recognizes just two Latin Americans, Argentinean Benito Lynch and Colombian José Eustasio Rivera, along with North American Bret Harte, in this fellowship of writers who understand the harsh and often violent experience of the frontier as the essential reality of modern life.[24]

Among the most revealing of these articles is "Un poeta del alma infantil," [A poet of the child-soul] published in *El Hogar* in August 1928.[25] In his homage to the "poet" of the title, Jules Verne, Quiroga reflects on colonial adventure fiction as a source of inspiration for children of his generation, which he nostalgically compares to the present one. Appropriating a gesture familiar to readers of Conrad's *Heart of Darkness* and *A Personal Record*, Quiroga explains that his early readings of Verne inspired him to pursue adventures catching lizards and constructing a shelter in what he describes as the "miniature jungle" of his childhood home, boyish pleasures that implicitly prefigure his adult ventures in the Chaco and Misiones. Each of these essays conveys Quiroga's chagrin that readers were no longer interested in the kind of narratives he excelled at producing: brief, compact fictions about the rigors of life on the tropical frontier. While expressing that anxiety, Quiroga also stakes a claim for the literary territory he occupies in the discursive space of colonial adventure.

It should be clear at this point that my project is not to trace the "influence" that either Kipling or Conrad may have had on Quiroga. Over the years a good deal of ink has been spent debating—and largely discrediting—Quiroga's assertions that Kipling was one of his literary "masters," a claim that has become all but inextricable from the untenable notion of the "cultural dependency" of the postcolonial world.[26] The question of affiliation first became an issue when Borges (who, as I have suggested, was one of Quiroga's detractors in the 1920s) ungenerously commented that Quiroga "wrote the stories that Kipling had already written better." Subsequent writers have come to Quiroga's defense; in asserting the value and originality of Quiroga's work, however, they have effectively negated its concern with imperialism. One of the most recent, Abelardo Castillo, suggests that Borges' remark "today would be equivalent to thinking that Quiroga only wrote those stories [*Cuentos de la selva*] or forgetting that they were stories for children."[27] Castillo's comment in turn implies that a talent for fable writing is all that Quiroga and Kipling shared. By describing scholarship that points to the relationship between them as "a frivolity," the critic, unintentionally perhaps, cordons off a crucial aspect of the historical and material context of Quiroga's writing: the reality of colonialism and informal imperialism in Argentina.

Rodríguez Monegal, to whom Borges' comment was originally addressed, came closer than most to the kind of approach to the relationship between Quiroga and colonial literature that interests me when he described the difference between Quiroga and Kipling with the remark, "Although Quiroga shows traces of the psychology of a *sahib*, there is none of that agressive imperialism that underlies certain of Kipling's books." But in order to understand why the author of "Los mensú" was willing to associate himself with the literature of the British Empire—beyond the potential for prestige—it is necessary to keep in mind, as few of Quiroga's critics have, that many British authors of the late nineteenth and early twentieth centuries, including Conrad and even Kipling, were actually ambivalent on the subject of imperialism and its benefits for both the metropolitan agent and his native subjects. Martin Green's book, aptly titled *Dreams of Adventure, Deeds of Empire*, describes the development of an "anxiety of possession" based on growing moral discomfort and an awareness of practical setbacks that demonstrated the unsteady progress of colonization: indigenous resistance to demands for their land and labor, low or unpredictable agricultural yields, seemingly uncombatable tropical diseases, declining forests, soils, and other natural resources.[29]

A brief comparison of "Una bofetada" (1916) and an incident in Conrad's *Heart of Darkness* will illustrate what I understand as the affinity between Quiroga's work and the British literature. Marlow, Conrad's narrator and protagonist, is contracted by a Belgian company to pilot a steamship on the Congo River; soon after arriving in Africa he learns that his predecessor, a Dane named Fresleven, was killed by a young African while relentlessly "hammer[ing] the chief of the village with a stick" over a minor dispute. "Oh, it didn't surprise me in the least to hear this," Marlow remarks, "and at the same time to be told that Fresleven was the gentlest, quietest creature that ever walked on two legs. No doubt he was; but he had been a couple of years already out there engaged in the noble cause . . . and he probably felt the need at last of asserting his self-respect in some way."[30] Quiroga's version expands an essentially similar story. "Una bofetada" exposes a large timber company's tactics of trapping local people in debt peonage and the beatings and dangerous working conditions to which they are subjected by following a series of encounters between an anonymous *mensualario* or *mensú* (so called because they were typically contracted on a month-to-month basis) and an overseer named Korner.[31] Korner's troubles begin when rum, which is prohibited among the workers because it fortifies them to rebel against the strict order of the camps, enters the *obraje*. "En los obrajes," Quiroga writes, "hay resentimientos y amarguras que no conviene traer a la memoria de los mensú. Cien gramos de alcohol por cabeza, concluirían con el obraje más militarizado." [In the work-camps there is resentment and bitterness of which it is better not to remind the *mensú*. One hundred grams of alcohol per head would ruin even the most militarized company] (204). One *mensú* in particular is singled out and beaten by Korner after a brief uprising of the workers; for subsequent "insolence" Korner banishes him from company territory. When the *mensú* reappears, the furious Korner fires a shot at him. The shot misses; the *mensú* overpowers and disarms Korner, then forces him on a trek through the jungle, rhythmically and unremittingly beating the overseer to death with his own whip.

The similarity between the two stories is striking: both are set in the colonial jungle, which they present as a place of real danger to the European. Rather than following the conventional pattern of representing the native as an unreasonable and unpredictable threat to the would-be civilizer, however, they show how colonial agents' abuse of power provokes natives to acts that are implicitly justified by the circumstances, accumulating detail to describe the beatings and humiliation that have driven the workers to violence. Both texts, in other words, work against centuries of Eurocentric prejudice by demonstrating that the true "savages" are not the natives so much as the Europeans who have come to exploit them. In discussing texts like *Heart of Darkness* and "Una bofetada," it may be necessary to differentiate between *colonial* and *colonialist* literature: the former I understand as literature that takes as its subject the experience and implications of colonialism, the latter as work that actively supports the colonial enterprise. Although it is at times understandably difficult—perhaps even impossible—to distinguish between the two, Quiroga's own writings make clear that what drew him to the British writers was both their choice of subject and the dynamic, complex representations of colonialism and its dubious benefits for colonizer, colonized, and the land between them that they frequently produced. For Quiroga, their (anti)colonial stories were crucial to his project of establishing the new language with which to describe the experience of the jungle, stripping away the idealized, romantic tropology of earlier eras and replacing it with an unsparing representation of the frontier as the contested site of Latin America's ongoing insertion into the international capitalist economy. "Una bofetada" and the texts discussed in the pages to follow—"Los mensú," "Los pescadores de vigas," *Una cacería humana en Africa*, "Los desterrados," and "El regreso de Anaconda"—mark a momentary convergence between Spanish American and British narrative, a moment when a disintegrating imperialism and an emergent postcoloniality briefly share discursive space, using the forms of colonial adventure fiction to contest the progress of colonization.

What develops in that discursive space is a dialogue about colonialism as Quiroga understood and desired it to be and the colonialism that thousands of Europeans were undertaking in Latin America and their nations' official empires overseas. In other words, Quiroga actively contests the Europeans' ability to establish the conditions of modernity in Latin America and other parts of the periphery and articulates his own ideas of a progressive, redemptive colonization. In his recent book *The Burden of Modernity*, Carlos J. Alonso describes Spanish American cultural discourse in terms of postindependence intellectuals' problematic relationship with the concept of the modern. The unique predicament of Spanish American writers, Alonso explains, develops from the inconsistency between a rhetorical commitment to "modernity"—always implicitly identified with Europe—that is intended to legitimate the elites' political and intellectual authority, and the unavoidably un-modern social reality of Spanish America. The resultant contradiction consistently threatens to deauthorize the intellectual's voice, forcing him to seek or create a discursive space that is "impervious" to the dictates of the modern. In the chapter dedicated to Quiroga, Alonso identifies what he sees as Quiroga's response to this compromising position in the contrast between his invocation of "modern" masters like Kipling, Maupassant, and Poe and his repeated transgression of the very standards those authors seem to establish. As a result the narratives lose their "exemplarity," but gain considerable force from the internal rhetorical struggle against "the death that comes with the threat of being an echo of someone else's voice."[32] Alonso's avowed purpose in *The Burden of Modernity* is to investigate the "rhetorical situation" presented by Spanish America's historical passage from Spanish colonialism to neo-colonial subjugation to Europe and the United States. To that end, his fascinating discussion is limited to consideration of "modernity" as a discursive construct, albeit, arguably, "the master trope of Western hegemonic authority, the one that provided the foundation for the countless other hierarchical arrangements of categories employed by the relentless *ratio* of the metropolitan discourse of domination."[33] I would argue, following Jorge Marcone's work on ecological criticism and sustainable development in the *novelas de la selva,* that Quiroga's *relatos de ambiente* actually challenge rather than evade the European discourses of the modern. Quiroga represents the material and social reality of Latin America less as an inherent underdevelopment or lack of modernity than as the result of an uneven and anarchic process of insertion into the international economy. In the stories that I am considering within the context of colonial literature, Quiroga counters the version of modernity that Europeans have imposed on the non-European world, and advocates a different kind of future for Latin America.

In the 1913 novella *Una cacería humana en Africa,* for example, Quiroga again engages that most emphatic exposition of modernity's destructive force, *Heart of Darkness,* and radically recasts it in order to recuperate a paternalistic colonialism as a way of establishing rational, humane labor relations. Quiroga makes the intertextual relationship clear from the first paragraph:

> Estamos en Africa, en plena Africa ecuatorial. La selva virgen, profunda, negra, inextricable, reina en el paisaje. Como una inmensa cinta de plata, el río Congo corre hacia el océano, arrastrando en su corriente enormes troncos, búfalos muertos, monstruosamente hincados y ya en descomposición, islas flotantes de juncos y pajas, y a veces piraguas tumbadas, en que alguna docena de negros naufragó.[34]

> [We are in Africa, in the midst of equatorial Africa. The virgin jungle, profound, black, inextricable, rules the landscape. Like an immense silver ribbon, the river Congo flows toward the ocean, dragging in its current enormous trunks, dead water buffalos, monstruously swollen and already

decomposing, floating islands of reed and straw, and occasionally a capsized canoe in which some dozen blacks have been shipwrecked.]

The narrative's opening words, designed to call up an established setting rather than describe an actual place, announce to the reader that this is a revision of an earlier writing on Africa. The passage that follows encapsulates the essential phrases of Marlow's descriptions of the landscape: his Congo is also "inscrutable," "immense," "so dark green as to be almost black." In *Heart of Darkness* death and putrescence also contaminate the waterways, and even the stench of decaying animal is familiar to readers of Marlow's inland journey.

Once this opening evocation is complete, however, the similarities between *Una cacería humana en Africa* and *Heart of Darkness* abruptly cease, as if Quiroga intended merely to call Conrad's text to mind before reworking it. References to Stanley Falls and the Mombasa–Victoria Nianza railroad make clear that this story is set in the same period as *Heart of Darkness*, but Quiroga has swept from the landscape the vast colonial enterprise that Conrad describes, the administrative and commercial centers, the railroad construction projects, even the gatherers of ivory and rubber. Quiroga's Congo is still a relatively unexploited place, to which his hero has come to enjoy "la vida, no salvaje, pero sí en países salvajes" [not the savage life, but life in a savage country] (93). In this and other ways the story resembles Quiroga's own experiences in Misiones. The hero Ruy Díaz, endowed with qualities Quiroga admired, is an amalgam of various types of adventurers: Díaz is Spanish by descent, and his name echoes that of Argentina's first colonial historian, Ruy Díaz de Guzmán. On the other hand, Díaz is explicitly Anglo-Saxon in appearance, "un hombre alto, de ojos celestes y barba rubia que le llega casi hasta el pecho. Viste kaky y sombrero de paja, tipo boer" [a tall man, with blue eyes and a blonde beard that fell almost to his chest. He wears khaki and a straw hat of the Boer type.] (93). Díaz is described as an adventurer and an expert hunter, but his purpose in Africa is scientific: educated in biochemistry at Oxford, he left that institution to study first at the Serotherapy Institutes of Pondictery (probably intended for Pondicherry or Pondichéry, in southeastern India) and British Guyana. He is in Africa to develop a serum for the virus carried by the tsetse fly, a project he is about to complete as the story begins.

Quiroga's Congo is, on the other hand, a colonized region whose native population is abused and tortured by European officials; the novella has Díaz protecting a native boy, Tuké, from two big-game hunters who threaten to use him as bait. Tuké's father, unable to protect the boy against the Europeans, implores Díaz to take him in, and the noble Díaz agrees to help the boy. The paternalism of the scenario could not be more apparent: the endangered African community is embodied in the semiarticulate, ingenuous boy, whose own impotent father gratefully allows himself to be supplanted by the brave, generous, and capable European. Clearly this is not Quiroga's best work; yet as a rewriting of what has become one of Europe's archetypal colonial narratives, *Una cacería humana en Africa* is indicative of his vision of colonialism in the ways in which he re-presents both the situation and its eventual solution. Unlike so many of Quiroga's stories, this one has a positive resolution: Díaz rescues Tuké from the villainous officials, then returns to Europe to testify against them in a court of law; when the officials are convicted, he returns to his Congolese friends and his philanthropic research. The relationship between Díaz and Tuké, as Juan José Beauchamp has suggested, is a model for a "positive" form of colonialism, one that offers the natives protection, emancipation, and a process of "modernization" that Quiroga very carefully outlines as the advancement of science and law over anarchy.

Quiroga was fervently anti-imperialistic, opposed to the capitalist exploitation of natural resources and commodification of the land and well aware of the connection between the extraction of surplus value and violence. Nevertheless, he believed passionately in the social and spiritual potential of what may be termed "colonization," precisely in the sense of pioneering or settling on land that is distant from the political and economic center of one's society and state. Near the end of his life, Quiroga urged his friend Ezequiel Martínez Estrada to join him as a *colono* in Misiones, describing the experience in utopian language:

> Creo que [el entendimiento] puede acaecer siempre que los dos amigos sigan la misma derrota—no espiritual, que sería lo de menos—, sino material. Por ejemplo si Vd. sintiera nacer en Vd. el amor a la tierra, al plantar, a hacer su casa, hacerla prosperar trabajando manualmente en ello, estoy seguro de que no se levantaría una nube sobre nuestras personas amigas.[35]
>
> [I believe that (understanding) can result, as long as two friends follow the same path—less the spiritual path than the material one. For example, if you felt born in yourself the love of the earth, planting, building your home, making it prosper through your own manual laboring, I am sure that not a single cloud would arise over these two friends.]

In the stories Quiroga vituperates the large-scale industries that rapid economic expansion brought to Misiones—and the Britons associated with them—for their exploitation of human beings and the land, but he continues to valorize colonization as a spiritually transformative experience uniquely capable of forming bonds of community among humans and the nonhuman environment.

If Quiroga is a colonial and antihegemonic writer, vehemently critical of capitalist exploitation and dedicated to the personal and communal rejuvenation he finds in the work of the settler or pioneer, that paradoxical positioning suggests a critique of imperialism that escapes the rigid narrative structure Abdul R. JanMohamed and others have recognized in the discursive forms imposed by formal imperialism and perpetuated even in postcolonial discourse.[36] In fact, *Una cacería humana en Africa* noticeably dislodges the Manichean oppositions that characterize Conrad's work. As is often said, *Heart of Darkness* presents a powerful subversion of the European mythology of empire, but that subversion depends rhetorically upon the use of irony to undermine the legitimacy of the colonialist perspective to which the narrator is explicitly committed. Though the relative value of the terms—Europe/Africa, civilization/savagery, black/white—is questioned ad infinitum, the poetics of the text nevertheless depends upon the continued interplay of opposites. (As Ian Watt points out, Conrad even went so far as to supress the role of Arab traders in aggravating colonial violence in order to maximize the aesthetic and moral force of the Manichean allegory.)[37] In Quiroga's work, on the other hand, the bipolar opposition is expanded back into a figure of three, with Ruy Díaz emerging as a positive alternative to the catastrophic colonialism of the past. Refusing to cathect the African landscape as symbolic "darkness," Quiroga shatters the essentialist identification between the land and its indigenous inhabitants, leaves metaphysics aside, and looks for positive solutions in Ruy Díaz's benevolent intervention between Tuké and, on the one hand, the colonial officials, and on the other, the deadly tsetse fly. Quiroga, in other words, is not locked into the bipolar models of identity that have so often been part of formal imperialism's legacy: Díaz is both a compromise and an escape route, an imaginary amalgam of Latin America's Spanish colonial past and a new paradigm of rational and humane colonialism.[38]

Quiroga's disregard for binary oppositions demonstrates a significant difference between the rhetorical structures produced in response to informal imperialism and the more frequently studied discourse of formal colonialism; in that regard his work is extremely relevant to the ongoing, interdisciplinary debate about Latin America's position in the field of postcolonial studies.[39] The triangulated and shifting forms he favors, which my introduction traced back to the days of Andrés Bello, correspond to the specific rhetorical situation created by Britain's informal imperialism in Latin America, where structures of internal and external colonialism mutually reproduced one another, and local elites frequently occupied an intermediary position between metropolitan centers of power and their countries' laborers and natural resources. The creoles' sense of their own colonial past was an available method of affirming their cultural identification with the metropolis; as Latin Americans became increasingly disenchanted with the neo-colonial order, however, it could also be used, as in the case of Ruy Díaz, to articulate progressive alternatives. With growing force in Quiroga's later work, the lack of Manichean absolutes opens discursive space for a fluid aesthetic and the emergence of a powerful third term, the role of nature and the land. Quiroga represents informal imperialism as a process of capitalist expansion that profoundly reorganizes the relationship between humans and nature within a given environment, empowering some while stripping others of their traditional livelihood, exposing them to exploitation, poverty, and disease. In the Misiones stories the typical colonial dyad becomes a triad formed by land, labor, and capital, and eventually disperses into the shape of a (bio)-sphere: what emerges in the dialogue between Quiroga and the British writers is a sense that for him colonialism was something other than an encounter or confrontation between racially and culturally opposed peoples. It was a new or different relationship between a heterogeneous human population and its physical environment.

Land, Labor, and Capital in Misiones

In Quiroga's texts land takes on the primacy Edward Said ascribes to it when he writes, "At some very basic level, imperialism means thinking about, settling on, controlling land you do not posess, that is distant, that is lived on and owned by others."[40] Land itself becomes the basis of the action and interaction of his characters in the colonial jungle. Quiroga's *cuentos del monte* may be roughly divided among three categories: those representing isolated colonists' struggle to survive amidst the perils of the jungle, those depicting local workers' exploitation by the timber and yerba mate companies, and those representing animals' response to development of the jungle. The importance of nature as the primary reality of the characters' lives is more visible in all three categories of Quiroga's stories than in the more "conventional" colonial literature Said discusses, which tends to focus on political or cultural conflict played out on the ground that is itself contested. In order to recuperate this suppressed materiality Said advocates a critical practice he calls a "geographical inquiry into historical experience"—but the same phrase might just as well describe Quiroga's authorial attention to the changing configurations of economic power, human freedom, and the use of land and natural resources.

These stories vividly convey the intense relationships among land, labor, and capital in the colonial jungle, where the power exerted by metropolitan capital extracts surplus value by deforming beyond all reason the "natural" interaction between local people and their environment. In "Una bofetada" Quiroga emphasizes the dangerous and inhumane working conditions of the *mensú,* who labor "bajo un sol de fuego, tumbando vigas desde lo alto de la barranca al río, a punto de palanca, en esfuerzos congestivos que tendían como alambres los tendones del cuello a los siete mensú enfilados" [beneath a fiery sun, felling trees and levering them down from the high cliff to the river in congestive efforts that pulled like wires the neck-tendons of the six workers in the line] (177–78). Later they stand shoulder-high in the Paraná River, tying together bundles of logs to be sent downstream: that job is so hazardous that the company supplies alcohol—otherwise strictly forbidden—to numb the workers to the danger and discomfort. In this emphasis on the role of nature within changing relations of production, and even as the instrument of exploitation, Quiroga's stories coincide with one of the most recent developments in Marxist critique, the move by scholars including Fernando Coronil, David Harvey, and Fernando Mires to integrate the "third term," land, more completely into the analysis of neo-colonial economic structures in the "developing" or postcolonial world.[41]

Marxists have traditionally neglected this crucial aspect of Marx's thought, expressed in the third volume of *Capital:*

> Just as the savage must wrestle with nature, in order to satisfy his wants, in order to maintain his life and reproduce it, so civilized man has to do it, and he must do it in all forms of society and under all possible modes of production. With his development the realm of natural necessity expands, because his wants increase; but at the same time the forces of production increase, by which these wants are satisfied. The freedom in this field cannot consist of anything else but of the fact that socialized man, the associated producers, regulate their interchange with nature rationally, bring it under their common control, instead of being ruled by it as by some blind power; that they accomplish their task with the least expenditure of energy and under conditions most adequate to their human nature and most worthy of it.[42]

Marx's dialectical, punning style subtly articulates the staggering effect that the process of capitalist expansion can have on laborers' changing interaction with nature in the economic periphery. With the development of the metropolitan economy the apparently unbridgeable distance between "civilized man" and "the savage" shrinks as the "realm of natural necessity" grows—both the scope of foods, raw materials, and consumer goods needed to support the worker and the geographical space in which they are produced. They meet, of course, in the colonial periphery, where the metropolitan settler goes about adapting the native to the system of disciplined labor that capitalism requires.

Another of Quiroga's most powerful stories, "Los mensú," traces precisely this process in the deculturation of two rural workers and their cruel apprenticeship as debt peons of the yerba mate industry.[43] The land that might have supported them has become the property of an export company, which is a cruel mediator between the workers and the natural environment, exposing them to storms, chill, and malaria while "teaching" them the value of the exorbitantly priced alcohol and tools sold by the company store. When they return to the mountain after a week of "recreation" below, the debts the *mensú* worked months to pay off have accumulated again, the result of "constantes derroches de nuevos adelantos—necesidad irresistible de compensar con siete días de gran señor las miserias del obraje" [constantly squandering new advances—an irresistible necessity to compensate with seven days of high living the miseries of the work station] (78). As autumn draws to a close, one of the *mensú* contracts malaria from the constant exposure to rainy weather: to purchase effective medicine Podeley would have to leave the camp, but the boss refuses to let him, preferring "hombre muerto a deudor lejano" [a dead man to a distant debtor] (83). Finally Podeley and Cayetano decide to leave the *obraje,* cutting what Deleuze and Guattari term a "line of flight" into the jungle. They manage to evade the overseer who chases after them, shooting and shouting, but Podeley's fever worsens and he dies the same night. He dies as the rain continues to fall, "la lluvia blanca y sorda de los diluvios otoñales, hasta que a la madrugada Podeley quedó inmóvil para siempre en su tumba de agua" [the white, deaf rain of the autumn deluge, until at dawn Podeley remained immobile for ever in his tomb of water] (87).

The dialogue between Quiroga and British colonial writers continues in another story from 1913, "Los pescadores de vigas," which represents the abuse of land and laborers in Misiones' timber industry.[44] Here the worker is a mestizo called Candiyú; the boss an English accountant referred to as Mister Hall. Hall hires Candiyú one evening to procure three logs in exchange for a gramophone and twenty records. Hall knows that Candiyú will illegally "fish" these logs out of the Paraná River when the logging company upstream sends them floating down to Buenos Aires; moreover he wants rosewood logs, which, as Candiyú explains, are only "sent down" in times of severe flooding. A prolepsis is inserted immediately after this first scene. An indefinite time has passed; we are told only that Candiyú has lived beside the Paraná for thirty years and that he is dying of liver failure brought on by successive bouts of fever. Only his hands, "lívidas zarpas veteadas de verde" [livid claws streaked with green], continue their monotonous motion, "con temblor de loro implume" [trembling like a featherless parrot] (116).

"The Freedom in the Field" 57

This story, brief and often overlooked, is uncommonly sharp in delineating, as Lafforgue and Baccino Ponce de León write, "the subject of modernity, and the first effects of modernity's arrival at the marginal world."[45] Beauchamp, similarly, reads "Los pescadores de vigas" as an allegory of the exchange (raw materials for manufactured goods) that characterizes neo-colonial economic structures.[46] In retrospect, it may be said that "Los pescadores de vigas" resonates with the symbolic meaning Beauchamp indicates: like the Buendía family's imported pianola in García Márquez's *Cien años de soledad,* Candiyú's gramophone gestures beyond the immediate context toward the overarching structure of export-led development. Nevertheless, Quiroga's ideological position differs from that of both García Márquez and his own contemporary José Carlos Mariátegui, whose *Siete ensayos sobre la realidad peruana* have become cornerstones of Marxist critique in Latin America. Though Quiroga published a brief, admiring eulogy soon after Mariátegui's death in 1930,[47] their approaches to social and political issues were divergent: Mariátegui developed a precise critique of Anglo-Saxon imperialism in Latin America out of his extensive knowledge of the region's history and his dedication to Marxist theory, which he had studied extensively in Europe. Quiroga, on the other hand, "does not theorize": he was skeptical about organized socialism, and based his critique of exploitation on a careful representation of local conditions.[48] Instead, the acuity of stories like "Los pescadores de vigas" and "El monte negro" results from Quiroga's certain knowledge of the power that foreigners wielded in the Río de la Plata and his implied analogy to Britain's activities in its official empire.

It is this comparison to the degenerate colonists of Kipling or Conrad's fiction that makes Hall stereotypically English, and transforms the individual character into an archetype of the abusive colonist: "como un inglés a la caída de la noche, en mangas de camisa por el calor y con una botella de whisky al lado, es cien veces más circunspecto que cualquier mestizo, Míster Hall no levantó la vista del disco. Con lo que vencido y conquistado, Candiyú concluyó por arrimar su caballo a la puerta" [since an Englishman at nightfall, reduced to shirtsleeves by the heat, his bottle of whisky by his side, is a hundred times more circumspect than any mestizo, Mr. Hall did not lift his eyes from the record. Defeated and conquered, Candiyú stopped his horse at the door] (114). Although the phrasing is different in subsequent versions, when "Los pescadores de vigas" was originally published the word "inglés" was almost immediately repeated: Hall takes a good look at the worker before him and becomes a recognizable national type: "La mirada turbia, inexpresiva e insistente de míster Hall se aclaró. El contador inglés surgía" [The turbid, inexpressive and insistent face of Mister Hall cleared. The English accountant appeared] (114).[49]

If his representation of the simple, heroic Candiyú betrays an indelible class bias, the power of the text as critical realism lies in Quiroga's attention to the physical details of the worker's experience. The perspective and positionality of the narrator show a flexibility and fluidity that surpass the expectations of colonial discourse, because Quiroga positions the narrator between the foreigner who commands local labor and the worker himself. As Jitrik explains, the shared experience laboring in and against the physical environment creates a sense of empathy and solidarity by heightening Quiroga's understanding of the workers' material conditions: "He approached the common man and understood him, he saw the reason and the consistency of his struggle against nature and understood the universality of his destiny" (78). To represent this physical struggle against nature in "Los pescadores de vigas," Quiroga narrates Candiyú's efforts in the surging river from a ground-level perspective like the one we have seen in "La insolación":

> Ahora bien, en una creciente del Alto Paraná se encuentran muchas cosas antes de llegar a la viga elegida. Arboles enteros, desde luego, arrancados de cuajo y con las raíces negras al aire, como pulpos. Vacas y mulas muertas, en compañía de buen lote de animales salvajes ahogados, fusilados o con una flecha plantada aún en el vientre. Altos conos de hormigas amontonadas sobre un raigón. Algún tigre, tal vez; camalotes y espuma a discreción—sin contar, claro está, las víboras. (119)

> [Now, when the waters of the Upper Paraná rise one finds many things before arriving at the chosen log. Entire trees, torn up from the ground, their black roots in the air like squid. Dead cows and mules, accompanied by a good lot of wild animals, all drowned, shot, or with an arrow still stuck in the belly. Tall cones of ants piled on a stump. Maybe a jaguar; *camalotes* and occasionally foam—not counting, of course, the snakes.]

In striking contrast to the elevated, panoramic view, the "sweeping visual mastery of a scene" that typifies colonial landscape description, Quiroga's narrator is located near the surface of the water, practically encountering with Candiyú the dead and decaying matter borne by the current.[50] The monstrous mixing of death and life is narrated from a position close to the man struggling to negotiate the river and not be pulled from his canoe into the sickening, disease-ridden water: details are described down to the horde of ants. The narrator, spatially aligned with Candiyú, is distanced from the "circumspect" Hall, who stays on the porch literally minding his own business. Hall looks on and directs the scene, while the narrator, Candiyú, and eventually the reader share this intimate knowledge of the hazards of the swollen river.

It should be said that this "ground-level" perspective is repeated in many of Quiroga's *relatos de ambiente* and becomes for this reader one of the most distinctive features of his narrative practice. In "El hombre muerto," for example, a man walking alone across his settlement suddenly falls to the ground, mortally impaling himself on the machete he carries; lying there prostrate and helpless, the man contemplates his imminent death.[51] The fascinating effect of the story is largely due to the fact that the narrative perspective follows the man's gaze wandering over the landscape he has labored to order according to his own will, projected from a position that is already aligned with the lowliest creatures and the earth itself: "Por entre los bananos, allá arriba, el hombre ve desde el duro suelo el techo rojo de su casa. A la izquierda, entrevé el monte y la capuera de canelas" [Among the banana trees, there above, the man sees from the hard ground the red roof of his house. To the left, he seems to see the mountain and the patch of cinnamon trees] (654). Quiroga's ability to sustain this ground-level view is also essential to his animal stories, including texts like "La vitalidad de las víboras," and "El pique" and longer works like the Anaconda stories to which we will soon turn.

In "Los pescadores de vigas," Hall's exploitation of the native worker is explicitly represented as a perversion or distortion of his "interchange with nature": far from the rational "common control" advocated by Marx, Candiyú is needlessly, senselessly exposed to the river at its most gruesome and fatal moment. Even the story's title—"The Log Fishers"—captures the ironic degeneration from a rational, humane use of the river to the practices of the British colonist. An ecological perspective complementary to Quiroga's critique of labor abuse emerges in the depiction of the logging outfit Castelhum and Company, which is juxtaposed with Candiyú's story. The legal employment of the company's workers is nearly as perilous as Candiyú's log fishing; they too (hence the plural of the title) are exposed to extremely hazardous working conditions, in "los esfuerzos malgastados en el barro líquido, la zafadura de las palancas, las costaladas bajo la lluvia torrencial. Y la fiebre" [ill-spent efforts in the liquid clay, the strain of the boards, the violent blows beneath torrential rain. And the fever] (118). The company, moreover, grossly wastes timber resources in a region where, as Eidt's *Frontier Settlement in Northeast Argentina* explains, the effects of deforestation on soil quality and erosion had been noted decades earlier.[52] In preparation for the flood they send one thousand logs downstream, a quantity so vast the river becomes clogged and the majority are lost before reaching Buenos Aires.

As I have suggested, critics have with some consistency recognized Quiroga's importance as a writer of socially critical realism; but this environmental or ecological discourse that his *relatos de ambiente* also formulate has less often been considered. In fact critics almost unanimously point to a fundamental conflict between human beings and the natural environment in Quiroga's fiction. For example, in his detailed and very convincing study of "underdevelopment, ideology, and worldview" in Quiroga's Misiones stories, Beauchamp writes: "In all of them . . . in one way or another, and sometimes indirectly, we perceive what Quiroga called his characters' struggles against poverty, or the struggle to conquer or at least survive against the hostile forces of nature."[53] I believe, on the contrary, that Quiroga's work deconstructs the strict opposition between humans and their physical environment that underlies both Beauchamp's remark and the conventional Marxist framework of his study. In much of Quiroga's fiction the natural environment is not represented as inherently "hostile" to human survival and happiness: the problem, on the contrary, is that capitalist industry brings radical changes to the Misiones ecosystem, destroying the balance of the bioregional community. If the protagonists of "A la deriva," "En la noche," and "El desierto" appear to be the hapless victims of a jungle infested with snakes and other deadly creatures, the conventionally anthropocentric focus of these stories is balanced by a different discourse, pluralistic and ecological, that explores from a range of perspectives the ways in which the settlers' efforts to extract surplus value from natural resources affect the human and nonhuman inhabitants of the frontier region.

In this regard Quiroga's aesthetic may be said to resemble the political ecology David Harvey outlines in *Justice, Nature and the Geography of Difference*. As Harvey explains, the contemporary fusion of Marxism and environmental concerns involves a critique of the instrumental view of nature that conventionally shapes Marxist ideas of emancipation from "social want" around the possibility of subjugating nature to human will. The necessary revision, he explains, incorporates a more dialectical understanding of the interdependence of human beings and the rest of the natural world in order to express both the environment's vulnerability to human destruction and (here drawing directly on Horkheimer and Adorno's critique of instrumental reason in *The Dialectic of Enlightenment*) "the connection between the domination of nature and the domination of others."[54] In many of Quiroga's stories, the problem is not the inherent malignity of the jungle, but the way that capitalist exploitation transforms local workers' reasonable relationship with the land into an irrational and mutually destructive situation.

Quiroga's critical observation of Hall and Castelhum is typical of the emergence of a new, ecological perspective on colonialism that environmental historian Thomas R. Dunlap sees developing in the early years of the twentieth century. As Dunlap explains, ecology signified a reconsideration of imperialism's fundamental assumptions about land and natural resources:

> Ecology's perspective challenges ideas inherited from Europe and rooted in settler culture by the experience of expansion. It speaks of limits, and shows how near they are. The settler societies have stressed the inexhaustibility of the land and built their dreams on the chance of wealth for all. It [ecology] sees people as part of the system of the land and speaks of us as citizens of a biological community. The settlers have spoken most often of conquest.[55]

Quiroga, like colonists in East Africa, Australia, and India, recognized the environmental havoc that imperialist enterprises had wreaked, noting problems ranging from forest depletion and wildlife scarcity to changing climate patterns. What seem most extraordinary in his response to the crisis are (1) his willingness to abandon the white settlers' conventional claims to the right to manage the conservation of those resources and (2) his desire to explore alternatives that do not overtly emulate indigenous practices but that protest the disenfranchisement of conquered peoples through their alienation from the land.

Los desterrados: Quiroga's Eco-Poetics

It would be a mistake to suggest that British colonial writers were incapable of grasping either the limitations of colonizers' endurance or expanding empires' effects on the environment; their exploration of the latter subject, however, is almost inevitably bounded by the Manichean relationship of colonizer and colonized. Rudyard Kipling's corpus provides some of the most sophisticated and creative examples of this probing, which may ultimately explain why Quiroga was so intrigued by his work. "The Bridge Builders" is one such text: what begins as a story about a feat of British engineering in India is deeply disturbed when latent forces of native / natural resistance irrupt into the surface of the text.[56] Its protagonist is an English engineer whose three-year effort to construct a bridge over the Ganges in northeastern India has led him to change "the face of the country . . . for seven miles around." Despite his extensive efforts to stabilize the terrain, a flash flood threatens to dislodge his work. Most important, a mythic subtext rises along with the surging river: as floodwaters engulf the bridge, Findlayson is led by his third-in-command, Peroo, on an opium-induced journey to meet the gods of popular Hinduism. Mother Gunga, goddess of the river, has gathered Kali, Krishna, Ganesh, and Hanuman to convince them to support her in destroying the bridge, which she sees as an offense against the gods and the people of India. "They fed me the corpses for a month," she says, "and I flung them out on my sand-bars, but their work went forward. Demons they are, and sons of demons! And ye left Mother Gunga alone for their fire-carriage to make a mock of" (179–180). After debate, Krishna convinces the others to allow the bridge to stand, because its temporary destruction would only waste more Indian lives. The gods disappear as Findlayson awakes, banishing the encounter to the realm of unreality and congratulating himself on the bridge's endurance of the receding floodwaters (164).

Here as elsewhere Kipling represents India in a series of attributes that are both attractive and threatening to the rational Western male—femininity, spirituality, nature—and that must be controlled if the colonial agent is to succeed, or even survive. But in linking the native people to their natural environment, his incursion into Hindu spirituality imparts an urgent critique of the British ambition to dominate nature rather than harmonize with it. While appearing to sympathize with the engineer, Kipling has made a series of authorial choices that trivialize Findlayson's work, even before Mother Gunga reveals its terrible human cost. When she does, the story shows that British scientism and will-to-power have distorted the natives' relations with the land so that their "exchange with nature" is now a dangerous, deadly necessity. In other words, Kipling reveals the issue "not far from the heart of all environmental politics," the problem of how the domination of nature becomes the domination of others.[57] "The Bridge Builders" resembles Kipling's most ideologically ambiguous fictions in that the narrative tension has as much to do with the success or failure of Findlayson's bridge as with the conflict between two opposite worldviews. Straining against the imperialists' conception of nature as a commodity to be exploited and transformed is a native cosmology that integrates nature and culture, humans, beasts, water, and soils in an interdependent whole. To the extent that Findlayson's dream is represented as a kind of fantastical, magical real, the text crosses over into an alternative subjectivity that is uneasily contained within the master discourse.[58]

Kipling nevertheless does restrain the irrupting native / natural discourse that threatens to dominate the narrative text; as a writer and a subject of the British Empire he has too much invested in Britain's national project to abandon it altogether (despite the sheer creative delight one senses in his representation of the Hindu gods). This conflictive, often creative dualism that animates Kipling's best work is "released" in Quiroga's Misiones stories as the colonists' struggle to subdue and transform the environment gives way to a sense of communal integration; in the later stories this often occurs in the death of the protagonist, as the human subject who has struggled to distinguish and defend himself from

"The Freedom in the Field" 63

the other elements of the environment encounters death as a kind of release into the inevitability of natural cycles. As Alonso remarks regarding "Las moscas," "the protagonist's decease is presented simply as a transition . . . The story thus projects a kind of materialistic pantheism that points to a survival of the spirit based on the indestructibility of matter even as it decomposes."[59] Martha Canfield describes at greater length Quiroga's "pantheism," which she sees developing particularly in the stories written after 1920:

> We can deduce that what is fundamental to the world-view that Quiroga has been constructing throughout his experience of the jungle is that each and every creature is irreplaceable until, in nature's constant process of becoming, it is replaced. In that moment the individual returns to the totality and is confused in the indeterminate unity, which in turn provides the origin of other determined and irreplaceable individuals. This is rooted in the inexhaustible energy of the life cycle.[60]

In *Los desterrados*, the 1926 collection on which my final remarks will focus, the sense of ecological equality Canfield describes animates the texts. Taken as a whole they represent Misiones as a "bioregional community," exploring the interrelated experiences of different human and nonhuman actors from their individual perspectives. "Tacuará-Mansión" and "Los destiladores de naranjas" consider the European expatriates who degenerate in Misiones, frustrated and disillusioned by the failure of their scientific and agricultural experiments. "El hombre muerto" considers humans' ultimate inability to separate themselves from the natural environment as a dying settler slowly watches the land he has worked to subdue slip from his control. "El regreso de Anaconda" looks at the effects of capitalist industry on the plants and animals of the upper Paraná, and "Los desterrados" presents two local workers who are fundamentally alienated from the land by the arrival of large-scale agriculture.

When *Los desterrados* was originally published in 1926, its full title was *Los desterrados: tipos de ambiente*. Idiomatically translated as "Exiles: frontier types," a more literal equivalent would read: "The unlanded: environmental figures." While Quiroga was undoubtedly interested in presenting his readers with what he calls the "tipos pintorescos" or "picturesque types" of the frontier region (especially in stories like "Los destiladores de naranjas" and "Tacuará-Mansión") the second, oxymoronic meaning is equally indicative of Quiroga's project in this, his most cohesive and critically successful collection, in which he represents the dispossession or alienation of persons who remain, essentially and inextricably, part of their environment. These stories in particular demonstrate the sense of balance in Quiroga's ecologism, which oscillates between careful attention to the natural environment and the crucial fact that the control of nature is ultimately always a question of social, political, and economic power: the control of other people. The story of Joao Pedro and Tirafogo, two Brazilian laborers who die on the border between Argentina and Brazil, unable to return to their homeland, was originally published as "Los proscriptos" (literally, "the forbidden," or "the banished"), but in editing the collection Quiroga changed the title to "Los desterrados."[61] As Lafforgue and Baccino Ponce de León write, the alteration tightens the text's political implications: the two men are not only exiles but, "the dispossessed of the earth, the landless," and their alienation from the *patria* is less a question of geographic location than—as we have seen in "La patria en la selva"—economic and environmental change.[62] (Quiroga's positive emphasis on the transnational qualities of the region, particularly in the spontaneous and "fuertemente sabroso" [strongly appealing] mixing of Brazilian Portuguese, Argentinean Spanish, and Guaraní, also suggests that their nostalgia for Brazil arises from something other than nationalism.) In fact what we learn is that these two men have been alienated from their customary relationship to the land by the arrival of large-scale yerba mate, ranching, and logging industries in Misiones. "Ahora el país era distinto, nuevo, extraño y difícil. Y ellos, Tirafogo y Joao Pedro, estaban muy viejos para reconocerse en él" [Now the country was different, new, strange and difficult. And they, Tirafogo and Joao Pedro, were too old to find themselves in it] (632).

Neither of them fits stereotypes of "native" innocence—Joao Pedro has killed at least three men, Tirafogo prides himself on his lack of legal identity—but they miss the old days in Misiones, when "no se conocía entonces la moneda, ni el Código Rural, ni las tranqueras con candado, ni los breeches" [currency, and the Rural Code, and fences, and breeches were all unknown] (631). As Leonor Fleming points out, the metonymic breeches indicate the arrival of the exploitative British colonists who wore riding pants on their plantations.[63] The present differs from the past, "como la realidad de un sueño" [like reality from a dream] and the men are nostalgic for the time "cuando no había límite para la extensión de los rozados, y éstos se efectuaban entre todos y para todos, por el sistema cooperativo" [there was no limit to the extension of the fields, and those were between all and for all, by the cooperative system] (631). Their nostalgia is antithetical to the positive value given to the standards of "progress" in one of the best-known Spanish American regional novels, Rómulo Gallegos's *Doña Bárbara* (Venezuela, 1929). For Gallegos's heroic protagonist, Santos Luzardo, legitimizing and securing private property by fencing in individual landholdings is the only way to incorporate Venezuela's llanos into the modern state.

"The Freedom in the Field" 65

A "modern" and seemingly rational response to the exploitation of the workers takes place in Misiones simultaneous to Joao Pedro and Tirafogo's attempted departure, in the form of an organized labor movement. The movement, however, which historically spread from Buenos Aires to the frontier in 1919, seems too foreign—and perhaps too urban—to have much success in Misiones. Quiroga ironically writes:

> Viéronse huelgas de peones que esperaban a Boycott, como a un personaje de Posadas, y manifestaciones encabezadas por un bolichero a caballo que llevaba la bandera roja, mientras los peones alfabetos cantaban apretándose alrededor de uno de ellos, para poder leer la Internacional que aquél mantenía en alto. Viéronse detenciones sin que la caña fuera su motivo—y hasta se vio la muerte de un sahib. (295–296)

> [There were strikes by peons awaiting the arrival of Boycott, as if he were someone from Posadas, and demonstrations led by a mounted shopkeeper carrying the red flag, while the literate workers sang, pressing around one to read the Internationale he held high. There were arrests completely unrelated to rum—and even the death of a sahib.]

The conspicuous choice of the term "sahib" for a foreign administrator killed during the protests indicates again Quiroga's desire to locate Misiones' history within the context of British imperialism, a hegemony that is being contested as much in the violence of the workers as in the narrator's own project. But the labor movement, misexplained and misunderstood by those it is intended to liberate, is uneasily juxtaposed with the nostalgic tone of the main narrative, as if to suggest that this is an "inorganic" and therefore unfeasible response to the problem of the dispossessed or displaced workers.

In "El regreso de Anaconda," as in "Anaconda," published two years earlier, and "La guerra de los yacarés," resistance to settlement and capitalist expansion is figured as the revolt of the natural world.[64] In "Anaconda" the snakes of the Upper Paraná band together to drive out the men who have come to develop the Serotherapy Institute, capturing poisonous snakes and keeping them in cages in order to extract periodically their venom for use in serum. Anaconda survives the general slaughter of the final pages to reappear in "El regreso de Anaconda" (1925), in which she leads a failed attempt to keep steamships out of the upper Paraná by blockading the river. In representing her efforts Quiroga constructs what Said calls a "geographical inquiry into historical experience," a dialectical representation of the historically dynamic relationships among the human, animal, and plant species that inhabit a given environment and the water, soil, air, and other resources they share. The story unfolds as a minute and particular examination of an ecosystem and the changes it undergoes when capitalist development enters the region. The story begins during a severe drought, a time of privation and also (as in Kipling's *Jungle Book*) a time when the animals cooperate to ensure the survival of the species. Anaconda convinces them to work together against their common enemy, man, rallying them in language that Quiroga rather playfully borrows from the contemporary labor movement:

> "¡Hermanos! . . . Todos somos iguales, pero juntos. Cada uno de nosotros, de por sí, no vale gran cosa. Aliados, somos toda la zona tropical. ¡Lancémonos contra el hombre, hermanos!"[65]

> [Brothers! . . . we are all equal, together. Each one of us, alone, is not worth much. Allied, we are all the topical region. Let's throw ourselves against man, brothers!]

When the deluge begins, she urges the animals to travel downstream with her to construct a blockade from the debris she knows will collect in the estuary. As the jungle and its creatures float along, Anaconda acquires a shelter, a lean-to that has been unearthed and is carried by the current. Inside a *mensú* lies dying; without knowing why, Anaconda defends him from the other creatures. When they arrive at the estuary her plan is defeated: the *camalotes*, immense water plants she hoped to mass together with the logs and other matter, drift off to the banks in order to bloom:

> Embriagados por el vaivén y la dulzura del ambiente, los camalotes cedían dóciles a las contra corrientes de la costa, remontaban suavemente el Paraná en dos grandes curvas, y paralizábanse por fin a lo largo de la playa a florecer. (622)

> [Intoxicated by the swaying and the sweetness of the atmosphere, the *camalotes* docilely succumbed to the countercurrents of the coast, gently drifted back up the Paraná in two great curves, and finally halted along the beach to flower.]

Defeated, Anaconda begins to lay her own eggs near the body of the man, and dies nearby when she is shot by one of the men on a steamboat.

By adopting the perspective of the boa, Quiroga explores a relationship with the environment outside the assumptions underpinning capitalism's exploitation of natural resources. In doing so, he addresses the Judeo-Christian "doctrine of dominion" expressed in the Genesis account of the Garden of Eden: "Then God said, 'Let us make man in our image, after our likeness; and let them have dominion over the fish of the sea and over the birds of the air, and over the cattle, and over all the earth, and over every creeping thing that creeps upon the earth'" (Gen. 26:1). In literature of the colonial jungle, the danger of poisonous snakes often elevates an ecological peril to a mythological, moral confrontation between good and evil, as is the case in Kipling's *Jungle Book:* the Rikki-Tikki-Tavi story, for example, has a native mongoose protecting an English family from the cobras that would rule the garden of their bungalow. In fact, scholars have described Kipling's rewriting of the story of humankind's expulsion from paradise as an idealized negotiation with India's indigenous society, from which Kipling himself had been expelled in early childhood.[66] If Kipling longingly stages a kind of prelapsarian reintegration into (Indian) Nature, Quiroga's depiction of the serpent as the wisest of creatures suggests a cosmology that transcends both the distinctions of good and evil in the Western tradition and the Manichean allegory of colonialist discourse.

According to Anaconda's worldview, it is the settlers' desire radically to transform the Misiones environment—the God-given right of "dominion" of the Judeo-Christian tradition—that inherently alienates them from the rest of nature. She recalls the arrival of the colonists:

> Un hombre, primero, con su miserable ansia de ver, tocar y cortar, había emergido tras del cabo de arena con su larga piragua. Luego otros hombres, con otros más, cada vez más frecuentes. Y todos ellos sucios de olor, sucios de machetes y quemazones incesantes. (610)

> [A man, first, with his miserable longing to see, touch, and cut down, had emerged around the sandbar with his long canoe. Later other men, with still others, each time more often. And all of them dirty-smelling, dirty with their machetes and their incessant burning.]

For Anaconda the process the settlers consider colonization is purely destructive. Quiroga's incorporation of the dying *mensú* into the narrative signals an important distinction between the local peoples' use of natural resources and the newcomers': the *mensú,* found in a poor shack, organically constructed and so lightweight that it is pulled along by the current upon a raft of *camalotes,* seems to have integrated his own activities into the natural biological order rather than pursuing the kind of large-scale deforestation the newcomers intend.

Despite Quiroga's jocular, ironic deployment of the egalitarian language of labor unions in the speech of the somewhat bullying Anaconda, he develops a system of representation that disperses the set of hierarchies, boundaries, and binary oppositions that commonly structure colonialist discourse, including Kipling's. The floodwaters that threaten to wipe out human endeavor are here a liberating force that lifts up the different species and takes them sailing downstream:

Había llegado la hora. Ante los ojos de Anaconda, la zona al asalto desfiló. Victorias nacidas ayer, y viejos cocodrilos rojizos; hormigas y tigres; camalotes y víboras; espumas, tortugas y fiebres, y el mismo clima diluviano que descargaba otra vez—la selva pasó, aclamando al boa, hacia el abismo de las grandes crecidas. (615)

[The time had come. While Anaconda watched, the entire region marched to the assault. *Victorias* born yesterday, and ruddy old crocodiles; ants and tigers; *camalotes* and snakes; foam, turtles and fevers, and the same diluvian weather let loose again—the jungle passed, calling to the boa, toward the abyss of the great floods.]

The joyful intermingling of species as they float downstream corresponds to the river's liberation from its banks and the great, unrestrained wash of water over the land. In their journey the narrative traces a complex and richly detailed geography of Misiones, all described as if through the gaze of the snake. The result is an awareness of place that is free of the topographical markers of Western rationalism: the precise, mathematical calculations of distances and demarcations of borders and property lines that legitimate and regulate colonial commodification of the land. The narrating voice is once again strategically located at ground level: "Toda serpiente de agua," Quiroga writes, "sabe más de hidrografía que hombre alguno" [Every water-snake knows more about hydrography than any man] (620).

Anaconda's sympathy for the dying *mensú* places him within the bioregional community from which the new arrivals are excluded. She finds him with his throat slashed, and pities him because he is "un desgraciado mensú. . . . Un pobre individuo, como todos los otros," [an unfortunate laborer. . . . A poor individual, like all the others] (619), a victim of violence and lawlessness. When the shelter on which he and Anaconda have been floating arrives in the estuary and draws near a steamship, one of the men standing on its bow shoots her. He claims as he does so that it is to avenge the death of the man inside:

—¡Allá!—alzóse de pronto una voz en el vaporcito.—¡En aquel embalsado! ¡Una enorme víbora!
—¡Qué monstruo!—gritó otra voz. ¡Y fíjense! ¡Hay un rancho caído! Seguramente ha matado a su habitante.
—¡O lo ha devorado vivo! Estos monstruos no perdonan a nadie. Vamos a vengar al desgraciado con una buena bala. (623)

["There!" another voice on the little steamer suddenly shouted. "On that raft! An enormous snake!"
"What a monster!" another voice shouted. "And look! There's a fallen shack! It must have killed the inhabitant."

"Or else she ate him alive! Those monsters don't forgive anyone. Let's avenge the poor guy with a good shot."]

In this final scene, the jocular, sportsmanlike attitude of the newcomers, combined with their location on the steamship, reiterate their alienation from the bioregional community formed by Anaconda and the laborer on his floating hut. Meanwhile Anaconda and the *camalotes* relinquish their own construction project. Rather than building a barrier across the Paraná, each gives in to the cycles of birth and death that seem to pull them away from their common purpose. The otherwise unaccountable sexual connotations of the language describing the *camalotes'* withdrawal from the estuary, for example, suggest an incipient maternal instinct: "la pasión de la flora había quemado el brío de la gran crecida" [the passion of the flowers had burned off the zeal of the great flood] (623). Anaconda, drawn by her sympathy for the dead *mensú* and strangely attracted to the warmth of his decaying body, draws near and deposits her eggs beside him so that his death will be "más que la resolución final y estéril del ser que ella había velado" [more than the final and sterile resolution of the being she had watched over] (622). Her own death, shot by the new arrivals, is a triumph of ultimate integration and creativity.

"El regreso de Anaconda" may present as clear a demonstration of Quiroga's politics as any of his stories, even though—and perhaps even because—the characters are nearly all animals. Not a fable (a representation of human qualities and relationships in animal forms), the narrative is a verbalization of the real relationships among Misiones' different species. As such, it stages the effects of capitalist development on Misiones' most disempowered inhabitants and demonstrates the kind of radical, epistemological change the ideal of political ecology entails. Quiroga's ground-level perspective is an important beginning, because it allows him to transcend the abstractions and valuations that characterize Western discourse on nature and to look at the environment instead as a dynamic system of minutely interrelated parts, and to conceptualize nature in such a way that humans are not excluded from or set against the environment but symbiotically located within it.

Quiroga's stories transcend the terms in which we ordinarily think about and discuss political issues, the categories of nation, class, gender, and race that structure cultural discourse in the nineteenth and twentieth centuries and subsequently our own often academic debates. Frequently cited as one of Latin America's first fully antihegemonic writers, Quiroga is also, as I have argued, a colonial writer, a writer whose literary production is profoundly shaped by informal imperialism and the modern experience of capitalist expansion. At the same time, his understanding of imperialism and colonialism is not structured by the stark opposition of cultures, races, or political regimes that typifies both colonialist and postcolonial discourses on formal imperialism. It is relatively free of what Said calls the "metaphysical weight" of the project of imperialism, the nationalistic, Eurocentric civilizing imperative that bore upon Kipling and Conrad—but also upon the positivist discourse that flourished in the Río de la Plata and is most fully embodied by Domingo F. Sarmiento's *Facundo: Civilización y barbarie*.[67] Instead, Quiroga's narratives are structured by more pluralistic configurations of power, which allow the geographical "subtext" of much colonial literature to rise to the surface, becoming not only the site and subject of violent confrontation but the source of a new sense of communal identity and resistance to the alienating effects of capitalist development. His sense of solidarity with local workers therefore grows: what begins as an essentially colonial project of adaptation to new environmental conditions expands to incorporate the region's indigenous human and nonhuman inhabitants. In the process, the capitalist's conception of territory as a commodity to be possessed and exploited is transformed into a vision of the land as a source of shared identity and ground for collective transformation.

2

The Geography of Resistance in Benito Lynch's El inglés de los güesos

Si a ella le hubieran dicho, por ejemplo, que El inglés de los güesos *se quedaría una hora más en el "puesto" bajo la condición expresa de que Inglaterra desarmase sus escuadras, diera su libertad a Irlanda, Jibraltar a los españoles y el Canadá a los canadienses, ella hubiese respuesto alzándose de hombros y tan extrañada y despectiva como el mundo: "¿Nada más que eso? ¡Oy, qué pavada!"*
—Benito Lynch, El inglés de los güesos

[*If they had told her, for example, that* The Englishman of the bones *could stay an hour more on the "post" under the express condition that England disarmed its squadrons, gave Ireland its freedom, gave Gibraltar to the Spanish and Canada to the Canadians, she would have responded by shrugging her shoulders, as amazed and scornful as the rest of the world: "Nothing more than that? Oh, what a cinch!"*]

Being a savage by birth, she took no trouble to hide her feelings, and the Englishman was amused.
—Rudyard Kipling

FROM THE SIMPLE STORY OF an English archaeologist who falls in love with the daughter of humble gauchos who shelter and feed him during his expedition on the Argentinean pampa Benito Lynch constructed a small masterpiece, his 1924 novel *El inglés de los güesos* [The Englishman of the Bones].[1] The book is at once a radical appropriation of the narratives so many British travelers wrote about their experiences in the Río de la Plata in the nineteenth and early twentieth centuries and an eccentric version of Argentina's most autochthonous literature, the poems, plays, and novels known as *literatura gauchesca*. Responding to both of these discursive traditions is crucial to Lynch's ideological work in *El inglés de los güesos*, which addresses both the past and present realities of its own historical moment, satirizing the discursive authority that some contemporaries attributed to the British travel-writers while critiquing the socioeconomic transformation their writing in many cases precipitated. In the process, *El inglés de los güesos* demonstrates the multivalent effexcts of Britain's informal imperialism in Argentina, linking the transculturation of the Europhile land-owning elite to the rapid modernization of ranching and agriculture by foreign capital and the impoverishment of the traditional working class.

The four novels Lynch wrote about Argentina's rural society—*Los caranchos de la Florida* (1916), *Raquela* (1918), *El inglés de los güesos,* and *El romance de un gaucho* (1933)—are all more critical of the pampa's socioeconomic structure than the conventional *novela gauchesca,* but *El inglés de los güesos* in particular shows the subtle, triangulated relationships among the influence of the thousands of Britons who lived, worked, and invested in Argentina in the late nineteenth century, the modernization of the cattle industry, and the exploitation of the disenfranchised descendants of the legendary gauchos. As a response to the genre of travel-writing, Lynch's most significant correction may be the final scene that he adds to the narrative, which demonstrates the consequences of the scholar's visit on the day after his departure, when the young woman's body is found hanging from a tree. By ending the novel with Balbina's suicide, Lynch extends the narrative beyond the limits of the English traveler's knowledge and experience, gesturing metonymically toward the far-reaching effects of his presence in the region, the consequences of which the visitor is and remains ignorant.

Unlike the other authors discussed in this study—Horacio Quiroga, José Eustasio Rivera, Rómulo Gallegos, and Ricardo Güiraldes—Lynch today is rarely read outside his native country. His work, however, is highly relevant to the study of regionalist fiction, as much for his thematic commitment to the nuanced exploration of place that defines the genre as for the outstanding literary quality of the handful of novels he produced. In the 1920s and 1930s he was widely considered one of Argentina's best novelists, and both Manuel Gálvez and Quiroga effusively praised his work.[2] Quiroga, in fact, was moved to publish an open letter directed to Lynch in the Buenos Aires magazine *Nosotros* after reading *Los caranchos de la Florida* in 1916. This letter, like the one addressed to the author of *La vorágine* a decade later, congratulates the young novelist's achievement and expresses the strong affinity Quiroga felt for another writer engaged in representing the real conditions and material struggle of life in the rural provinces. "Yo vivo en Misiones, en pleno bosque, y desde hace varios años," the letter begins. [I live in Misiones, in the middle of the forest, and have for several years.] It continues:

> En primer término, debo confesarle que muy pocas veces hallé en relatos de la vida del campo cosa alguna que me satisfaciera. No es, como usted sabe,

porque no se nos hubiera martillado los oídos con venganzas de jóvenes, rencores de viejos, idilios de una y otra edad, todo sobre un fondo de siestas, inundaciones y sequías.

Pero yo no veía en tales psicologías nada característico y pujante, ni en las enumeraciones (no me atrevería a decir *descripciones*) del fondo, veía el campo, que bien que mal conozco. ¿He sido yo el único descorazonado? Creo que no. Y aquí cobra cierto valor el grito *nuestro*—digamos—ante *Los caranchos de La Florida.*[3]

[In the first place, I should confess that very rarely have I found in tales of life in the country anything that satisfied me. This isn't, as you know, because our ears are not hammered with the vengeance of youths, the rancor of old men, idylls of every age, all drawn against a background of siestas, floods and droughts.

But I never saw in those psychologies anything characteristic and forceful, nor in the enumerations (I wouldn't dare say *descriptions*) of the setting did I see the countryside as I know it to be. Am I the only one to be so discouraged? I don't think so. And that adds some weight to *our*—let's say "our"—enthusiasm for *Los caranchos de la Florida.*]

The book in question, *Los caranchos de La Florida*, was Lynch's first rural novel. It describes the Oedipal struggle between two ranchers, a father and son who clash over the beautiful daughter of a tenant family. Elements that Lynch was to take up again in *El inglés de los güesos* are already present in *Los caranchos de la Florida*: the "vultures" of the title are don Pancho and don Panchito, who share the same autocratic temperament and control the land and the people who work it like feudal lords, despite their shared interest in modernizing production (the son, don Panchito, returns from studying agriculture in Germany as the novel begins). Not surprisingly, given his own aversion to the conventional rusticity of Spanish American *costumbrismo,* Quiroga singles out the sustained force of characterization and the truthful representation of the land, which Lynch communicates not by overwhelming the reader with local color but by providing the detail that produces what Quiroga calls "*sensación* de campo," the *feeling* of the countryside.[4]

The high critical opinions of Quiroga and Gálvez were met by popular success as well: *El inglés de los güesos* was a best seller in the 1920s and became the basis of a movie in 1941. Though Lynch's renown endured into the 1950s and 1960s, when Roberto Salama and Ulíses Petit de Murat each published book-length studies on him,[5] Lynch and *El inglés de los güesos* fall into oblivion soon after: a pair of articles are all the attention they have received in recent years. Given its literary quality, psychological acuity and sociopolitical relevance, the disappearance of *El inglés de los güesos* raises important questions. The most obvious explanation is that Lynch himself vanished from the literary scene of the Río de la Plata long before his death in 1951; during the last years of his life he intentionally blocked the republication of his work. Even earlier Lynch had shown little interest in promoting his literary career, generally refusing interviews; during the few he did grant, he shifted the topic of conversation onto other subjects, such as his enthusiasm for boxing.[6] As Gálvez remarks, Lynch avoided "literary" conversation and never wrote the essays and articles of literary criticism that kept writers like Quiroga, Ezequiel Martínez Estrada, Jorge Luis Borges, and others in the daily press.[7]

On the other hand, the obscurity into which Lynch has fallen is even more significant in comparison to the posthumous success of Ricardo Güiraldes, his compatriot and contemporary. Güiraldes' *Don Segundo Sombra*, published a year before his death in 1927, has become one of the most admired texts of the period. It, too, is a somewhat belated *novela gauchesca*, telling the story of an orphan boy who runs away from the oppressive guardianship of his aunts in Buenos Aires to learn the life of the gauchos from his new mentor, Don Segundo. Under Don Segundo's tutelage Fabio is initiated into the practical and spiritual knowledge of the pampa, learning to skin a steer, for example, and to contemplate the majestic beauty of the land. The famous surprise ending of *Don Segundo Sombra* arrives when Fabio, now a young man, is told that his deceased biological father was a wealthy rancher, whose property Fabio is about to inherit. Fabio clearly regrets that his new position will separate him from his beloved Don Segundo, but the old gaucho rejects his impulsive desire to divide his new property among many and points out that he now has the knowledge and skills to manage the land wisely.

As Beatriz Sarlo has written, one key behind the lasting success of *Don Segundo Sombra* is that it manages to fuse disparate and conflicting elements of Argentinean society at a time when many felt the national community was being threatened by both massive immigration and economic modernization. The text synthesizes the nationalistic, nostalgic impulses inspired by the celebration of the centennial anniversary of Argentina's independence from Spain with the new, modernist poetics of the avant-garde, but it also projects a nostalgic fantasy that erases class conflict on the pampa and "unifies the culture of the bosses and that of [their] subordinates."[8] As Sarlo explains, Güiraldes achieves this fusion within the traditional framework of the pastoral, proposing in the "return" to the rural setting a return as well to the organic unities of nature and society denied by life in the modern metropolis. She adds that the background of modern pastoralists like Güiraldes "usually aligns them with members of the established order evoked in the pastoral and not, it is clear, with the groups whose labor served as their support and who suffered because of its very concrete impositions."[9] In fact Lynch and Güiraldes were both working within a well established tradition of nativist or *criollista* literature, which had its roots in the nineteenth-century gauchesque poetry of Bartolomé Hidalgo, Hilario Ascasubi and José Hernández, author of the classic *Martín Fierro*. Although gauchesque poetry had a strong political component, the prose fiction that later evolved out of the same tradition was closely connected with romantic *costumbrismo,* and tended to idealize the folkloric and "picturesque" aspects of rural life. These later gauchesque writers—Eduardo Gutiérrez, Eugenio Cambaceres, and others— were (like Güiraldes) generally sons of the landowning elite whose aristocratic view of life on the large ranches rarely questioned or revealed the changing social order.[10]

Lynch also belonged to "the established order." Both sides of the Lynch family, of Irish and Spanish ancestry, had been in the Río de la Plata for generations; the distinguished writer Miguel Cané was a cousin. Nevertheless, Lynch's depictions of rural society consistently resist the aesthetic and ideological fusions of Güiraldes' work in order to reveal class conflict and the socioeconomic transformations of the time. As Sandra Contreras has recently written, Lynch "confronts" the nostalgic pastoral tradition by evoking "the signs of modernization that were increasingly obvious after the turn of the century—just what Güiraldes decides *not to see:* barbed wire fences, windmills, the ever more apparent presence of immigrants, projects of agricultural modernization."[11] Historians tell us that the changes Contreras describes—the mixed blessings of modernization— were stimulated by British capitalists' large-scale investment in the ranching industry, which began in the mid-nineteenth century.

The situation on the pampa, like Quiroga's beloved Misiones a few years later, corresponds to the articulation of a "double" colonialism that I see as particularly characteristic of Britain's informal imperialism in Latin America, in that the pressures of the international market and the massive investment of foreign capital led to the perpetuation and exacerbation of a colonial land-tenure system that in many areas had existed since the years of Spanish rule. The *Conquista del Desierto*, the military operation undertaken by the Argentinean government in 1879 to exterminate the remaining Indians of the pampa and assume control of the territory, resurrected a centuries-old logic of white, European domination in the service of modern capitalist expansion: an influx of British investment resulted in the construction of six thousand kilometers of railroad track between 1870 and 1890 and improved port facilities in Buenos Aires harbor, developments that both facilitated the mission and motivated its speedy completion by laying the groundwork for increasing trade with Europe. The new infrastructure first spurred a boom in cereal production in the rural areas surrounding the capital, then the construction of British and U.S.-owned meatpacking plants outside Buenos Aires made the traditional creole business of ranching lucrative: high-quality stock was imported from Britain, and by the time Lynch was a young man Argentina had become that country's largest supplier of beef. The rapid expansion of trade meant that properties granted to creole families during the independence era and all but ignored since were suddenly extremely valuable.[12]

John Foster Fraser, an Englishman who visited Argentina during the period Lynch depicts, describes the new prosperity of the region:

> the wealthy Spanish Argentine is not the creator of his own wealth. I heard of only one case of a Spanish Argentine owing his great fortune to commercial enterprise. The fortunes of most of these Argentines come from land. Their grandfathers got immense areas by the easiest means. Properties were so enormous that extent was not reckoned in acres, or even square miles, but by leagues. But a hundred leagues, however good for cattle or sheep, or wheat growing—what was its value a couple of hundred miles from a port? Then came British railways. They pierced the prairies. The land bounded in value, tenfold, a thousandfold.[13]

Fraser, of course, has mastered the smug rhetoric of business imperialism, representing the landed creoles as a degenerate, parasitic class, and the enterprising English investors as active, diligent men, the only men virile enough to "pierce" the virginal prairie. Like the "capitalist vanguards," the British travelers of the post-Independence era Mary Louise Pratt analyzes in *Imperial Eyes: Travel Writing and Transculturation*, Fraser emphasizes the creoles' neglect of the natural resources around them in order to legitimate the intervention of the British.[14]

While property values soared thanks to those industrious Englishmen, native laborers frequently found themselves replaced by imported machinery or the European workmen who were deemed more efficient by *estancieros* and their administrators. Many migrated to the cities, competing with millions of immigrants for jobs in service or Buenos Aires's incipient manufacturing industry. Farther out on the pampa, the rapid increase in land values, coupled with a decline in real wages, meant that the thirty thousand hectares annexed by the Conquista del Desierto were divided among established landowners rather than being sold as family farms as earlier statesmen like Bernardino Rivadavia, Juan Bautista Alberdi, and Domingo F. Sarmiento had intended. Many of those large properties were subdivided, according to modern agricultural science, into sections where tenant farmers were employed in growing wheat or alfafa on a rotating basis. *Puesteros,* like the family of the fictional Balbina Fuentes, lived an ironic contrast between their stationary existence and the legendary mobility and freedom of the gauchos: confined to a limited portion of land referred to as a *puesto,* the tenant farmers themselves were *puestos* in the adjectival sense, staying "put" because they were confined to a strictly delineated territory.[15]

Lynch's novel simultaneously confronts the nostalgic pastoral tradition of the Argentinean *novela gauchesca* and the accounts of rural society written by scores of British travelers during the nineteenth and early twentieth centuries. Lynch offered a rare commentary on his work during an interview that Petit de Murat quotes extensively in *Genio y figura de Benito Lynch.* When the anonymous interviewer asks about the genesis of *El inglés de los güesos,* Lynch responds:

> O bien: ¿Darwin, Munster, Haigh, los Robertson? ¿Sería posible que esos simpáticos, ilustrados y andariegos mozos ingleses, que tan a conciencia recorrieron nuestras pampas y que tan largamente convivieron con sus habitantes no tuvieran con alguna muchachita de campo su aventura de amor? ¿La protagonista? . . . ¿Quién podría ser? . . . Esta o aquélla o la de más allá . . . ; cualquiera de esas interesantes chinitas que conocí alguna vez en alguna parte, hace años.[16]
>
> Well: Darwin, Munster, Haigh, the Robertsons? Would it be possible that one of those friendly, enlightened and vagabond English boys, who so conscientiously covered our pampa and lived at such length among its inhabitants had his love adventure with some young country girl? The heroine? Who could it be? This or that or the other one. . . . Any of those interesting *chinitas* I once met, somewhere, years ago.

What intrigues me in Lynch's response—even beyond the list of sources—is his willingness to blur the line between British and creole accounts of the pampa. The British travel narratives often have a surprising amount in common with the Argentinean *gauchescas,* as Britons like Darwin and Francis Bond Head also experienced the pampa as a "return" to a simpler and more authentic culture, despite the scientific and "modern" (very often capitalist) nature of their missions. Certainly the limited span of their visits prevented them from developing a more profound understanding of gaucho society and its history. Lynch will confront this attitude on the part of the British in *El inglés de los güesos;* he will also indict the equally dismissive and proprietary attitude of the creole elite to which he himself belongs, summed up in that casual "cualquiera de esas interesantes chinitas que conocí alguna vez en alguna parte, hace años." One of the central concerns of *El inglés de los güesos*, which this chapter will explore in detail, is precisely this problem of the Argentinean creole's ambiguous positioning between the British capitalists and the traditional working class of the pampa, which involves both their shared modes of representation and the economic collaboration that systematically disenfranchised the gauchos.

El inglés de los güesos confronts the nostalgic pastoral, in its British and Argentinean varieties, through a technique that seems uniquely appropriate to convey Lynch's vision of the Invisible Empire: it captures the ironic contrast between the appearance of Argentina's accelerated export-led development and the realities of informal imperialism, including both the country's increasing economic subordination to Britain and the disenfranchisement of the traditional rural population. The plot achieves this trajectory by adding a chilling epilogue to the story of the Englishman's sojourn on the pampa: Grey returns to England, savoring the memory of his romantic idyll, but the reader is made to understand the story beyond the ending, which is the grim fact of Balbina's suicide. In this regard *El inglés de los güesos* is closer to William Henry Hudson's *The Purple Land*, published nearly forty years earlier, than to *Don Segundo Sombra*. As Borges wrote, *The Purple Land* is a novel about *acriollamiento*, the story of an English subject who becomes acculturated to local values and customs while fighting in Uruguay's civil war.[17] Soon after his return to Montevideo, the narrator learns that his beautiful young wife, whose decision to elope with him has, perhaps permanently, alienated her from her family, is dying of consumption. In *The Purple Land*, then, the protagonist Richard Lamb becomes acculturated and acquires a sense of responsibility to his new community almost simultaneously.[18] Lynch's James Grey, on the other hand, abdicates his responsibility to Balbina and pragmatically returns to Britain to pursue his academic career. Despite the hero's refusal to participate in the process, *El inglés de los güesos* is nonetheless, in its own way, a narrative of *acriollamiento*. In this case the transculturated subject is the reader, who stays behind for one final revelation after Grey has departed and learns to appreciate the passionate nature of the abandoned girl and to understand her family's cultural, social, and economic vulnerability.

At the level of the sentence, the contrast between the ideology of informal imperialism and its reality is deliberately set up by Lynch's pattern of rhetorically invoking the romantic strains of the pastoral tradition—in which I include both Argentinean and British-authored versions—and deflating them through a sharp return to realist discourse. The result is what may be called a failed pastoral, a romantic return to nature that is disappointed by the intrusion of a social realism that insists on describing the material conditions experienced by its working-class protagonists. Any one of several passages would illustrate the rhythm of the failed pastoral, but the following sentence is particularly concise:

> Desde el día aquel en que el doctor Paláu, que le asistía, declaró a míster James fuera de peligro, agregando que *El inglés de los güesos* debería tener "sept vidas com es moix," hasta la fecha, en que doña Casiana creyó descubrir confianzas excesivas entre el huésped y su abnegada enfermera, habían florecido ya más besos en las manos morenas de La Negra que margaritas rojas en las diez mil hectáreas de campo bien cabales que encerraban los alambrados de "La Estancia Grande." (132)

> [From the day when Dr. Paláu, who attended to him, declared Mr. James out of danger, adding that *The Englishman of the bones* would have "seven lives, like a cat," to this one, when doña Casiana discovered what she took for excessive confidences between the house guest and his devoted nurse, there had flourished on the brown hands of La Negra more kisses than red daisies on the ten thousand hectares of good land enclosed by the barbed-wire fences of "La Estancia Grande."]

This passage, rambling in syntax and uneven in tone, encapsulates the whole trajectory of the narrative, which traces a path from the comic realism of the first few pages to the romantic pastoral of the love story and its starkly realistic conclusion. The Catalonian country doctor making his sanguine prognosis appears as a comic character; then, more seriously, Balbina's mother Doña Casiana introduces one of the central concerns of realist fiction, the social and sexual vulnerability of young women of the working class. But her motherly, practical concern that Grey will "take advantage" of Balbina is quickly superseded by the narrator's modulation into the lyrical language of the pastoral, which he uses to figure their relationship in rhetoric that masks its economic and social asymmetries with an image of the natural beauty of the pampa. The narrator's reference to a vast tract of land, picturesquely dotted with flowers, draws on the literary mythology of the pampa as a place of freedom from the constraints of modern society. But in this passage, as in the novel as a whole, the pastoral is invoked only so that it may be deflated by a stinging return to realistic discourse. The final phrase quoted above—"que encerraban los alambrados de 'La Estancia Grande'"—debunks the traditional myth by revealing the realities of rural society at the turn of the century. By then the seemingly limitless land of the pampa was almost entirely divided up into private holdings, not as small family farms but in an anachronistically feudal arrangement that concentrated enormous expanses—the property euphemistically called "The Big Ranch" comprises ten thousand hectares—in the hands of a few wealthy proprietors and foreign corporations, while families like Balbina's earned a humble living as tenant farmers or *puesteros*. Barbed wire was an important innovation of the late nineteenth century, and the fences that criss-cross "La Estancia Grande" seem to hold its human inhabitants in along with the owner's cattle. If barbed wire seems innocuous enough today, we might recall the gruesome death of a boy who becomes entangled in it in Quiroga's "El hijo" (The son).

Lynch's Differential Geographies

Lynch's deflated pastoral, by invoking and rejecting the obfuscatory rhetoric of capitalist ideology, reforms the romantic pastoral into a narrative structure that might be called a geography of resistance. In *Justice, Nature, and the Geography of Difference,* David Harvey develops the notion of a politicized geography as a kind of ideological resistance to what Karl Marx famously identified as "the fetishism of commodities."[19] In the first volume of *Capital,* Marx explains how the market economy simultaneously creates and occludes a network of social relationships between the producers and consumers of goods and services. The determination of exchange value, in other words, replaces both the "physical properties" of the thing being sold and the conditions under which it was produced with a monetary amount so that complex material and social relations are reduced to an exchange of one "thing" (money) for another (the commodity). Marx writes, "There is a definite social relation between men that assumes, in their eyes, the fantastic form of a relation between things."[20]

Harvey, whose contributions include integrating a traditional Marxist commitment to social justice with the contemporary environmental movement, emphasizes the need to uncover the geographical relations obfuscated by commodity fetishism. Although most interpretations of the passage consider only labor issues, Marx's initial statement of the problem clearly indicates that the values and meanings lost in the commodity form are both human and *natural*:

> It is as clear as noon-day, that man, by his industry, changes the forms of the materials furnished by Nature, in such a way as to make them useful to him. The form of wood, for instance, is altered, by making a table out of it. Yet, for all that, the table continues to be that common, every-day thing, wood. But, so soon as it steps forth as a commodity, it is changed into something transcendent.[21]

As Harvey suggests, consumers in the globalized society of today are often ignorant of "a relations of dependence upon a whole world of social labor conducted in many different places under very different social relations and ecological conditions of production."²² The goal of social justice, comprehensively articulated, requires recovering these occluded relationships and tracing "the whole intricate geography and sociality of intersecting markets." In Marx's relatively simple example of the table, recovering the kind of geography Harvey advocates would require tracing the origin of each of the component parts of the table and the tools or machines used to produce it, from the wood to the saw, hammer, nails, and so forth. Harvey's geography would then need to follow the table through all the stages from production to consumption (and beyond), through modes of transportation (railroads, ships) with their own implications for workers and the environment, through merchants to retail stores and into someone's home, considering at each stage the equity of the interactions.

El inglés de los güesos, I will argue, confronts the pastoral tradition as represented by both the conventional *novela gauchesca* and the British travel writers' accounts of the Río de la Plata, revealing the asymmetrical power relations among Argentina's landowning elite, the British capitalists of London and Buenos Aires, and the traditional working class of the pampa. Ironically, rural poverty only increases along with the modernization and capitalization of agricultural production. The remainder of this chapter will explore each of the three component parts of Lynch's analysis of informal imperialism in *El inglés de los güesos*: (1) the use of material detail, through which Lynch most forcefully conveys the growing socioeconomic imbalances of the triangular beef trade; (2) his engagement of British travel writers, through which he challenges their discursive authority in Argentina and critiques Britain's positivist, imperialist ideology; and (3) the tentative emergence of a discourse of cross-class and interracial solidarity through which Lynch seeks to fortify Argentina's weakened defenses against the economic and cultural effects of informal imperialism. Before exploring the geography of resistance in *El inglés de los güesos*, however, I turn to Lynch's little-known first novel, *Plata dorada*, which anticipates many of the central concerns of his more mature work.

Lynch made his first attempt at creating a differential geography like that which Harvey describes in 1909, when he published his first book, called *Plata dorada* ("Gilded silver").²³ Unlike his subsequent works, *Plata dorada* is primarily an urban novel; it is also almost entirely unknown today. Though inferior in quality, *Plata dorada* anticipates several of the central concerns of *El inglés de los güesos*, including the collaboration between landowning elites and British capitalists that was rapidly corrupting Argentina's upper class and impoverishing its rural laborers. Back in the 1880s, Lynch's kinsman Miguel Cané had the following to say about economic modernization in Argentina:

> Nuestros padres eran soldados, poetas y artistas. Nosotros somos tenderos, mercachifles y agiotistas. Ahora un siglo, el sueño constante de la juventud era la gloria, la patria, el amor; hoy es una concesión de ferrocarril para lanzarse a venderla en el mercado de Londres.[24]
>
> [Our fathers were soldiers, poets, and artists. We are grocers, hucksters, and speculators. A century ago, the constant dream of youth was glory, the fatherland, love; today it is a railroad concession to sell on the London market.]

The novel corresponds to most of what is known today about Lynch's early life, and biographer Petit de Murat writes that Lynch later expressed discomfort with the degree of personal disclosure in the text.[25] The first-person narrator is Williams Fernández, whose story begins when he is ten years old and sobbing on a train en route from the family ranch to the city of La Plata where he and his sister are about to begin school. Nostalgia flows through the early chapters of *Plata dorada*, which describe the child's resistance to his new surroundings and the routine demanded by the English school he attends. The mood continues as Williams grows up and becomes increasingly convinced that in comparison to the pampa the city is a decadent environment where he and his creole peers are rapidly degenerating. When Williams finally returns to the countryside near the novel's conclusion, however, his nostalgic expectations are disappointed by the realities of life on the pampa, which combines the worst elements of modernization with cruelty and the semifeudalism of the past.

The education Williams's father has planned for his son is decidedly unsentimental. Not only is the boy denied the outdoor life and the contact with the gauchos of the family ranch he enjoyed as a child; he is also enrolled in an English school where he is expected to learn English manners and customs—such as drinking whisky and walking alone through the city streets—along with the basic requirements of a career in business or engineering. The elder Fernández, as Williams explains, is afflicted by "inglesitis agudo" (a bad case of English-itis) and has decided that his son will be successful only if he is stripped of creole habits and learns to imitate the attitude of the independent and energetic Britons. Williams describes an encounter between his own father and his new schoolmate's:

> "Es mi deseo—dijo—es mi mayor deseo; quisiera convertirlo en un inglés verdadero y he de conseguirlo."
> "Te gusta la raza sajona"—le preguntó entonces el señor Foster.

"¡Vaya si me gusta!—repuso con calor mi padre.—Es una gran raza, es la que va a dominar al mundo con el tiempo." (107)

["It is my desire," he said, "it is my greatest desire; I would like to make him a true Englishman and I must do it."
"You must like the Saxon race," asked Mr. Foster.
"Oh, do I like it!" my father ardently responded. "It is a great race, it is the race that in time will dominate the world."]

Though the elder Fernández is financially ruined by his blind faith in the probity and brilliance of the English businessmen—he loses the family ranch by investing with a British company—his admiration for the British and desire to transform Argentina in imitation of England are unwavering.

Fernández's aversion to his creole heritage is not unique in *Plata dorada*. The title, which translates literally as "gilded silver," refers to the superficial sheen put on by the upwardly mobile middle class in its effort to win the approval of the British capitalists and imitate their success. La Plata, which is located some sixty kilometers from Buenos Aires, was founded in 1882 (eight years before the Lynch family moved there) so that the province of Buenos Aires would have a political capital separate from that of the republic. In Lynch's rendering, the city was created by and for the transatlantic trade, and developed extremely quickly with the profits from beef and cereals. Things English are all the rage among the young creoles: boys and girls attend English schools, speak perfect English, and imitate British manners, customs, and dress. Williams wears corduroy trousers, smokes a pipe and—like the biographical Lynch—practices *el box* in an effort to become as fit and disciplined as his English peers. Blue-eyed and fair, by the time he reaches adulthood Williams is able to "pass" as an Englishman in La Plata, but his father's failure makes him doubt the possibility of truly assimilating English habits.

Like many Spanish Americans confronting Anglo-Saxon imperialism in the early twentieth century, Williams begins to formulate an oppositional Latin American identity in response. Unlike the defiant discourses writers such as José Martí, José Enrique Rodó, and José Vasconcelos produced in response to the aggressions of the United States, however, Williams's sense of the Latin "race" is pessimistic, and he falls into a language of gloomy racial determinism that more closely resembles less celebrated works like Sarmiento's "Conflictos y armonías de las razas en América" and Alcides Arguedas's *Pueblo enfermo*. Of his father, for instance, Williams laments, "El pobre ignoraba el poder de la sangre, la imposibilidad de esa transformación que no podrán operar nunca ni el ambiente, ni la educación, ni las costumbres impuestas, ni aun esa buena voluntad de nuestra raza latina hacia las grandes modificaciones, hacia los grandes progresos y sobre todo hacia aquello que nos viene de afuera y que es exótico" (17) [The poor man didn't know the power of the blood, the impossibility of that transformation that cannot be achieved by environment, education, imposed customs or even the goodwill of our Latin race toward great changes, toward great progress and above all toward that which comes from outside and is exotic.]

The last few chapters of *Plata dorada* focus on the love affair between Williams and another Argentinean, the beautiful Manuela Belgrano (neé Belgrani), the daughter of Italian immigrants who attempts to "pass" as a descendant of one of Argentina's most illustrious families. Once an outsider among creole high society, Manuela becomes the protegée of rich Mr. Linck and transforms herself into "the perfect Englishwoman." Linck takes Williams into his protection as well, putting him in charge of the creamery he is developing on open land near the Paraná River to the north. The story seems to be approaching a happy ending when Manuela visits Williams at the creamery and agrees to marry him, but their love is doomed by what Williams describes as the conflict between their passionate instincts and the physical and emotional restraint demanded by the English. When Linck and his associate Sylvan discover the couple in their first sexual encounter, Manuela dives into the Paraná and attempts to swim away, only to be gruesomely killed by that nineteenth-century icon of trade and progress, the British steamer.

Plata dorada anticipates *El inglés de los güesos* in connecting the "contamination" of Argentina's urban middle class by British capitalism to the degeneration of the social structure of the countryside. The young protagonist, seeking relief from the fetid air of the metropolis, finds that the nostalgia he has nursed since childhood cannot be satisfied by returning to that lost Eden, because Eden itself has become infected with the disease of English-itis. A metropolitan bank foreclosed on the family ranch years ago, and now Williams's position on the pampa is dependant upon his acquiescence to the dictates of the British. Significantly, it is *Sylvan* and *Linck* who intrude upon his relationship with Manuela, as if to remind Williams that even this rustic territory is inseparable from the new rules of the metropolis; even the bucolic idyll is bounded by their authority.

It is in *Plata dorada*, in other words, that Lynch first shows the insalubrious links between the capitalization of the city and the exploitation of the countryside. The clearest example occurs one evening during Williams's tenure at the creamery: he and the English overseer relax outside their office awaiting the arrival of a messenger from La Plata. Williams is watching the stars, dreaming about Manuela and listening vaguely as Mr. Barley describes the "admirable progress that European industry makes each day," when finally a rider appears. It is not the messenger they expected, but rather a gaucho who asks, following a long-standing tradition of the pampa, for permission to spend the night among the working men of their establishment. Barley quickly rebuffs the supplicant, directing him toward a public hotel two leagues away. Williams informs us that the man made little attempt to elicit his sympathy, convinced in all likelihood that he was English too (346). Then he confesses:

> Me pareció que aquel hombre era la encarnación de mi raza, la triste imagen de mi raza débil, que desalojada por la conquista mansa, pero firme, volvía la espalda a lo suyo para hundirse por los siglos de los siglos en el misterio insondable de la nada...
> —Estos pícaros se creen que ésta es una estancia de gauchos—murmuró míster Barley.
> Y yo sentí frío en el corazón y vergüenza de mi mismo.
>
> [It seemed to me that that man was the embodiment of my race, the sad image of my own weak race that, ejected by a mild but firm conquest, turned its back on its own to bury itself for centuries in the impenetrable mystery of nothingness . . .
> "These jokers think this is a ranch of gauchos," murmured Mr. Barley.
> And I felt cold in my heart and ashamed of myself.]

This scene anticipates Lynch's treatment of the disenfranchisement of rural laborers in later texts, such as *Los carranchos de la Florida, Raquela,* and *El inglés de los güesos:* the propertyless gaucho forced to pay for a night's lodging in a commercial hotel rather than be given shelter by a paternalistic *estanciero* epitomizes the alienation of traditional rural society by the modern, foreign commodification of labor.

Williams's sudden ambivalence toward his own identity is also significant: up to this point he has delighted in his nickname, "El inglés," and his acceptance by the British community of La Plata. In this case, however, the gaucho's (presumed) assumption that he is English prompts Williams to imagine momentarily a creole or Argentinean solidarity that transcends class divisions: "It seemed to me that that man was the embodiment of *my race,* the sad image of *my own weak race*" (emphasis added). Sustaining this inclusive identity beyond the momentary impulse that prompts it, Williams realizes, would mean renouncing both the traditional advantages of his class and the new privilege of his association with Linck. He finds himself uncomfortably, if gainfully, employed as the mediator between foreign capital and the rural poor of his own country.

El inglés de los güesos also creates a differential geography like the one Harvey describes by demystifing the economic distortions of ranching and the international beef industry and translating the relation between things back into human form. It is in many ways a more sophisticated and subtle novel than *Plata dorada;* the explicit commentary on British imperialism that is occasionally heavy-handed in the earlier novel is kept to a minimum here. Instead, Lynch conveys his social and economic concerns more obliquely, through the strategic use of material detail that, as Quiroga wrote, is one of the outstanding characteristics of his style. The most obvious contrast is that of the material and psychic universes inhabited by Balbina and James Grey. Grey is a rising young academic from Oxbridge; Balbina is an illiterate girl from an unnamed spot on the pampa. Her home is a rough *ranchito,* furnished with piles of leather skins and "el vetusto mueble que doña Casiana denominara pomposamente cómoda, y que del mismo modo se usaba para guardar ropas femeninas íntimas como artículos de almacén o productos de la huerta" [that ancient piece of furniture that doña Casiana grandly called a bureau, and which was used to hold intimate articles of feminine clothing right along with groceries and produce from the garden], (119). Grey arrives with all of the gear of a nineteenth-century man of science, exotic items that fascinate Balbina:

> Inmóvil, y con una mano apoyada en la mesa, la niña lo observaba todo; la cama de míster James, cubierta con un poncho leonado; el *winchester,* que pendía de la pared; la caja del microscopio, las botas de caucho . . . y, por último, allá en el rincón junto al lavabo, aquel gran baúl misterioso, forrado en cuero de vaca, y en el cual al decir de Bartolo, "el míster escuendía todas sus *macanitas.*" (121)

> Immobile, and with a hand resting on the table, the girl observed everything; Mister James' bed, covered with a tawny poncho; the winchester rifle, hanging from the wall, the microscope in its box, the rubber boots . . . and finally, there in the corner by the washbasin, that great mysterious trunk, bound in cowhide, in which as Bartolo said, "Mister hid all his little things."

Opening the trunk, Balbina finds even more objects, all representing for her the strange and alluring life that James enjoys in the metropolis: books, letters, eyeglasses, medicine, and photos of his university classmates and even an English dance-hall girl, blond and "toda desnuda" (all naked) in her skimpy evening dress. The novel's treatment of the material differences between James's world and Balbina's is often fairly lighthearted: when Balbina pouts about never having seen such a thing as an evening dress, for example, the narrator comments: "Se hubiese dicho, al oírla, que míster James tenía la culpa de que ella y tantos otros millones de hermosas muchachas estuviesen condenadas a morir sin gustar nunca jamás de tales maravillas. Pero *El ingés de los güesos,* que no podía advertir esas sutilezas, agregó en seguida riendo: 'Cuando Babino vaya en Buenos Aires pone también así.'" (106) [One might have said, hearing her, that Mister James was to blame for the fact that she and so many other millions of lovely girls were fated to die without ever having enjoyed such marvels. But *The Englishman of the bones,* unaware of such subtleties, added laughing: "When Babino goes to Buenos Aires, she'll dress that way too"] (106). As the narrator's ironic tone conveys, Lynch saw the dance halls and other degraded and degrading spectacles of London's turn-of-the-century popular culture as a small loss to the beautiful, "barbarously innocent" Balbina, who embodies the more wholesome diversions of Argentina's traditional rural culture.

In fact, much of what we see of the developing relationship between Balbina and James is recounted through the same lightly ironic and amused tone, as if the narrative were written in direct imitation of the style of the British travel writers. This style is repeatedly interrupted, nonetheless, by the abrupt intrusions of realist discourse that characterize Lynch's deflated pastoral. Particularly in describing the social and material conditions of Balbina's peers, Lynch segues into the stark, naturalist tones of *Los caranchos de la Florida* and *El romance de un gaucho*. The young gaucho Santos Telmo, for example, is first introduced in the humorous role of Balbina's persistent, hangdog suitor; but he soon becomes a compelling image of the impoverishment and social disintegration of rural society. We learn through free indirect discourse that his hopeless love for Balbina, illusory as it is, is the one positive element in an otherwise bleak existence:

> Santos Telmo era varón, y además de varón, dos veces "guacho" . . . ¿Qué podía esperar del mundo con flaquezas? ¡La ternura del retorcido poste de *ñandubay* en que se apoyaba, la ternura de aquel hombre de pera tordilla, que mientras él sufría andaba por allí descolgando unos cueros con la misma cruel indiferencia con que, veinte años antes, ensilló su caballo una mañana, para irse a otros pagos, abandonando al horror de su destino unos bellos ojos de mujer, suplicantes y enrojecidos de llorar, porque el que se había atrevido a ser padre no se atrevía a ser marido! (116)

> Santos Telmo was a male, and besides male, an orphan twice over. . . . What could he expect from this meager world? The tenderness of the twisted *ñandubay* post he leaned against, the tenderness of that gray-bearded man, who while he suffered went around picking up hides with

the same cruel indifference as twenty years earlier, when he saddled his horse for other pastures, abandoning to the horror of their destiny the beautiful eyes of a woman, begging and red from crying, because the man who had dared to be a father did not dare to be a husband!

Santos Telmo is a juvenile delinquent, about to become an attempted murderer: he stabs Grey in a jealous rage, and Lynch does not blink in revealing the social, affective, and economic realities that have led to his criminality. The gauchos' world, particularly that of the younger generation, is a world in decay. The young men have no prospects to look forward to in "el mundo con flaquezas," and only broken homes to turn to for comfort and support. The group of young gauchos who are depicted in the novel waste their time on useless and often destructive pursuits: Bartolo Fuentes digs holes with his dog; Deolindo Gómez dreams up malicious gossip to amuse his unmarried, vengeful sisters; and Santos Telmo nurses his unrequited love. Violence and the threat of violence are all around them: Santos Telmo stabs Grey, Deolindo's sister is menaced by her would-be lover, and Balbina eventually kills herself. Although Balbina is generally described in the lighthearted tones associated with James Grey, she belongs to the bleak and narrow world that Santos Telmo inhabits—and she proves this by her suicide in the novel's final pages.

While the main action of *El inglés de los güesos* unfolds almost entirely in the Argentinean interior, again in contrast to *Plata dorada,* Lynch very precisely contextualizes the developing relationship between Balbina and James within the triangulated structures of informal imperialism: the would-be lovers are brought together by none other than the owner of the enormous ranch where Balbina and her family make their meager living, "un señor metropolitano que se sorbía la vida y que se llamaba don X" [a metropolitan gentleman who sipped at life and who was known as don X] (72), who imposes Grey on the Fuentes family in order to impress his recommender, an anonymous British minister. The mysterious Don X spends as little time as possible on La Estancia Grande, preferring the luxuries of the city. He spends his evenings at a social club where his time is largely taken up by card games and the complications of his numerous infidelities. In describing Don X and his wife Chelita, the third-person narrator adopts the sarcastic strains of the social satirist, which Lynch had first practiced in his days as society columnist for a local newpaper and in an ill-fated play called *El cronista social*.[26] We meet Don X and Chelita just as their typical evening has been spoiled by the news of Santos Telmo's stabbing attack on Grey:

> En el momento en que oprimía con un dedito muy rollizo el timbre, disimulado entre las complicadas molduras del friso de caoba, la señora dijo

con una entonación de mimosa ternura, muy sincera sin duda, pero que, por desgracia, no se avenía con la adiposa madurez de su físico:

—¡Pero *Bebe,* no te pongas así!

Pero el *Bebe* no advirtió, o no quiso advertir, aquel reflorecimiento romántico, y después de replicar, entre malhumorado y risueño, con un "No, ¡si me voy a reír!", se quitó los guantes y se puso a escribir con lápiz y en una hoja de agenda el borrador de un despacho telegráfico para el administrador de "La Estancia", y en el que ordenaba no se reparase en gastos para atender debidamente a *El inglés de los güesos,* ya trayéndole a la capital, ya llevándolo a la ciudad más cercana.

Redactaba con tanta rapidez que, aunque escribió, es cierto, 'impugne' por 'impune', y 'peliar' por 'pelear', antes de un minuto ya tuvo hecho el telegrama. (144)

> [At the same time that her pudgy little finger pressed the bell, hidden among the complicated moldings of mahogany wainscoting, the wife said with a tone of indulgent tenderness, very sincere no doubt, but unfortunately a bit inappropriate for the adipose maturity of her physique, "Baby, don't get up*set*!"
>
> But "baby" didn't notice, or didn't want to notice, that romantic flourish, and after answering, between grouchy and amused, "No, I'm going to laugh about it!" took off his gloves and set about drafting in pencil and on a page of his appointment book a telegram to the administrator of "La Estancia," in which he ordered that no expense be spared in attending to *The Englishman of the bones,* either by bringing him to the capital or by taking him to the nearest city.
>
> He wrote so quickly and freely that, while he did put "impugne" instead of "impune" and "peliar" for "pelear," within a minute the telegram was ready.]

In a few deft strokes Lynch shows us that the wealthy landowners of *El inglés de los güesos* are as corrupt and degenerate as the creole upper class in *Plata dorada*. They bear the physical signs of decadence in the corpulence of the indolent, infantilized Chelita, the elegant gloves of Don X, and the expensive wooden wainscoting of their home. They are entirely dependent on the servants whom Chelita is about to summon with the elegantly embedded bell. What is more, their wealth and decadence are both linked to the English, who dominated the economic and social life of the Río de la Plata in the early twentieth century: Chelita's pet name for her husband is the English "baby" rather than the Spanish "bebé," and Don X's Spanish shows lexical and phonic confusions not unlike those of James Grey, as if to suggest that constant exposure to English has begun to erode his native language.

Grey's presence among the gauchos, brokered by the wealthy, "metropolitan" Don X, telescopes the tripartite sectors of the beef trade: British consumers hungry for high-quality chilled meat, the nexus of foreign capitalists and Argentinean landowners headquartered in the city of Buenos Aires, and the rural society of the pampa, increasingly disenfranchised by the capitalization of the industry. Despite Grey's apparent lack of interest in economic affairs, his trajectory demonstrates the social and ecological relations behind what the logic of commodity fetishism represents as purely economic transactions: the weight of Britain's status as the preeminent imperial power, the Argentinean elites' desire to modernize the country after the European model, and the land-tenure system that concentrated natural resources in the hands of the privileged few.

Hombres de marcha (Men on the Move)

El inglés de los güesos engages the issue of Britain's infiltration of Argentina's developing national discourse less explicitly than *Plata dorada*, but nevertheless takes part in a rhetorical struggle for national self-determination. In *El inglés*, Lynch accomplishes this more subtly, by deriding the discursive authority of the British travelers, whose view of nineteenth-century Argentina was beginning to occupy a central role in national historiography, and developing an alternative, more locally grounded perspective. As it is, the writing of *El inglés de los güesos* coincided with a local boom in British travel narratives: no fewer than fifteen of these volumes were published in Buenos Aires between 1910 and 1925. Doubtless the celebration of Argentina's centennial in 1916 sparked a fresh interest in the independence era, which for many was satisfied by the history included in volumes such as Alexander Gillespie's *Buenos Aires y el interior: observaciones reunidas durante una larga residencia, 1806 y 1807, con relación preliminar de la expedición desde Inglaterra hasta la rendición del Cabo de Buena Esperanza, bajo el mando conjunto de Sir David Baird* and Sir Francis Bond Head's famous *Las pampas y los Andes, notas de viaje*.[27]

Following the 1992 publication of Mary Louise Pratt's *Imperial Eyes: Travel Writing and Transculturation,* scholars have produced valuable research exposing the relationship between the writings produced by nineteenth-century travelers and the project of empire building.[28] Some of these travelers were directly employed by the governments of Britain, France, Belgium, Germany, the United States, or other countries as scouts seeking valuable natural resources as well as trade routes and possible political alliances; others were hired for similar tasks by private enterprises.

Some, archaeologists and anthropologists, for example, were sent on missions whose usefulness for empire building was not immediately apparent, but even these carried with them an implicit sense of Europe's superior culture and technological advancement that in their minds and many others justified their presence and intervention in foreign countries. As Gillian Beer writes,

> Although the nineteenth-century journeys that set out from Britain to survey the seas and coasts around the world were not piratical, not part of that unconcerned predation that earlier centuries justified as exploration or discovery, they were nevertheless an expression of the will to control, categorize, occupy, and bring home the prize of samples and of strategic information.[29]

Lynch's *El inglés de los güesos* shows how the actions of the British travelers reflected that sense of superiority and economic privilege in terms of the technology at their disposition and their mobility. At the same time, Lynch presents an implicit critique of the attitude of Argentinean elites who have learned of the rural, working people of their nation only through the lens of European travel writing; he opens up an alternative discursive space that combines the education and discursive capacity of the elites with the social and ecological experience of the working class.

To understand Lynch's achievement in appropriating and revising the genre of the travel narrative, it is necessary first to consider the prestige those texts commanded both at the time the novel was written and in subsequent decades. As Samuel Trifilo writes in his comparative study, *La Argentina vista por los viajeros ingleses: 1810-1860*, the years surrounding World War I saw an upsurge in interest in British accounts of the pampa. Their principal attraction for local audiences, in his opinion, was the objectivity and rigor of the British observers. "Along with the enormous quantity," he writes, "is the fortunate discovery that the English narratives were also, as a general rule, of very good quality. Distinguishing themselves from travelers of other nationalities, the English as a group tried to be objective, to see their surroundings clearly and not exaggerate excessively."[30] In 1936 Carlos Cordero, author of the compendious *Los relatos de los viajeros extranjeros posteriores a la Revolución de Mayo como fuentes de historia argentina: ensayo de sistematización bibliográfica*, enthused:

> So much surprising information, such unhoped-for visions, what finds, what unimagined treasures in these pages! How they enrich our understanding of the historical past—men, deeds, things—through the observation, the sensibility, the culture and the emotional state of an industrialist, a botanist, a naval officer, a university professor, the director of a mining

92 NATURE, NEO-COLONIALISM

company, a general, a consular agent, an adventurer! That vivid, exuberant, no doubt contradictory image contains raw materials the historian will certainly know how to extract and utilize.[31]

If Cordero's enthusiasm and confidence in the testimony of those myriad British businessmen, soldiers, and scholars seems somewhat naive today, it was nonetheless corroborated by Borges, who wrote in his 1941 "Sobre *The Purple Land*": "Percibir o no los matices criollos es quizá baladí, pero el hecho es que de todos los extranjeros (sin excluir, por cierto, a los españoles) nadie los percibe sino el inglés: Miller, Robertson, Burton, Cunninghame Graham, Hudson." [Perceiving creole nuances or not may be a trivial matter, but the fact remains that of all the foreigners (not excluding, of course, the Spanish), no one perceives them but the English: Miller, Robertson, Burton, Cunninghame Graham, Hudson.][32]

More recently Roberto González Echevarría has studied the influence of European travelers and scientists on Spanish-American prose in general and on one of Argentina's most important national narratives, Domingo F. Sarmiento's *Facundo: Civilization and Barbarism*. As González Echevarría writes, the texts of scientific travelers like Alexander von Humboldt, Francis Bond Head, Charles Darwin, and others established "a new masterstory" that has resonated among Latin American intellectuals since the early nineteenth century.[33] He continues:

> Backed as they were by the might of their empires and armed with the systemic cogency of European science, these travelers and their writings became the purveyors of a discourse about Latin American reality that rang true and was enormously influential. Their entire discursive activity, from traveling itself to taxonomical practices, embodied truth and exuded authority through its own performance. The influence of this travel literature was immense, not only on political developments within the very reality they described, but on the conception of that reality that individuals within it had of it and of themselves. (228–29)

As evidence of that influence, González Echevarría refers to *Facundo,* one of the most influential texts of the nineteenth century. *Facundo,* first published in 1845 as *Facundo: Civilización y barbarie. Vida de Juan Facundo Quiroga y aspecto físico, costumbres y hábitos de la República Argentina* [Facundo: Civilization and barbarism. Life of Juan Facundo Quiroga and the physical features, customs, and habits of the Argentine Republic], is a voluminous, hybrid text, a biography of the caudillo Facundo Quiroga, that is also a sensational novel, a political diatribe, and a historical treatise on the Rosas regime. Anxiously asking the question, "civilization or barbarism?" *Facundo* is often credited with establishing the categories that would polarize political discourse in Argentina and much of Latin America throughout the nineteenth and twentieth centuries. However, as González Echevarría points out, Sarmiento's own knowledge of the pampa was acquired largely through books, especially Francis Bond Head's *Rough Notes Taken during Some Rapid Journeys across the Pampas and among the Andes,* which he repeatedly quotes in French. "The self-discovery in *Facundo* is thoroughly mediated by texts, just as the texts of the travelers are mediated by scientific discourse," he writes (237).

Of all the Englishmen who traveled to Argentina in the nineteenth century, none had more influence on science and society than Darwin, whose *Journal of Researches* describes the South American voyage made by the H.M.S. *Beagle* in 1832. While the ship sailed slowly up the eastern coast of South America, Darwin, who suffered intensely from seasickness, preferred to travel by land, meeting up with Captain Fitzroy and the crew at successive harbors. In the intervals Darwin explored the flora and fauna, the wildlife and human inhabitants of the region, often lodging (like the fictional James Grey) with local families. He describes his encounters in considerable detail in the *Journal of Researches,* conveying the same forebearance and condescending good humor as the fictional Grey. He gratefully describes the local custom of offering lodging to travelers, and explains that he "repaid them for their hospitality" by entertaining his hosts with the marvels of European science, demonstrating in particular the workings of his pocket compass. Darwin, like Grey, is often amused by the ignorance of his hosts:

> I was asked whether the earth or sun moved; whether it was hotter or colder to the north; where Spain was, and many other such questions. The greater number of inhabitants had an indistinct idea that England, London, and North America, were different names for the same place; but the better informed well knew that London and North America were separate countries close together, and that England was a large town in London![34]

Darwin's impact on Argentina continued long after his departure from South America: Sarmiento became his outspoken admirer, as Giaconda Marún has shown in a recent article, and during his term as president of the republic (1868–74) actively supported the study of evolution in Argentinean schools and fostered the advancement of the natural sciences by sponsoring a series of prominent researchers invited from Europe.[35] Sarmiento and the young scientist Eduardo L. Holmberg made speeches at a memorial service organized by the Medical Circle of Argentina soon after Darwin's death in 1882. In his address the former president expresses enthusiasm for Darwin's work and claims to have met the young naturalist and the rest of the *Beagle*'s crew when the ship was docked off the coast of

Chile.³⁶ He speaks with pride of Darwin's South American sojourn, and of the pampas' importance in his scientific researches:

> ¿Por qué no habremos de asociarnos a los que en el resto del mundo tributan homenaje a la memoria de Darwin, si todavía están frescos los rastros que marcan su paso por nuestro territorio, *y es uno de nuestros propios sabios*? (emphasis added)³⁷
>
> [Why shouldn't we join those in the rest of the world who pay tribute to the memory of Darwin, since the tracks that mark his journey through our land are still fresh, *and he is one of our own scholars?*]

With characteristic vigor Sarmiento stakes a claim for Argentina's share in Darwin's scientific achievement. His remark is an implicit rejection of the role Victorian scientists frequently ascribed to Latin America and Latin Americans as passive objects of European study, asserting instead that Argentina was a willing participant in the voyage of the *Beagle*. What at first glance appears to be a defiant, anticolonial gesture, however, is in reality based upon the perpetuation of a dynamic that must be described as internal colonialism: Sarmiento's identification of the collective national "us" with Europe and the United States is founded upon the marginalization of the uneducated and "uncivilized" indigenous and mestizo populations who were the object of the European gaze. In this case, as it turns out, Sarmiento's personal will to dominate and subdue the internal Other greatly exceeds that of the European "master" he claims to emulate. Darwin gratefully acknowledges the assistance of the caudillo General Juan Manuel de Rosas—Sarmiento's archnemesis is the only Argentinean mentioned by name in the *Journal of Researches*—who personally provided Darwin with a local passport. Darwin extols Rosas's discipline and leadership skills, and protests against the extermination of the pampa Indians, which Sarmiento aggressively advocated.³⁸

In contrast to Sarmiento's technique of discursive empowerment through identification with European authority, Lynch develops an alternative strategy of aligning the narrating voice with the rustic inhabitants of the pampa and turning the inquisitive gaze upon the European scientist himself. His narrator speaks the refined, educated Spanish of the elite, but in terms of perspective the voice is as often positioned with the humble tenant farmers as with the English traveler. The first paragraph of *El inglés de los güesos*, for example, describes the Fuentes' reaction to their first encounter with Grey:

> La llegada de míster James, o mejor aún de *El inglés de los güesos*, como le apodaron todos, provocó en los habitantes del "puesto" de "La Estaca" la más risueña curiosidad y la más franca chacota.

> Y por cierto que no era para menos. Apareció de repente, allá por el bajo de la laguna, jinete en el petiso de los mandados de "La Estancia", más cargado de bártulos que el imperial de una diligencia y desplegando al tope de su alta silueta, nítidamente recortada sobre el fondo gris de la tarde lluviosa, un gran paraguas rojo . . . (30)
>
> [The arrival of Mister James, or better yet of *The Englishman of the bones*, as everyone called him, provoked in the inhabitants of the "post" of "La Estaca" the most piquant curiosity and the frankest laughter.
> And with good reason, to be sure. He showed up all of a sudden, there by the low area of the lagoon, a horseman riding a yearling of the bosses of "The Ranch," more loaded-down with bundles than a diligence and unfurled at the top of his tall silhouette, sharply standing out against the grey background of the rainy afternoon, a large red umbrella . . .]

From the very first sentence the narrating voice resides with the rustic gaucho family, and describes Grey's appearance so that the reader sees him as they might have. Reversing the perspective of conventional travel literature, Lynch casts the Englishman in the position of the Other. Moreover, the text not only describes the Fuentes' experience for the reader but replicates it by defamiliarizing what would otherwise be a recognizable image of a naturalist arriving to conduct his research. The sophisticated equipment that to an audience educated in Western science might have inspired respect is instead represented as an eccentricity, a cumbersome burden that makes Grey's awkward figure even more ungainly. He is introduced, similarly, with the enigmatic and somewhat absurd nickname "The Englishman of the bones," which casts a bizarre, fetishistic quality to his scientific endeavor. When one of the locals is described, in contrast, his potentially comical appearance is presented as an asset and a function of his occupation: "Y manos sobre el vientre y esparrancadas sus piernas de domador congénito, [Bartolo] se reía con unas risotadas agudas como relinchos" [And, hands upon his belly and legs spread apart like a born horsebreaker, Bartolo laughed with cackles as sharp as a whinny].

The scene has all the ideological force that Mikhail Bakhtin associated with the celebration of carnival, during which humor is used to destabilize the power of established authority. Bartolo's belly laugh represents an eruption of "the people's laughter which characterized all the forms of grotesque realism from immemorial times and was linked with the bodily lower stratum."[39] Spatially, Lynch represents the scene as a confrontation between high and low, not unlike that of Don Quijote and Sancho Panza: the tall, elongated figure of James Grey, mounted on horseback and extended even further by the ridiculous red umbrella, stands before the bandy-legged boy, whose earthiness is accentuated by his stance. That "laughter that degrades and materializes" endows the boy with a kind of discursive power, rooted in his physical being and experience, which confronts and challenges the authority of the cerebral Englishman.

While he undermines the conventional authority of the scientific observer, Lynch simultaneously constructs an alternative discursive space by implicitly aligning the reader with the family of gauchos. As if in answer to Sarmiento's claim to elite identification with European scientism, Lynch creates a narrating voice that is firmly rooted in *place,* by articulating Bartolo's relationship to his environment through the earth, the animals, and his work as a ranch-hand, in a language that is readily accessible to an educated reading public. He draws readers into that discursive space from the very beginning by inviting us to share the joke: "¡Vean, vean!" [Look, look!] shouts the boy, calling us, along with his mother, sister, and friend, to join him.

The identification established in this first scene appears intermittently throughout the novel. While most of the travel writers gloss over their inability to communicate in Spanish, Grey's stammerings are rendered phonetically, so that his mistakes and mispronunciations become a running joke between writer and reader, a joke not unlike the tricks Balbina and Santos Telmo plot to take advantage of Grey's unsteady command of Spanish. The deficiencies of the *puesteros,* on the other hand, are treated much more sympathetically. Balbina in particular holds the narrator's affection from beginning to end: even when her teasing of Grey becomes outright malicious she is represented tenderly, as a robust and charming beauty: "La Negra, con sus diez y ocho años bien cumplidos, con sus mejillas morenas teñidas de sangre sana, con los rizos alborotados de su cabellera de seda negra, con aquellos ojos profundos, cargados de interrogaciones, de nostalgias y de misterios" [La Negra, with her eighteen well-spent years, her dark cheeks with a healthy, sanguine tinge, the riotous curls of her hair of black silk, those profound eyes so full of questions, of nostalgias and of mysteries (29–30). As Contreras astutely points out, the "savage" beauty of Balbina directly challenges the terms laid out in Sarmiento's *Facundo*.[40]

The intimacy between James and Balbina deepens when Grey, incapacited after the attack by Balbina's jealous suitor, Santos Telmo, is confined to his room to recuperate. The narrative's emphasis in these pages is on Balbina's innocent coquetry, her efforts to pronounce his name correctly, and the rapt attention with which she listens to his stories of England:

> Y en tal manera seducían a la moza estos inocentes relatos, que a menudo, y cuando *El inglés de los güesos* acababa de referirle, por ejemplo, cómo una vez su padre estuvo a punto de ser aplastado por un tren, ella,

después de suspirar levemente, le decía sonriendo como una chicuela engolosinada con el relato de una fábula:
—¡Ah, ah! Cuentemé otro, míster, ¡otro! (137)

[And those innocent stories so seduced the girl that often, and when *The Englishman of the bones* had finished telling her, for example, how his father was once nearly run over by a train, after sighing lightly she said, smiling like a little girl enchanted by the telling of a fable:
"Oh, oh! Tell me another one, mister, another one!"]

Mobility arises here as an important element of the imbalance between the two characters. Grey, as a privileged citizen of the British Empire, has access to power and knowledge of most of the world: he has traveled not only in Argentina and Uruguay, but in Africa and Asia as well, and his privileged position vis-à-vis all of these regions is emblematized by the book to which he is contributing, volume 54 of the encyclopedic *History of the Savage Men*. Balbina, on the other hand, is unschooled in the geography of maps, uncertain (we are told) whether London is farther off than Buenos Aires; to her it seems almost inconceivable that Grey will return to that distant island. Like the young woman in a pink dress lying in the burnt brown grasses of a seemingly endless field in Andrew Wyeth's painting *Christina's World*, Balbina's experience and the horizon of her imagination are both defined by her confinement to a stretch of land where little novelty arrives to disrupt the monotonous continuity of days. The psychic poverty of the *puesteros* is brought home in Balbina's drastic response to Grey's impending departure: because she can imagine no way of life other than that of the pampa—Grey's England, after all, is a fairy tale to her, and Buenos Aires equally unreal—her only response to the crisis is to beg him to stay where she is.

Even while introducing the imbalance of power that underlies the relationship between Balbina and James, Lynch also undertakes a subtle analysis of the ideology of neo-colonialism by critiquing the function of stoicism within Victorian culture. Her incontinent intolerance of pain, presented humorously at first, foreshadows Balbina's eventual suicide. When Balbina tells him that she is unusually sensitive to physical pain and would rather die than experience an earache again, the response delivered in James's pidgin Spanish is equally ominous, "¡Eso mala, Babino! ¡Es mucho mala! Vida todo trabaca, todo sufirmienta, y osted tiene que acostumbra per fuerza" (140). [That's very bad of you, Babino! Very bad! Life is all work, all suffering, and you must force yourself to get used to it]. The stoic acceptance of personal suffering that James expresses here reiterates the virtues that young Williams Fernández, the protagonist of *Plata dorada*, was taught by his British peers and schoolmasters. Once again Lynch opposes British stoicism and restraint to the more overt emotionality of the creoles. In *El inglés de los güesos,* however, Lynch develops the initial contrast between British restraint and creole passion into a brilliant unveiling of the imperialist ideology behind the thoughts and actions of the apparently disinterested scientist, revealing how Grey's stoic commitment to duty serves to mask the egoism of his ambition and the ethnocentrism of his avowed humanism.

James gets his marching order in the form of a letter from "none less than the illustrious anthropologist and Cambridge professor, Mr. Douglas Amstrong," who demands his immediate return and the results of his investigation. Balbina is inconsolable, and her frightened mother approaches Grey to enlist his help in easing the pain of the separation, asking him even to lie to Balbina if necessary. Grey responds by indignantly denying his responsibility to Balbina and her family, refusing to accept what in his mind represents a gross impropriety: "¡Mí viene a esto tiera per trabaca, no per ingana siñorito; mí un *gentleman,* siniora!" [I came to this country to work, not to seduce a young man (*sic*); I am a *gentleman,* señora!] (175). Here Grey hides behind the privileges of his race and class, which are proudly asserted in his native language and at least in his own mind seem to offer him a kind of immunity. Under the circumstances, James's ungrammatical Spanish—punctuated by the resounding phrase, "mí un *gentleman"*—becomes less the sign of his vulnerability that it was when he arrived than a mark of enthnocentrism and his refusal to transcend the limits of his own cultural horizon. His mistaken masculinization of Balbina's name and his odd choice of the word "siñorito" betray Grey's insensitivity to local interdependencies of race, class, and gender, and simultaneously tie in to the local kids' habit of labeling Grey as "raro" or queer.[41]

Throughout most of the novel the use of free indirect discourse is limited to developing the subjectivity of the tenant farmers, exploring their ideas about each other and their impressions of the Englishman lodged among them. In the scene following Grey's encounter with Doña Casiana, however, the focalization comes to rest on Grey in order to communicate his more private thoughts on the subject. Alone at the archaeological site, he takes a skull in his hand to contemplate, Hamlet-like, his situation. Here Lynch reveals that Grey is in fact more upset than he allows himself to appear, and that he is suffering pangs of sincere sympathy for "aquel sufrimiento de una obscura muchachilla semibárbara y hasta ayer completamente desconocida para él" [the suffering of an obscure little half-wild girl till yesterday completely unknown to him] (176). Considering Balbina's anguish and the possibility of his own, Grey redoubles his commitment to duty:

[E]l no podía detenerse . . . , porque *El inglés de los güesos,* "hombre de marcha" de la Humanidad, por nacimiento, por educación y por costumbre, tenía como un compromiso moral contraído consigo mismo, y por razón de quién sabe qué arrepentimientos ancestrales, de caminar, de caminar siempre, recta y pausada y metódicamente, para cubrir en la vida la mayor distancia que le fuera posible sobre un largo camino de antemano elegido y jalonado por el cálculo. (179)

[He could not be detained . . . because *The Englishman of the bones,* in step with the "march" of Humanity, by birth, by education, and by custom, had a moral obligation to himself, brought about by who-knows-what ancestral guilt, to proceed, to proceed always straight forward, with an even and methodical step, to cover in life the greatest distance possible on a long road of progress chosen and calculated beforehand.]

Grey's thoughts rehearse a long stream of Victorian and positivist catch-phrases as justification for the pain he is about to inflict on Balbina. He speaks, in this most private moment, an oddly public discourse that at once discredits the sincerity of Grey's personal interrogation and suggests that Lynch is criticizing not only the individual character but the culture and society that have informed his personality (including the guilt-stricken forebears Max Weber discussed in his famous essay on the Protestant work ethic). Grey's commitment to duty and the progress of Humanity might seem credible enough in a different context, but for the fact that Lynch has already trivialized the project in which Grey is involved: a fifty-odd volume *History of the Savage Men* that is entirely removed from the reality of contemporary life and reduces the diversity of human societies to fragmentary remains of the distant past. Similarly, when Grey's positivist dedication to the "long road of progress" is juxtaposed with his decision to leave Balbina, it suggests that he has conflated an admirable notion of service to an abstract universal "humanity" with a more narrowly personal ambition.

The case against Grey becomes more damning a few pages later, when Balbina, encouraged by the advice of the *curandera* doña María, manages to pretend she is indifferent to his departure. At this point a return to free indirect discourse reveals that Balbina's nonchalance disturbs him even more deeply than her suffering:

¡Ah! . . . El sería un loco, un miserable, todo lo que se quisiera; pero habría sido tan feliz yéndose con la seguridad absoluta de que al irse se llevaba consigo y para siempre, arrancado de cuajo, el único corazón de mujer que había hecho acelerar los latidos del suyo, aquel único y dolorido e ignorante corazón virginal que en un rancho obscuro de un país remoto le hiciera experimentar las emociones más hondas de su vida, le dejara entrever las maravillas de un mundo nuevo, en cuya existencia no había creído en serio nunca, a pesar de haberle sido garantizada tantas veces por sus sabios maestros y por las formidables bibliotecas de Oxford. (239)

[Oh! Perhaps he was crazy, desperate, anything, but he would have been so happy to leave with the absolute certainty that in leaving he took with him and for ever, torn out by the root, the only woman's heart that had ever made his own beat faster, that unique, aching, and ignorant virginal heart that in an obscure ranch in a remote country made him experience the most profound emotions of his life, had let him see the wonders of a new world, a world he never seriously thought existed, despite having been guaranteed to him so many times by his wise teachers and the formidable libraries of Oxford.]

Grey's thinking falls into the old colonialist habit of dividing the world between the conventional reality of England or northern Europe and the romantic, mysterious south. In his fantasies Grey indulges in a kind of sentimental primitivism, a carryover from romanticism that was common to British and North American discourse on Latin America and Italy in the early twentieth century. Like the travelers in E. M. Forster's *A Room with a View* (1908), Virginia Woolf's *The Voyage Out* (1915), and D. H. Lawrence's *Plumed Serpent* (1926), Grey wants to experience an emotional intensity unknown to him or off-limits at home in England without feeling the personal responsibility of one whose relationship to the local community is permanent.[42] Unlike the above-mentioned British authors, however, Lynch insists that in the colonial context Grey's longing for emotional intensity slips all too easily into the belligerent attitude of conquest, as the violent image of an innocent heart "torn out by the root" immediately reveals.

Taken all together, Lynch's characterization of the English naturalist James Grey warns against the prestige and authority that British observers of the pampa had acquired among Argentina's educated elite. More than the popularity of their translated travel writing, a worldview and a vision of society were at stake: Lynch implicitly argues against accepting a view of rural society that was mediated by the values and experiences of the itinerant British observers. His work in rewriting and redressing the conventional drama of the British travel narrative is essential to his project of tracing a geography of resistance: travel writing, especially in the era of high imperialism, is based, like commodity fetishism, on the suppression or suspension of human relations and social responsibility between subjects in different economic zones. The traveler's relationship to his or her "travelees" is by definition a limited engagement, an encounter that is bounded in time by the inevitable return to the metropolis.[43] As Richard Kerridge writes, "The itinerary is fixed, and the timetable for closure—for return and re-entry into the atmosphere of home—is drawn up in advance."[44] Lynch demonstrates, through the actions and ideas of James Grey, the degree to which the travelers' insights were conditioned by ethnocentrism and mobility, and posits in opposition to a false, consumerist cosmopolitanism that sees the world in fragments and fails to understand its geographical connections, a sense of identity and a cultural discourse that are firmly rooted in the politics of place.

Balbina's World: Neo-Colonial Intersections of Race, Gender, and Class

The writings of the Britishers who visited the pampa may have sparked Lynch's imagination with the hints they give about the interactions between traveling Englishmen and the women of the pampa; some of them depart from mundane notes on the local political situation, travel conditions, labor, and natural resources to comment on the protagonists' encounters with local women. Darwin was one of those "friendly, enlightened and vagabond English boys" who crossed the pampa in the early 1800s, frequently lodging with local families as he did. The descriptions of the Indians of the pampa in his *Journal of Researches* express a remarkable attraction to the women and an appreciation of their dark, healthy beauty that finds an echo in Lynch's depiction of Balbina: "Among the young women or chinas, some deserve to be called even beautiful. Their hair was coarse, but bright and black; and they wore it in two plaits hanging down to the waist. They had a high colour, and eyes that glistened with brilliancy; their legs, feet, and arms were small and elegantly formed; their ankles, and sometimes their waists, were ornamented by broad bracelets of blue beads."[45] The passage is teasing, enigmatical: the speaker's emotion is vividly conveyed, but we have no information about what brought Darwin's party into contact with the Indians or how long the meeting lasted. All we know about the encounter is that Darwin was close enough to the women to notice their jewelry.

Sir Francis Bond Head, author of the famous *Rough Notes Taken During Some Rapid Journeys Across the Pampas and Among the Andes,* was less evasive about his meeting with a young girl of the pampa:

> I was therefore going to lie down for a few minutes among the long grass to rest myself, when passing the corner of the hut I saw close before me a female figure pounding corn. She was the only daughter and eldest child of

Don José (who was a widower), and she was about sixteen years of age. Her whole dress consisted of a coarse woolen petticoat, and over her bare shoulders was loosely thrown (as a shawl) an old scarlet poncho. . . . As soon as I appeared before her, with one hand she closed her poncho in front, and continued to pound the corn with the other; however, as soon as I asked her a few questions about the corn, she began earnestly and with great naiveté to explain to me the whole operation, and then working the pestle with both her hands, she illustrated her art both by practice and theory, pounding and expounding at the same time; and although I cared but little how the corn was pounded, yet it was impossible to help admiring the artless simplicity and innocence of the girl's countenance, manners, and appearance.

By describing the girls' movements, Head presents the reader with a visual dirty joke, an image of himself ogling the exposed breasts of a girl who earnestly explains the task she is performing. The scene might be described as a kind of eroticized colonial pastoral: his enjoyment of the native girl's "artless simplicity and innocence" combines the nostalgic pleasure of an imaginary return to an earlier, less complicated era with the sexual power endowed to the male colonial subject by virtue of his economic advantage.

But the implications of Head's encounter with female labor are much more complex. He concludes the vignette with the remark, "before I mounted my horse, I took a little memorandum book from my pocket, and wrote in it 'Black woman skinning a cow', for the rest of the scene I thought I should remember."[46] The bizarre code Head applies to the encounter refers back to his initial impression of the scene: "Arrived at a post hut, and found its owner, Don José, skinning a cow which he had just killed—he was assisted by a black woman of about fifty." The cryptic phrase reduces the family's activity to what for Head were the only essential elements: the stark description of the mature black woman at her grisly task, he is sure, will be enough to remind him of the nubile white woman. His confidence in the nmemonic device suggests that Head senses a kind of correspondance between these two images. In fact, as Sander Gilman has explained, the system of imperialist and racist stereotypes that circulated among nineteenth-century Europeans often led to the pairing of white and black women in aesthetic representations: it was commonly understood that the presence of the black woman signified the sexual deviance or availability of the white.[47] In this case there is an even stronger visual rhyme in the pairing of the two images: the white woman exposes her breasts to the British spectator, while the black woman performs a more gruesome strip-show for Don José. The relative castes of the two women are strongly invoked in the kinds of labor they perform: in Head's imagining, the relevance of the white woman's labor is the sexual charge it provides him; while the older, black woman is identified with a grotesque, baroque image that seems to conflate her age, race, gender and class.

Head's attitude toward these two working women is even more remarkable if it is compared with his admiration for the male gauchos, for which he is often cited as one of the most open-minded of neo-colonial travelers.[48] Head defends the men from European misconceptions, explaining that what is often mistaken for "indolence" is in fact an austere and admirable simplicity; regarding the women, on the other hand, he remarks, "they have literally nothing to do . . . *their* lives are very indolent and inactive" (15). He adds, without a trace of irony, that "they have all, however, families, whether married or not; and once when I inquired of a young woman *employed* in nursing a very pretty child, who was the father of the 'criatura,' she replied, 'Quién sabe?'" (15; emphasis added).

Both of these scenes, including Head's responses to them, reveal the dialectical interdependencies of the categories of race, class, and gender in the (neo)colonial context. As McClintock has written, "Gender here, then, is not simply a question of sexuality but also a question of subdued labor and imperial plunder; race is not simply a question of skin color but also a question of labor power; cross-hatched by gender."[49] In other words, Head's valuation of Argentinean labor is sharply gendered (men's work is valuable and productive, women are engaged in sexual activity only), but his interpretation of gender is strongly dependant on race (in the text only the young white woman is represented as truly "female") and his observation of the entire scene is predicated on his own position of economic dominance over all of these Argentineans, including the superfluous patriarch Don José. The scene is representative of the complex dynamics that appear when gender enters the accounts of business imperialism: real and imaginary orders of race, class, and gender overlap here as Head's patriarchal and neo-colonial view confronts a scene that is already informed by the colonial and gendered legacies of rural Argentina.

One more visitor to the Argentinean pampa must be drawn into the discussion alongside Darwin and Head. In this case the observer is not a European but a creole: Benito Lynch himself. At the beginning of the previous section I quoted an interview in which Lynch was asked about the inspiration behind *El inglés de los güesos*. After identifying several of the Europeans who wrote about their travels in Argentina, he says, "The heroine? Who could she be? This or that or the other one. . . . Any of those interesting *chinitas* I once met, somewhere, years ago."[50] At first glance, Lynch's language in this passage seems to contradict the sympathy for Balbina and her class conveyed by *El inglés de los güesos:* the term *chinitas* is pejoratively used to refer to the mixed-race working-class women of the pampa, and his vague reference to the names and locations of those women replicates the dismissive, irresponsible language of the colonial texts criticized by the novel. On closer examination, however, this gratuitous autobiographical turn, from an author as famously reticent as Lynch, is revealing: he projects himself into the space of encounter with an unprecipitated willingness to cast himself in the position of the foreign interloper. This odd self-consciousness, I argue, corresponds to a willingness to expose the exploitative relationship between the national landowning class—the socioeconomic group to which Lynch himself belongs—and the rural poor. In the novel, as in his remark to the interviewer, Lynch resists the temptation to represent Balbina's story as a simple encounter between two individuals, one British and the other Argentinean. Instead, he depicts neo-colonialism in terms of a more complex, triangulated dynamic, in which the creole landowner—not foreign-born, but not quite a native of the pampa either—is implicated as a mediator between local workers and the European capitalists.

Like Head's narrative, *El inglés de los güesos* raises the related issues of the nature of women's labor in a patriarchal, neo-colonial society and women's place in the conflict between capital and labor under neo-colonialism. In his response to these issues Lynch diverges significantly from the conventions of the regionalist novels, which commonly deal with the problem of labor in agricultural production as it is played out in the more visible, masculine space of confrontation between bosses and workers. When women do appear in texts like *Don Segundo Sombra, La vorágine* and, most notoriously, Rómulo Gallegos's *Doña Bárbara* (1929), they are represented as either unwelcome intruders or embodiments of an essentialized "feminine principle" that confuses women with the natural environment. If women are not directly employed in farming or tending livestock in *El inglés de los güesos*, Lynch carefully delineates their roles in the reproduction of labor. With regard to gender, this novel shows the inverse of the conventional regionalist novel by focusing on the interior of the frontier home as the space in which labor is continually reproduced through women's work as providers of food, comfort, and rest, as well as the reproductive capacities of their sexual bodies. The male characters come and go, but the background of nearly every scene has Doña Casiana and / or Balbina involved in their daily domestic labors—cooking dinner, tending the vegetable garden, cleaning, mending torn clothing, and so forth. Stripped down to its economic essentials, *El inglés de los güesos* represents two women at work in carrying out the ranch-owner's command to shelter and care for the English visitor. In fact the first sign of conflict or unease appears when Doña Casiana voices her fear that the family's limited resources will prevent her from carrying out the boss's orders: "Vea don 'Yemesgré'.... Yo no sé a qué comodidades estará hecho usted....

El patrón lo manda, es cierto; pero como nosotros somos pobres, quién sabe si podemos atenderlo a satisfacción en estos ranchos" [Look, Mr. Jamesgray.... I don't know what comforts you're used to.... The boss orders it, it's true, but poor as we are, who knows if we can tend to you to your satisfaction in these shacks] (33).

Lynch astutely establishes Balbina's location within two social hierarchies that intersect and overlap when Grey arrives on the pampa. The text is particularly sharp in representing her vulnerability to men of her own class and country as well as the English traveler and develops a contrast between James' discreet, almost unintentionally manipulative behavior and the more overt aggressions of the creoles. In contrast to them, Grey's behavior is dangerously ambiguous; it resists interpretation according to the social and sexual codes of conduct understood by the inhabitants of the pampa. Her only potential mate among the local men is Santos Telmo, the alternately demanding and supplicant suitor whose aggressive behavior prompts the intervention of Balbina's father and later the indignation of Grey ("¡Aoh! ¡Schooking!" he says when he learns of Telmo's plan to carry Balbina off on the back of his horse.) Any comedic touches involved in the portrayal of Telmo vanish when he attacks Grey in a rage of jealousy and frustration, brutally stabbing him at the archaeological site.

Santos Telmo is the only potential partner who appears from among Balbina's companions on the pampa, but another threat arrives in the figure of the ranch's owner, Don X, who visits Grey two weeks after the stabbing, and is dismayed to find that Grey has refused his offer of transport to an urban hospital. As he enters the room in which Grey is recuperating, Don X pauses in the doorway to stroke the cheek of Balbina; she naively misconstrues his intentions. But the narrator lays bare the interacting dynamics of race, class, and gender at work in the scene:

[Balbina] no podía sospechar jamás, en su bárbara inocencia, que aquel hombre le tocaba la cara porque ella era 'ella' solamente, y que aquel mismo hombre no se hubiese atrevido a tocársela nunca si, en cambio, hubiera sido Florencia Wilson, por ejemplo, aquella otra virgen de dieciocho años, cuyo padre—un señor muy intransigente—opuso al patrón tantas dificultades, tres lustros antes, cuando éste gestionaba su admisión en el círculo casi hermético del "Pocker Club." [sic] (147)

[Balbina could never suspect, in her barbarous innocence, that the man touched her face because she was simply "her," and that the same man would never have dared to touch her if she had been, in contrast, Florencia Wilson, for example, that other eighteen year-old virgin whose father—a very intransigent gentleman—put up so many obstacles, fifteen years ago, when the owner applied for admission to the hermetic circle of the Poker Club.]

The text presents an ironic chiasmus in this confrontation between the hypercivilized predator and the "barbarous innocence" of the rural girl. While reiterating the disapproval of the economic and social privileges enjoyed by the English community in Buenos Aires that is expressed in the earlier novel, the present scene complicates the situation by introducing the issue of gender: in the social space where two sharply patriarchal societies meet and interact, the economically empowered Wilson is able to protect his daughter in a way that the gaucho and *puestero* Don Juan Fuentes cannot. Don Juan's interdiction is only effective against Santos Telmo, and even there only to a certain point.

The narrator's attention to the social significance of names is also crucial here, and will help to tie in Lynch's acquaintance with those "interesting *chinitas*" with the encounter between Balbina and Don X, who is evidently too well-known in Buenos Aires to be named in the text. A name, especially a powerful English patronym like "Wilson," endows a woman with a social identity and a degree of security. Balbina, in contrast, is identified by the estanciero only as "her," as if to suggest that she has no role or function in his worldview outside the reproductive capacity of her gendered body. Yet Grey's clumsy mispronunciation of her name as "Babino," which he never rectifies, corresponds to his well-intentioned willingness to know her as an individual and his utter incomprehension of the local sex-gender system. We are told very little of the conversation that ensues between Grey and Don X, but as the interview ends the landowner suggests, "with a meaningful, libertine wink" to convey his approval, that Grey and Balbina are lovers. Grey, of course, is scandalized, and responds with his familiar defense, "¡Aoh! ¡No! ¡Mí un *gentleman*!" As the hypocrisies of the sentimental tourist are conveyed alongside the aristocrat's archaic sense of droit du seigneur, Lynch more clearly than ever casts the creole landowner into the position of willing intermediary between the rural poor and the abuses of foreign capitalists. Here it is not the male gauchos who are exploited and alienated by changes in the land-tenure system and relations of production, but the woman whose body is offered to the demand of the English.

The encounter between Balbina and James can also be seen as a sanitized version of the colonial pastoral described by Head, in which the sentimental primitivism of the prudish naturalist replaces the more overt eroticism of the rough-and-ready ex-soldier. In fact, Lynch emphasizes that the physical relationship between James and Balbina was limited to those impassioned but chaste kisses on the hand: "Por fortuna para ella y para el candor de su novela," the narrator declares, "*El inglés de los güesos* era 'tan raro' en su modo de ser y de pensar, que con sólo la mitad de sus rarezas hubiese bastado para hacer desternillar de risa a Deolindo Gómez y a todos los Deolindos de cincuenta leguas a la redonda de 'La Estancia Grande'" [To her good fortune and for the innocence of her novel, *The Englishman of the bones* was "so odd" in his way of acting and thinking that half of his oddities would have been enough to make Deolindo Gómez and all the Deolindos within fifty leagues of "The Big Ranch" burst out laughing] (135). Again homophobia and xenophobia are linked, this time by Deolindo Gómez. On the one hand, this metafictional moment turns the text into a kind of palimpsest, by invoking all of the other stories that cannot be told with "candor": stories of country girls who were seduced or raped by itinerant foreigners and stories like the brief encounter Head describes are also encoded into the sentimental tragedy of the innocent Balbina. By protecting the chastity of the heroine even in the face of death, Lynch remains faithful to a convention of sentimental literature and avoids plunging the novel into a starker naturalism than he was willing to pursue. At the same time, he nonetheless evokes the narratives that remain hidden from view, creating a powerful sense that what cannot be said is also paradoxically present in the text, straining against the story that is told.

When "race" enters the conceptual framework, Lynch's handling of gender becomes more clear, because *El inglés de los güesos* presents its characters as belonging to particular racial categories that are visibly constructed in relations of fluctuating interdependence with gender and class. The romantic attraction between James and Balbina, for example, is consistently figured in terms of their complementary physical types: one or more elements of James's physical makeup—blue eyes, blond hair, ruddy skin—is often counterposed to Balbina's features. James's most specifically Anglo-Saxon feature, his blue eyes, are always implicitly gendered masculine by the use of adjectives including "cold," and "penetrating," just as Balbina's large dark eyes are romantically described as expressive of "a woman's" love and sorrow, as if to suggest that they are "feminine" and "Latin" at once. Conventional gender roles, in other words, are fused with racial terminology that is also strongly marked by indications of power and subordination linked to social class and relative economic strength. The constant repetition of Balbina's nickname, "La Negra"—a traditional term of endearment among Spanish American families—underscores the contrast between James and herself and serves as a mark of racial difference, an outward sign of that innocent inward "savagery" the narrator admires in her.

I believe Balbina can be seen as Lynch's figure for a new "Latin" identity that transcends the old colonial class system by reconciling laborers and landowners in opposition to the neo-colonial invasion. If Lynch tentatively and pessimistically took up the same theme in *Plata dorada*, it is treated with more subtlety and confidence here. The sympathy the educated, elite narrator extends to her is an important part of this identification, which is made more specific in the account of the night of the *curandera*'s visit. In regard to Balbina's brother Bartolo, who complains of hunger while waiting for Doña Casiana to cook dinner, the narrator remarks:

> Para que se cumpliera esa práctica ancestral de nuestra nerviosa raza latina, que no come en cuanto una emoción ingrata le escarbabajea en los plexos, allá fue el pobre Bartolo, abochornado y triste, a tender su recadito en el ángulo más obscuro de la vasta cocina y a rumiar el dolor de la casa. (224)
>
> [In order to fulfill that ancestral practice of our nervous Latin race, which does not eat when an unpleasant emotion rakes around the solar plexus, away went poor Bartolo, ashamed and saddened, to lay out his little saddle in the darkest corner of the vast kitchen and to ponder the sorrow of the house.]

Previously the narrator's discourse has signaled the differences between the literate and worldly culture he implicitly shares with the reader and that of the humble, isolated gauchos, but in this scene, which occurs relatively late in the novel, he marks instead an identification with "our nervous Latin race." In comparison to the stoic and cerebral Grey, Balbina has most of the attributes that Lynch identified as creole or "Latin" in *Plata dorada*—passion, loyalty, honor, and emotionality.

Because Balbina's character must remain conventionally "pure," another figure enters the text as a kind of complement to her and the embodiment of the range of experience—independence, mobility, labor, sexuality—that is carefully segregated from her. Like the black woman in the anecdote recounted by Francis Bond Head, Doña María figures the "true" subaltern woman whose presence symbolically complements that of the beautiful *morena* who is represented as the white males' object of desire. But if the "black woman skinning a cow" is a pejorative gloss on black female labor, the *curandera* Doña María is a kind of local saint, whose science or "cencia" and her devotion to her neighbors have earned her the love and admiration of the entire community. Doña María embodies traditional communal ties, traveling about on horseback with her herbs and homemade medicines, bringing news of the neighborhood and conducting a kind of socialist economy. (Her patients pay her in produce, which she frequently redistributes around the neighborhood.) She is repeatedly represented by metonymic reference to her "black hands," a compound image that alludes to her powers as a healer, based on her connection to the earth and her African heritage, as well as to her physical labor-power and her independence. The phrase closely links her to Balbina, "La Negra," and becomes a sign of Balbina's own subalternity vis-à-vis the creole elites.

In comparison to Balbina's "innocence" and the exaggerated refinement of Grey, Doña María is more than willing to get those hands dirty in the labor of loving and healing the community. As a healer she is Grey's antithesis, with her homemade medicines called *yuyos* and the folk spirituality of her treatments. She is also characterized by a kind of moral ambiguity that challenges the rigidity of the Englishman: her service to the community transgresses the official mores of the time, as she is known for healing *mal de amores* (lovesickness) and providing abortions to women facing unwanted pregnancies. (As her indiscreet grandson makes clear, Doña María arrives at the ranch under the impression that Balbina is pregnant.) Although Doña María is regarded within the community as a holy woman, her acceptance of others' foibles introduces a note of moral ambiguity that counters Grey's rigidity and seems to touch the others in her presence. The "gargantuan" grandson who accompanies her on all of her housecalls, for example, is an unabashed glutton who takes advantage of the Fuentes' anxieties to gorge himself at their expense while they await Doña María's report on Balbina. And as if the mere proximity of Doña María were enough to tinge Doña Casiana's reputation as well, we are reminded soon after Doña María arrives that her common-law husband, Don Juan Fuentes, is known in the community as "el engañado" (the cuckold).

With her healing power and her earthy good humor, Doña María seems to represent the possibility—perhaps the viability—of the kind of reckless, passionate love Balbina embodies. She represents the physicality and the impulsiveness that Grey eschews; she is at home in the realm of the sexual, the spiritual, the emotional. And she dies just before Balbina does, reinforcing the implicit bond between the innocent, passionate young woman and the wise old one who embraced all of this realm of life that restraint, stoicism, and modernization would suppress. The scene of Grey's departure powerfully demonstrates how the integral, rural community represented by Doña María is being rapidly superseded by the new order dominated by foreign capital. As Grey boards the sulky of the ranch administrator who has come to escort him to the train station, Balbina tensely watches him for a sign that he has decided to stay. Her hopes are finally disappointed when their eyes meet and Grey remains silent. At this point the narrative focus of the scene changes dramatically: the two protagonists recede into the background—Grey literally withdraws into the carriage—and the action is moved forward by "external" forces. The efficient, impatient administrator Don Lucas directs the human actors, and his decisions are clearly based on the new class structure of the pampa. When a horseman appears on the horizon, riding toward the ranch at breakneck speed, Don Lucas hesitates a moment to see who it is before departing. He delays because he thinks it may be Mr. Jewel, one of the foreigners who runs the neighboring ranch of

110 NATURE, NEO-COLONIALISM

La Indiana—"¡Pero diga, hombre!: ¿es míster Jewel o no es míster Jewel?" [Tell me, man! Is it Mr. Jewel or isn't it?], he exclaims—but when he finally discerns that the rider is not an Englishman but Pantaleón, grandson of the *curandera,* he impatiently spurs the horse to start. Pantaleón arrives a moment later, bearing the news that his grandmother is dead. The rapid succession of these three linked events—James' final decision to suppress his love for Balbina, Don Lucas's attention to the demands of the foreigners rather than the needs of the locals, and the death of the rustic matriarch—affirms with grave finality the establishment of a new economic and social order that subordinates the romantic if imperfect rural community to the dictates of foreign capital.

The novel's conclusion brings a radical change to the narrative: as if to underscore the immensity and artificiality of the new order, the final chapter is narrated from the perspective of the lowliest members of the regional community. Diamela, the Fuentes family's dog, is sniffing around the yard: first she finds an overturned stool and one of Balbina's shoes lying beneath a tree, then she digs up the box in which Balbina, following the *curandera*'s instructions, had buried an old toad a few days before. As Doña Casiana looks toward the same tree and realizes that her daughter has taken her life, she cries out in anguish, "primero como un alarido salvaje, después como el ulular de una fiera" [first like a savage yell, and then like the howling of a wild animal] (270). The narrating voice maintains the same impersonal tone as the focalization now switches to the toad, who has taken a few shaky hops across the grass. He rests beneath a quinoa plant,

> y desde allí se puso a contemplar con sus ojillos socarrones el soberbio espectáculo del nacer del día, la pompa extraordinariamente magnífica que la Naturaleza desplegaba aquella mañana, como si hubiese querido distraer, a fuerza de luz y de colores, la atención de los hombres y de las bestias, para que no pensaran, para que no dudaran, para que siguieran confiando siempre en la equidad de sus leyes y en su poder soberano. (270)

> [and there he sat contemplating with his cynical little eyes the superb spectacle of the birth of the day, the extraordinarily magificent pomp that Nature displayed that morning, as if wanting to distract by the force of light and colors, the attention of men and beasts, so they would not think, so they would not doubt, so they would continue to trust always in the equity of their laws and in their supreme power.]

The introduction of a radical new perspective on these pages seems a departure from the rest of the text. On the contrary, Lynch is only radicalizing—in the literal sense of getting to the root of the problem—the scrutiny of land tenure and use that was begun much earlier in the novel. His lowering of the narrative perspective to the level of the dog and the toad resembles the adaptation of a ground-level perspective in the stories of Horacio Quiroga, who, as I have argued, repeatedly uses this viewpoint to reassert the ecological interdependency of human and nonhuman species in the face of capitalist commodification of nature. Lynch's strategic adaptation of the ground-level perspective, like Quiroga's, serves to check the hubris of a national and international elite that monopolized control of land and other natural resources while becoming increasingly distant from the region and its inhabitants.

No less important, that long last sentence also revisits and re-creates the failed pastoral we have seen earlier in the text. As in the sentence analyzed earlier, the novel's final phrases recapitulate the rhythm and tone of the narrative as a whole, with its modulation from the comedy of the first encounter between James and the tenant farmers through the romantic interlude to the stark realism of the end. Here, however, the narrator explicitly warns against succumbing to the deceptions of the pastoral by allowing the "superb pomp" of dawn to distract attention from the iniquities of human societies and by accepting the beauties of nature as a sign of social justice and harmony. The deflation of the romantic pastoral in the untempered severity of these final words brings to *El inglés de los güesos* a sense of consequence that corresponds to the novel's ongoing interrogation of the ethics of travel writing, mobility, and even the fetishization of commodities on the international market. All of the individuals endowed with socioeconomic power—the administrator Don Lucas, the landowner Don Luis, and most important, Grey himself—have left the site of the ranch, which they will probably continue to evoke with nostalgic, romantic memories. The terrible result of Grey's visit remains behind, unbeknownst to them. Only the *puesteros,* the immobilized descendants of the gauchos, will live with the consequences.

3

La Vorágine
Dialectics of the Rubber Boom

FOR MANY READERS THE MYSTERY of José Eustasio Rivera's *La vorágine* (1924) is the fate of its protagonist, Arturo Cova, who disappears in the Amazon jungle somewhere near the Rio Negro in northwestern Brazil. The only explanation in the text is in the novel's famous last words, presented in the form of a telegram from the Colombian Consul in Manaos:

> "Hace cinco meses búscalos en vano Clemente Silva.
> Ni rastro de ellos.
> ¡Los devoró la selva!" (385)[1]

> [For five months Clemente Silva has searched for them.
> Not a trace remains.
> The jungle devoured them!]

Though I cannot claim to have recovered the lost steps of Arturo Cova, I find myself more intrigued by a different disappearance: that of the scandalous Peruvian Amazon Company, which *La vorágine* at once exposes and almost entirely conceals.

As many of its readers know, *La vorágine* combines two different stories, one largely fictional and the other closely based on documentary sources. The first is the personal odyssey of narrator Arturo Cova, a well-known poet who flees Bogotá and an incipient scandal with his lover Alicia. After the pair spend several weeks on a cattle ranch in the rustic province of Casanare, Alicia leaves with the notorious slave trader Narciso Barrera, and Cova pursues them into the jungle, accompanied by a small party of ranch-hands. As Cova enters the jungle, his personal, fictive narrative becomes intertwined with the second, largely historical story, which is based on the scandal of the Peruvian Amazon Company, a consortium of British and Peruvian interests that in the early twentieth century was accused of exploiting the indigenous tribes of southwestern Colombia. The Peruvian Amazon Company, which began in the last years of the nineteenth century as a small rubber-trading outfit run by Julio C. Arana, took brutal advantage of the lawlessness of the region known as the Putumayo—a stretch of disputed land on the Peru-Colombia border—to terrorize both would-be competitors and local indigenous tribes, gradually establishing a monopoly on labor and natural resources there. In 1907 Arana's business became multinational: it registered on the London Stock Exchange, received more than one million pounds sterling in investment, and became formally known as the Peruvian Amazon Company. Several Britons held seats on the company's board of directors and others were installed as local agents in South America when accounts of atrocities began to appear in the British press in September 1909. Britain's Foreign Office sent Sir Roger Casement, the Irish humanitarian who had been instrumental in exposing the horrors of imperialism in central Africa, to investigate the company's labor practices. The report he ultimately submitted to Parliament describes a pseudolegalistic system of debt-peonage that was enforced by terror and violence: as Casement attests, workers were tortured and murdered for failing to bring in enough latex, for refusing to surrender their women and children to the company's thugs, or merely for the sadistic pleasure of their oppressors.[2]

What surprises and intrigues me is the contrast between the initial denunciations of the Peruvian Amazon Company written by Casement and others and Rivera's representation of it in *La vorágine*. British accounts of the Putumayo scandal emphasize the responsibility of the London investors who supported and profited from Arana's activities; *La vorágine*, on the other hand, does not mention a single Englishman or even allude to the company's investors overseas. What is more, Rivera's "oversight" was almost certainly intentional, as much of the British material was translated and published in Bogotá between 1910 and 1915 and Parliament's investigation of the Peruvian Amazon Company was closely followed by the Colombian press. From Casement's point of view, the exploitation of the Putumayo was a particularly cruel and uncontrolled instance of Europe's depredation of non-Western peoples and territories, differing only superficially from formal imperialism.[3] Casement had been instrumental in drawing international attention to the atrocities committed in King Leopold's Congo Free State, which he investigated in 1890, briefly crossing paths with the future author of *Heart of Darkness* (1899), Joseph Conrad. Like W. E. Hardenburg, the young American engineer who first broke the story in the British press, Casement repeatedly compares the Putumayo to the Congo:

> This Putumayo Slavery is, indeed, as Hardenburg said, and as I laughed at when I read it a year ago in *Truth*, a bigger crime than that of the Congo, although committed on a far smaller stage and affecting only a few thousands of human beings, whereas the other affected millions.

The other was Slavery under Law, with Judges, Army, Police and Officers, often men of birth and breeding even, carrying out an iniquitous system invested with monarchical authority, and in some sense directed to public, or so-called public ends. It was bad, exceedingly bad, and, with all its so-called safeguards, it has been condemned and is in process, thank God, of passing or being swept away.

But this thing I find here is slavery without law, where the slavers are personally cowardly ruffians, jail birds, and there is not authority within 1200 miles, and no means of punishing any offense, however vile. Sometimes Congolese "justice [sic] intervened, and an extra red-handed ruffian was sentenced, but here there is no jail, no judge, no Law.[4]

The map reproduced here (figure 1) dramatically represents the correlation between imperialism in Africa and Asia and the situation Hardenburg referred to as "The Devil's Paradise: A British Owned Congo." It is reproduced from a document known as *El libro rojo*, the anonymous "Red Book" that was first published in London in 1913, translated into Spanish and republished in Bogotá soon after.

The map shows the Putumayo region, located on the border between Colombia and Peru, bounded by the Putumayo and Caquetá Rivers and near the headwaters of the Amazon. Although the only city on the map is Iquitos, in northeastern Peru, the map shows the degree to which rubber stations were established throughout the Putumayo. The rivers are dotted with them, squeezed closely together to absorb the intensive activity among traders and the Indians who did most of the work of harvesting rubber from trees scattered throughout the jungle. What fascinates me about this map are the heteroglot names inscribed upon it, names that create a verbal and visual history of the region. The rivers are still called by the names given them by indigenous societies long ago—Caquetá, Putumayo, Igaraparaná, Caraparaná—perhaps so that native guides could more easily be used to navigate the regions' bafflingly complex waterways. Most of the rubber stations, on the other hand, bear Spanish names like Nueva Granada and Santa Bárbara. Some, like Esperanza, Providencia, and Encanto, unendingly recite the ambitions and expectations of their long-dead settlers; Matanzas (Killings) evokes some bloody event of the past. But two even stranger names are found on the lower Igaraparaná, "Africa" and "Indostan"; and straight to the north of "Africa" is a place called "Abisinia." More than simply cosmopolitan, these last three names are unmistakably colonial, as if selected out of some nineteenth-century atlas of European empires.

What are Africa, Hindustan, and Abyssinia doing on a 1913 map of the Putumayo? Casement, who also mentions a place called "La China,"

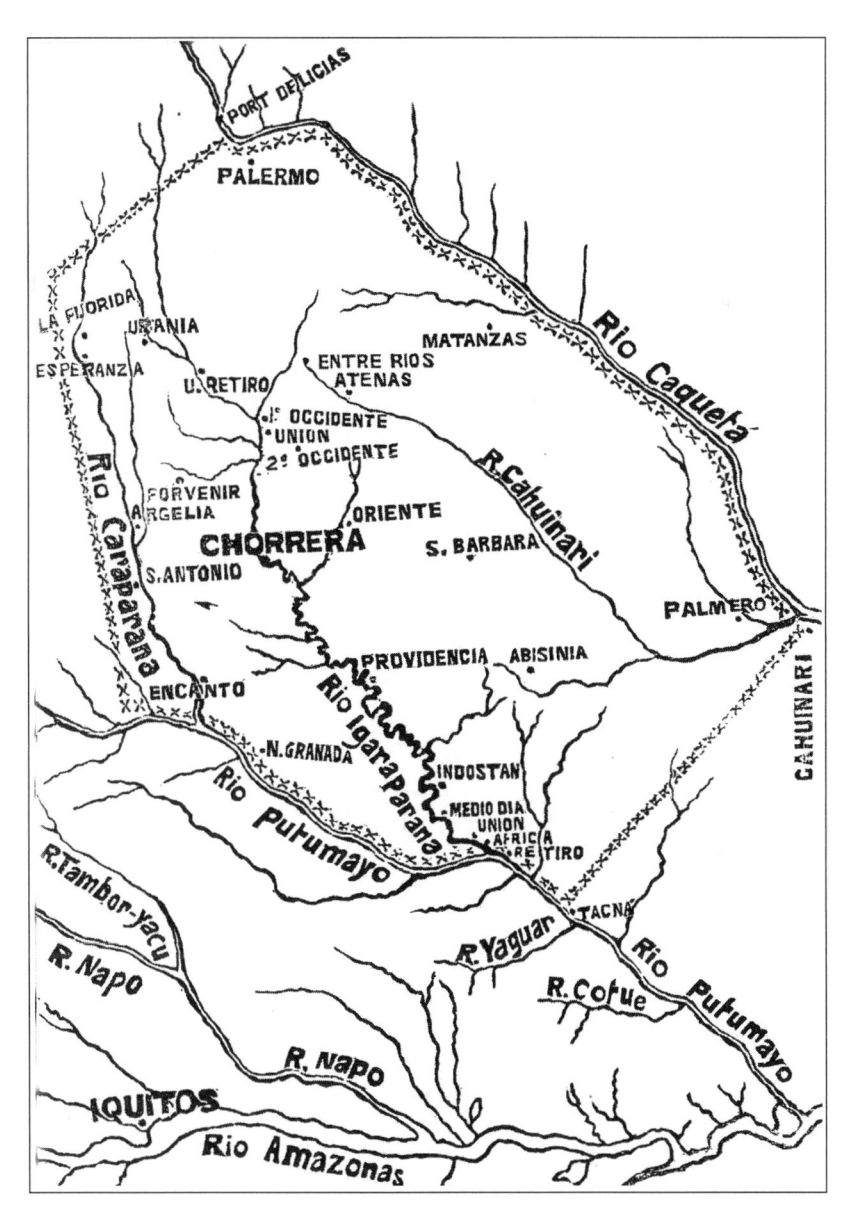

FIG. 1. "Principales secciones caucheras" [Principal rubber-gathering areas]. From *El libro rojo del Putumayo* (Bogota: Arboleda & Valencia, 1913), xi. Courtesy of Stanford University Libraries.

remarks that the rubber stations were "capriciously named." Today we have little way of knowing who was responsible for these names, how long they had been in place, or why they were selected. But the names reveal the colonial or, more appropriately, neo-colonial dynamics of the rubber-boom, explicitly locating the trading posts of the Peruvian Amazon Company within the context of the plundering of tropical jungles in Africa and Asia. Whoever chose those names did not follow the usual colonial practice of naming the newly founded cities in the New World after beloved places in the Old; instead they created an appropriately *neo*-colonial toponomy by borrowing the names of Europe's long-established official colonies. The miniature "colonies" of the Peruvian-Amazon Company that dot the 1913 map cynically repeat the names of other places and peoples already subjugated to the demands of industrial capitalism.

Names on a map, as J. Hillis Miller writes, are a palimpsest, layer upon layer of inscribed meanings that can tell the history of a place: "All the place names on a map in their systematic interrelation tell obscurely the story of the generations that have inhabited that place. In living they have left the traces of their lives behind in tombstone inscriptions and in names given to houses, villages, fields, roads, or streams."[5] Miller's assurance that the landscape will honor the memory of the dead sounds like wishful thinking when applied to the bloody and chaotic history of the Putumayo, the site of a frenzied holocaust in which tens of thousands of Indians were killed by rubber traders and the private armies they maintained in the first decade of the twentieth century. But as Miller suggests, the science of "topology," the knowledge of places, includes both the study of its physical features, or *topography*, and the study of the names inscribed upon it, its *toponomy*.[6] Combining both studies, perhaps, we may get a more complete story, one that tells us how heterogeneous human populations have explored, settled on, and harvested the natural resources of the region, suggesting if only vaguely the social relationships—cooperative and relatively benign or bloodthirsty and exploitative—that have developed among and on those many rivers and in the dense tropical jungles.

In order to understand better the carefully constructed topography of *La vorágine*, let us compare the map included in *El libro rojo* with one printed in *La vorágine,* as the text traditionally includes a map of southern Colombia, Venezuela, Brazil, and Peru, showing Cova's circuitous path from Bogotá to the Rio Negro. This second map (figure 2) is from the ninth edition of *La vorágine*, which Rivera closely supervised up to the time of his death in New York City in 1928. It shows at least as much detail as the map from *El libro rojo,* but the toponomy, in contrast, is entirely Latin American: all the place-names on Rivera's map are of clearly indigenous or Hispanic origin, and there is no evidence to suggest that

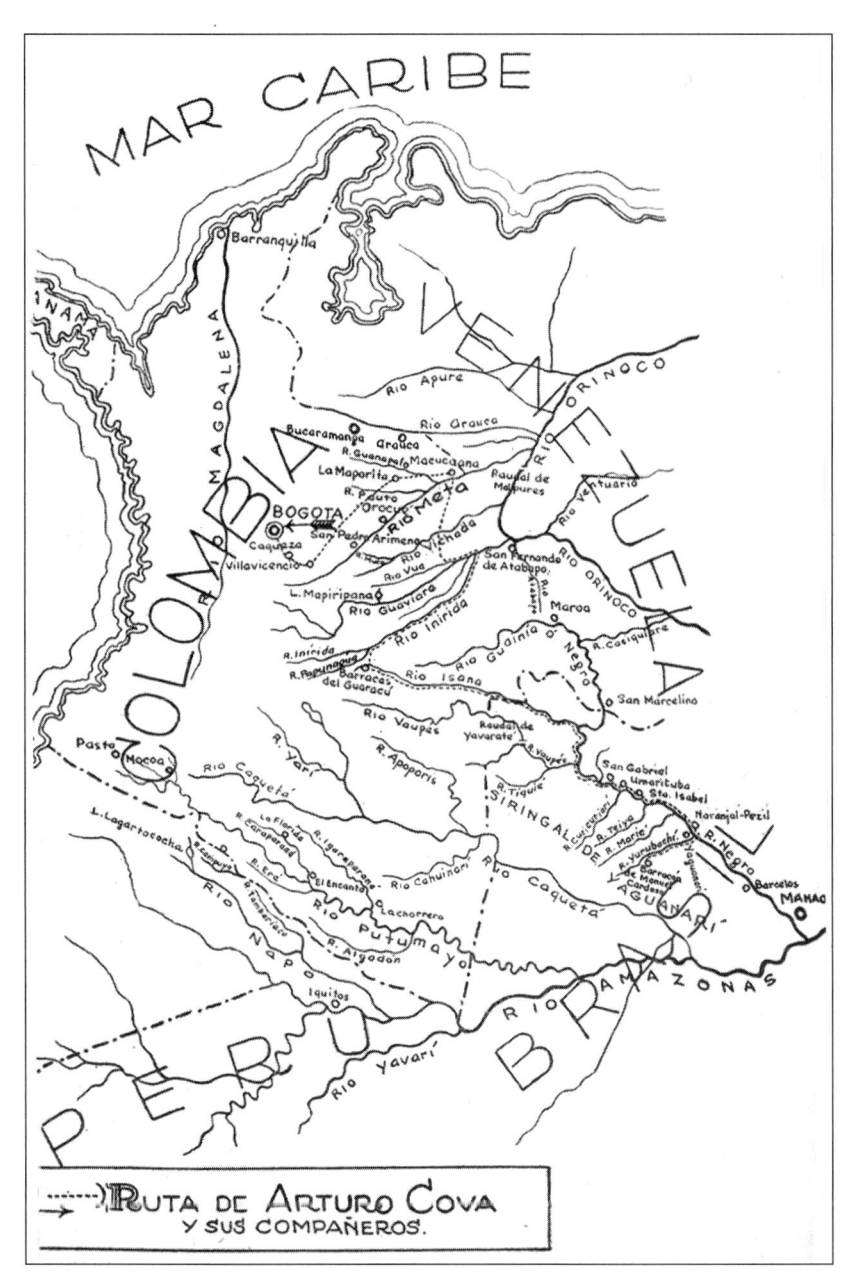

FIG. 2. Ruta de Arturo Cova [Arturo Cova's route]. Map from José Eustasio Rivera, *La vorágine* (New York: Editorial Andes, 1929), 341. Courtesy of University of Minnesota Libraries.

Englishmen were involved in the region at all, or that the tumultuous and tragic Putumayo so closely resembled the geography of empire.

If names on a map describe the human history of a given place, then clearly the maps presented in *El libro rojo* and *La vorágine* are telling two different stories. One locates the exploitation of the Putumayo within the context of European imperialism and the other reads the same events within the history of Hispanic penetration and colonization of the South American interior. Rivera, I will argue, chose to tell one version of the story rather than the other, deriving his historical information from sources close to Casement while electing to suppress the British presence in the Putumayo altogether.

Similarly troubled by the novel's historical inconsistencies, Carlos J. Alonso has raised the issue of why Rivera would bother so zealously to denounce labor practices that had all but ended a decade before, when British consumers shifted their interest to the plantations of southeast Asia, where a cheap and reliable supply of rubber was being produced on British-owned plantations. Alonso suggests that Rivera develops an implicit contrast between the economic and ecological rationalism of the plantation rubber industry—which had been established using specimens of *hevea brasilensis* surreptitiously exported from the Amazon and cultivated in London's Kew Gardens—with the relatively unprofitable and unsustainable wild rubber industry in South America.[7] Undoubtedly the efficiency of the Asian plantations contributed as much as the moral outcry against the Peruvian Amazon Company to British stockholders' en masse divestment in 1911. Nevertheless, Rivera's nonliterary writings—to which we shall soon turn—show that the economic, social, and environmental abuses in southern Colombia were still a timely concern in 1921; Julio Arana continued to operate in the region long after the liquidation of the Peruvian Amazon Company. Roberto Simón Crespi has also suggested that the European crisis of World War I lowered the humanitarian standards of the British government, which hypocritically fed its insatiable wartime demand for rubber with "the black and bloody gold of Arana."[8]

Crespi, one of the first to dedicate his investigation exclusively to an analysis of *La vorágine*'s contradictory politics, is clearly frustrated by the absence of the Peruvian Amazon Company: "Neither Cova nor Rivera nor the countless others who had condemned the crimes of the Putumayo understood that, among other supports, the Peruvian, Colombian, and European investors and other businessmen were the true benefactors and defenders of Arana and the system they had helped to construct."[9] Crespi's vigorous Marxist analysis criticizes Rivera for failing to grasp the significance of the international capitalist market and individual investors' responsibility for the exploitation of the Putumayo. The present analysis, which in many respects builds on Crespi's, must nevertheless begin by asserting that many of Rivera's contemporaries, and certainly many of those who denounced the Putumayo abuses, *did* understand the relationship between capitalist investment and neo-colonial exploitation. Furthermore, there is considerable evidence to suggest that Rivera himself had that information by the time he wrote *La vorágine*.

In 1939 Eduardo Neale Silva, author of what remains the definitive biography of Rivera, wrote that Casement's report was "one of his main sources for the section dealing with the Putumayo."[10] Whether or not Rivera had access to that very document, information on Casement's mission and the inhumane practices of the Peruvian Amazon Company was disseminated in Colombia in exposés including *El libro rojo del Putumayo* and *Putumayo caucho y sangre*. The story was closely watched in Colombian newspapers, including the Bogotá dailies *El Tiempo* and *El Espectador*, both of which were popular among Rivera's liberal intellectual associates.[11] On November 23, 1912, for example, *El Tiempo* published an article with the sensational headline, "La barbarie inquisitorial del hombre blanco. Crímenes monstruosos y horrorosas atrocidades" [The inquisitorial barbarism of the white man: Monstrous crimes and horrific atrocities]. The lengthy article enumerates in considerable detail Casement's accusations against the Peruvian Amazon Company, at times quoting directly from the *Blue Book*. Many of the accusations repeated in the article, and attributed to Casement, will appear again in *La vorágine*:

> En su informe, dice Sir Casement, que varios empleados de la Compañía mataron a tiros, por distraerse, a niños indios, que mujeres y niños han sido azotados con látigos, hasta que murieron hechos una pura llaga; que se hace morir de hambre a hombres y mujeres; que cuando los empleados están aburridos, atan a estacas a los indios y los convierten en blanco de sus rifles; que otras veces entretiénense dichos empleados en cortar las orejas a los trabajadores indígenas, y cuando un indígena no lleva a la Compañía el caucho que se les había encargado, se le dan doscientos palos, o se le hace sufrir una espantosa y dolorosísima mutilación.
>
> ... En el Alto Amazonas, Distrito del Putumayo, la Compañía tiene 45 centros, donde trabajan unos 50,000 indígenas. Estos se dedican a la recolección del caucho; ese caucho que, como dice Luis Bonafoux, sirve para los automóviles en que banqueros y cocotas atropellan al campesino en la ruta y al obrero en la calle.

> [In his report Sir Casement [*sic*] writes that several employees of the company amused themselves by shooting Indian children to death, that women and children had been whipped until they died, utterly covered with wounds;

that men and women are starved to death, that when the employees are bored they tie the Indians to posts and make them the targets of their rifles; that other times they entertain themselves by cutting off the indigenous workers' ears, that when an indigene fails to bring the company the quantity of rubber he was ordered to collect, he is given two hundred strokes, or made to suffer a horrific and extremely painful mutilation.

... In the Upper Amazon, District of the Putumayo, the company has 45 centers, in which 50,000 indigenes labor. They dedicate themselves to the collection of rubber; that rubber that, as Luis Bonafoux says, serves for the automobiles in which bankers and prostitutes run over the peasant in the road and the laborer in the street.]

The article quoted above is part of a long series dedicated to the Putumayo scandal and official attempts to improve the situation. In November 1911, *El Tiempo* ran an article describing plans to liquidate the Peruvian Amazon Company as investment trickled out. On September 6, 1913, *El Tiempo*'s "Páginas Literarias" were dedicated to an essay by R. B. Cunninghame Graham, the radical Scottish aristocrat who as a member of Parliament had witnessed Hardenburg's testimony.

What is more, *El Tiempo* presents the revelations about the Peruvian Amazon Company in the context of growing public mistrust of Great Britain: its pages suggest that Britain's nineteenth-century image as a seemingly benign financial "partner" to a developing Colombia was wearing thin. The paper's most prominent advertisers during the years investigated, it should be noted, are merchants offering British imports ranging from genuine "Collins" tools (on sale at the Casa Inglesa) to Dr. Williams's "Píldoras Rosadas" (pink pills) and the latest in London tailoring for men and women. Much of the news, especially during the crisis of World War I, comes from Europe and particularly London. There are reports from British Foreign Secretary Sir Edward Grey, a regular column entitled "Noticias del Gobierno inglés," and human interest stories such as a note on the "fearsome" suffragist Emmeline Pankhurst. If *El Tiempo*'s interest in and access to the news from London seem surprising, this apparent goodwill is countered by a number of articles that are skeptical, even suspicious, of Britain's interest in Latin America. In August and September 1911, while Parliament continued its investigation of the Peruvian Amazon Company, *El Tiempo* reports conflicts between the Colombian government and two British companies, the London and South Western Bank, Ltd, and the Santa Marta Railway Company, Ltd, which failed to construct major railway lines for which the Colombian government had already paid. The news of British business imperialism is reflected in *El Tiempo*'s features and editorials. "La República está sola," written by

La vorágine: Dialectics of the Rubber Boom   121

Jaime Gutiérrez and published May 8, 1911, suggests that Colombia's European allies are unwilling to protect the country from U.S. aggression, and cites reports from the London *Daily Mail* and *Daily Chronicle* that support Washington's deployment of North American troops in Mexico and the Caribbean. "La guerra europea y el porvenir de Colombia" [The European war and Colombia's future] (August 12, 1915, anonymous) contests the common belief that once the war is over the influx of foreign capital will develop Colombia's natural resources to such a degree that "in a word, we will find ourselves in circumstances similar to those of Argentina in the first stage of its economic bloom." It suggests, in contrast, that "competition in everything and for everything will eventually mean the dominance of the strongest with grave consequences for the weak. And are we prepared for that?"

The sharpest accusations are formulated in an anonymous editorial titled "Inglaterra contra nosostros," published November 18, 1915. The author writes in response to a complaint filed by one Guillermo [*sic*, probably William] Boshell, a British subject who accuses the Colombian government of fraudulent practices in the Caquetá region eight years earlier. Boshell's charges and his claim to 250,000 pesos in damages, determined to be spurious by a special committee of the Colombian Senate, are aggressively backed by the British Foreign Office and its agent in Bogotá. The editorialist, linking the current action to the Foreign Offices' support of the London and Southwestern Bank in the ongoing Puerto Wilches scandal, accuses the British government of using its unmatched military power to support "adventurers" intent upon robbing "a poor, weak country." The article's forceful conclusion is worth quoting at length:

> En el gran drama que hoy se juega en el mundo, la opinión colombiana ha sido en su mayoría favorable a los aliados, y nosotros no hemos ocultado la viva simpatía que su causa nos inspira, simpatía que no nos impide sentir una inmensa admiración por las energías y la fuerza gigantesca del pueblo alemán. Pero debemos reconocer que Inglaterra nada hace por merecer nuestro afecto y muy al contrario, llegará con sus procedimientos a hacernos odioso un país cuyo gobierno es el principal sostén de quienes tratan de cebarse en nuestra debilidad y de explotar ferozmente nuestros errores o nuestras ligerezas.
>
> Y en estas circunstancias, debemos recordar que antes que ninguna otra cosa, estamos en el deber de ser colombianófilos, de negar nuestro apoyo moral a quienes sólo tratan de hacernos mal y no se acuerdan de nosotros sino para imponernos su voluntad y para chupar nuestra escasa sangre.
>
> [In the great drama being played out in the world today, Colombian opinion has largely sided in favor of the Allies, and we have not hidden the

lively sympathy their cause inspires in us, sympathy that does not prevent us from feeling an immense admiration for the energy and the gigantic force of the German people. We must recognize that England does nothing to merit our affection and on the contrary, will commit such acts as to make hateful to us a country whose government is the principal support of those who try to feed on our weakness and ferociously exploit our errors or our shortcomings.

And in these circumstances, we must remember that above all we must be Colombianophiles; we must deny our moral support to those who try only to do us harm and who remember us only to impose their will on us or to suck what little blood we have.]

The idea that Rivera was unaware of the links between the Putumayo scandal and the British government or the growing Colombian resentment against Britain is untenable, not only because of the similarities between Casement's report and *La vorágine*, but because of the prominence of the story in the Bogotá press during the years when Rivera was living in the Colombian capital as a law student and a fledgling poet. An individual who was completely withdrawn from public life might have managed to miss the scandal as it unfolded in late 1913, but Rivera was consistently engaged in politics and current events. What is more, he published the sonnet "Tierra de Promisión" in the October 11, 1913, edition of *El Tiempo*'s "Páginas literarias," just three weeks after the same feature ran Cunninghame Graham's essay on Hardenburg. Surely Rivera was not unaware of the British ties to the Peruvian Amazon Company, nor of the general climate of public outcry against Britain's informal imperialism in which the scandal developed. Nevertheless, the British-owned Peruvian Amazon Company disappears from Rivera's jungle even more mysteriously than Cova himself.[12]

In this regard *La vorágine* is very different from the texts we have examined in the previous chapters. Whereas Quiroga and Lynch overtly criticize the actions of British neo-imperialists in the Río de la Plata, explicitly engaging Britain's colonial literature to draw out parallels between the situation in their countries and in the formal empire, Rivera instead has detailed information on Britain's involvement in the exploitative rubber industry, and yet refuses to introduce it into his novel. His decision to occlude this seemingly vital information from *La vorágine* is closer to Andrés Bello's response to the work of Spaniard Juan María Maury y Benítez. As I explained in the introduction, Bello rewrote Maury's "La agresión británica" (1806) as his famous "Oda a la agricultura en la zona tórrida" back in 1826, building on Maury's idyllic images of the Latin American countryside while suppressing what the Spaniard recognized as

Britain's neo-colonial desire to control the region. To understand Rivera's decision, we should take into account the dramatically different historical circumstances of Colombia and the countries of the Río de la Plata. In both cases Britain had built up a strong economic presence in the last quarter of the nineteenth century: although Colombia's political instability prevented investment from reaching the same proportions as in Argentina and Uruguay, the telegraphs, railroads, and other infrastructure that supported the flourishing coffee industry were largely built using British technology and labor, while imported manufactures and luxury goods were almost entirely supplied by British merchants, as the pages of *El Tiempo* and *El Espectador* attest. While dependence on British capital and technology undoubtedly weakened the Colombian economy and exacerbated class differences, at the same time, Colombia and the other nations of the Caribbean and Central America were vulnerable to a much more direct and immediate threat to national sovereignty: the United States. For these nations, Britain and the United States presented very different threats: in contrast to the subtle economic dominance exerted by the Invisible Empire, the United States all too often meant military force, territorial invasion, and direct political control. Like Andrés Bello, Rivera might have chosen to occlude the British threat in order to concentrate his compatriots' energies on more immediate enemies; he might have even had some aspiration of enlisting British aid against both the hemispheric tyrant and the more local problem of Peruvian and Venezuelan incursions.

I suspect, however, that his motives were quite different. As reported in the pages of *El Tiempo, El Espectador,* and *El libro rojo,* the story of the Peruvian Amazon Company is almost as much about the power and prestige of English law as it is about informal imperialism or capitalist exploitation. The first significant reports feature Sir Roger Casement firmly at the helm of the investigation; subsequent reportage details the atrocities committed by agents of the Peruvian Amazon Company, but always in the context of the British Parliament's pursuit of justice, which eventually led to the dissolution of the corporation. While the board of directors may have been made up of Englishmen, the individuals most directly accused of murder and mutilation were South Americans. Thus Rivera, in writing about the Putumayo scandal, faced a catch-22: either write the British into the story and run the risk of polishing up Britain's somewhat tarnished reputation for justice and moral rectitude, or write them out altogether. It little mattered, under the circumstances, that Casement's work in the Putumayo and the Congo were, in the words of Edmund Morel, "the only two [occasions] in which British diplomacy rose above the commonplace."[13] Nor did it matter that by 1917 Casement was dead, executed by the British government on charges of treason for his work on behalf of

Irish home rule. Neither of those pieces of information could be accomodated within the scope of Rivera's novel, and so he chose to write the British out altogether, suppressing the profit-mongering of company shareholders along with the humanitarian labors of Casement. (Hardenburg, the U.S. citizen who first exposed the situation in the British press, was an even less likely candidate for Rivera's novel.) The photographer Eugenio Robuchon is the one European who does make it into the text, as the humane "mosiú" murdered by Arana's henchmen; it is logical that Robuchon should appear, given the contrast between the neo-colonialism of the Anglo-Saxon countries and the relatively unaggressive agenda France was pursuing in Latin America in the same period.

In other words, if Rivera had tried to give a more complete version of the Putumayo scandal in *La vorágine,* he would have found himself in the undesired position of propping up a narrative that in Colombia and other parts of Latin America was already on the verge of collapse, a narrative of heroic Anglo-Saxons bringing justice and the rule of law to the barbaric peoples of the tropical jungles. Given Rivera's patriotism and his sensitivity to the ongoing risk of neo-colonialism, that possibility was unacceptable to him, so he told a version of the story in which a Colombian intellectual, Arturo Cova, plays the role that historically belonged, collectively, to the British: that of the exploiter turned whistle-blower. At the same time, Rivera is far from turning a blind eye to the international or transatlantic issue of informal imperialism: the narrative account of Cova's transformation is constructed so as to dismantle almost completely the ideological structures that had supported Britain's economic hegemony for nearly a century—by which I mean both the Latin American elites' cultural Eurocentrism and the colonial relationship to the continent's indigenous people and natural resources that for decades had enabled them to mediate between those resources and British capital.

In order to do justice to the ideological and rhetorical complexities of *La vorágine*—and more completely situate the novel in its equally complex historical context—I should say that the novel offers two somewhat contradictory responses to the problem of informal imperialism, one of which may be called a *liberal* response, and the other a *radical* one. The liberal response, characterized by a desire to extend national sovereignty into Colombia's geographic periphery, is apparent in Rivera's collection of sonnets (*Tierra de Promisión*), his nonliterary work as a government official sent to investigate the Venezuelan border, and *La vorágine*'s topographic drive. Rivera's liberal response, while aimed at fortifying Colombia's borders against foreign incursion such as occurred in Panama and the Putumayo, offers little protection against the more insidious invasion of British capital. On the contrary, incorporating more of the country's outlying territories under the sway of a Eurocentric and profit-driven national government would only perpetuate the interlocking structures of internal and external colonialism that, as I have argued, characterize British hegemony in Latin America. So *La vorágine* also articulates a contradictory radical response that aims at undermining the Eurocentric and capitalist assumptions of the Colombian elite and establishing a new, nonexploitative relationship between the country's government and its human and natural resources. In order to understand how this uniquely positioned novel responds to U.S. *and* British informal imperialism, including the problem of internal colonialism, we shall look first at Rivera's liberal response and then at the more radically anticolonial, anticapitalist critique of *La vorágine*.

Losing Ground: The Topographic Response

As Hilda Soledad Pachón Farías writes, Rivera's provincial origins made him particularly sensitive to the vast differences—geographic, economic, cultural—that separated the southern and eastern regions from the Colombian capital.[14] He was born in 1888 in the region known as Huila, a remote ranching area south of Bogotá that did not become an official department until 1905 and remained isolated from the rest of the country until the 1950s. According to Pachón, during Rivera's childhood Huila was conservative, staunchly Catholic, and financially desolate after the events of the Thousand Days' War. Rivera was expelled from the local private school he attended and then sent to boarding school in Bogotá. He returned to Huila with a college degree in 1909 and served as school supervisor of Ibagué and Neiva until 1911, when he was fired for criticizing the district's conservative policies on female education. At that time Rivera returned to Bogotá, matriculated as a law student, and began his successful career as a poet. In 1919, soon after graduating from law school, Rivera made the famous journey to Casanare in Colombia's eastern plains where he (unsuccessfully) argued his first legal case and gathered material that would later be incorporated into the first section of *La vorágine*.[15]

These peregrinations must have made Rivera particularly aware of the isolation and vulnerability of the distant provinces. The threat of U.S. imperialism was unavoidable: like all his generation, Rivera had come of age feeling the weight of the 1902 partition of Panama, which was kept alive in Colombian politics by the controversy over treaties to legalize the separation. In fact, Rivera's political activism seems to have begun in 1909, when he led his classmates in protesting against General Rafael Reyes' approval of a treaty that legalized the separation, granting the United States the right to drill in Colombian oil fields in exchange for the twenty-five million dollars originally promised as reparations.[16] Pachón rightly emphasizes these two pieces of biographic information—Rivera's childhood on Colombia's geographic periphery and his adolescent protest against the ratification of Panama's secession—because they indicate his early and profound sensitivity to Colombia's vulnerability to territorial dismemberment. By the same logic, she understands Rivera's literary achievement as a response to this concern: "Part of his greatness lies in having contributed to the unity of the nation by integrating vast territories that remained in oblivion by making them known to his compatriots."[17]

Tierra de Promisión, the collection of poems Rivera published in 1921, may be considered his first attempt to create a literary topography of Colombia in response to neo-colonialism. Its very title, which translates into English as "The Promised Land," announces the text's intention of rhetorically claiming at last the vast unsettled stretches of Colombia's national patrimony. Its fifty-four sonnets are divided, like the map of Colombia, into three sections, corresponding to the jungle, the mountains, and the plains. Each of the sonnets represents a different scene in the wild, describing animals, plants, and topography in intimate detail and emphasizing the minute interactions among them with a scopophilic pleasure to rival contemporary nature programs on television.[18]

> Sobre el musgo reseco la serpiente tranquila
> fulge al sol, enroscada como rica diadema;
> y en su escama vibrátil el zafiro se quema,
> la esmeralda se enciende y el topacio rutila.
>
> Tiemblan lampos de nácar en su roja pupila
> que columbra del buitre la acechanza suprema,
> y regando el reflejo de una pálida gema,
> silbadora y astuta, por la grama desfila.
>
> Van sonando sus crótalos en la gruta silente
> donde duerme el monarca de la felpa de raso;
> un momento relumbra la ondulante serpiente,
>
> y cuando ágil avanza y en la sombra se interna,
> al chispar de dos ojos, suena horrendo zarpazo
> y un rugido sacude la sagrada caverna.[19]
>
> [Upon dry moss the tranquil serpent
> lies resplendent in the sun, coiled like a rich diadem;
> and among its vibrating scales the sapphire burns,
> the emerald ignites and the topaz glows.

> Flames of nacre tremble in the red pupil
> that spies out a buzzard, the supreme snare,
> and strewing the reflection of a pale gem,
> whistling and astute, it files through the grass.
>
> Its rattles are heard in the silent grotto
> where the monarch of silken seclusion sleeps;
> the undulating serpent pauses, dazzling, for a moment,
>
> and when it agilely advances and penetrates the shade,
> winking its two eyes, a horrendous blow is heard
> and a cry shakes the sacred cavern.]

Critics often attribute the contrast between the orderly and highly aestheticized depiction of nature in *Tierra de Promisión* with the chaotic and hostile environment of *La vorágine* to the fact that Rivera did not visit either the plains of Casanare or the Amazon jungle until after the poems were completed. Rivera's shock—and perhaps embarrassment—at the contrast is reflected in these oft-quoted lines of Arturo Cova: "¡Nada de ruiseñores enamorados, nada de jardín versallesco, nada de panoramas sentimentales!" [No loving nightingales, no garden of Versailles, no sentimental vistas!] (296).[20]

While that is undoubtedly true, the poem quoted above also demonstrates a lordly and colonial attitude toward nature that parts 2 and 3 of *La vorágine* will thoroughly subvert. Like nearly all the sonnets of *Tierra de Promisión*, this one represents a space that is devoid of human inhabitants, scarcely populated by two wild animals. This emptiness allows the imaginative power of the speaker to dominate the scene.[21] The speaker, standing alone, maintains an aloof distance from the conflict that develops; yet his gaze penetrates the space to take in details of the animals' appearance. As a result the scene described is an extraordinary combination of *modernista* aestheticization and a naturalist's attention to ecological detail: the poet looks on, imaginatively transforming the snake into a collection of glittering gemstones that reflect his own sophistication and desire. He allows the elemental conflict between snake and buzzard to recede into a rich display of cultural allusions, drawn from orientalism and medieval Christianity—that surround the act of killing like the silken tapestries of a royal bedchamber. This worldly observer orders each scene and provides the continuity among them all, incorporating Colombia's wealth of geographic expanses into a framework established by the erudite voice of the poet. The speaker himself appears in several of the poems, participating like the others in this strangely ritualistic struggle for survival. In two he is described as a hunter, shooting a squirrel and allowing his dogs to devour a living tapir. In the most disturbing, a "malicious" (male) Indian brings an indigenous girl to his tent: inside they struggle, but the sobbing child is "caught by my desire" [presa de mi deseo] and quickly overpowered. The poem concludes: "Pobre. . . . Ya me agasaja! Es mi lecho un andamio, / mas la brisa y la noche cantan mi epitalamio / y la montaña púber huele a virginidad" [Poor thing . . . Already she tries to please me! My bed is a scaffold / but the breeze and the night sing my epithalamia / and the pubescent mountain smells of virginity] (poem 7, p. 25).

In *La vorágine* the topographic response initially articulated in *Tierra de Promisión* becomes a more strategically precise defense against foreign encroachment and a protest against the Colombian government's failure fully to establish sovereignty in the geographic periphery. Between the writing of *Tierra de Promisión* and *La vorágine* intervened not only the sojourn to Casanare but also a 1922 expedition into southern Colombia as secretary of a special government commission to investigate the disputed Venezuelan border. Accompanied by engineers and geographers from the national Oficina de Longitudes in Bogotá, Rivera descended southeast from the capital to the territory that Arturo Cova would later explore in *La vorágine*: the dense jungles where the territorial limits of Colombia, Venezuela, and Brazil meet. There they met up with their Venezuelan counterparts to investigate the situation. The Venezuelan problem was similar to the still-unresolved issue of the Putumayo: foreigners, some of them working for Julio Arana, were accused of encroaching on Colombian territory, abusing local tribes, and exploiting the region's remaining rubber trees.

The expedition ended in frustration and a disagreement that continued for months afterward: Rivera accused several of the other officials, including his direct superior, Justino Garavito, and the commission's leader, Julio Garzón Nieto, of unpatriotic negligence in failing to perform their duties and the commission separated into two groups before returning to Bogotá. Two months after setting out, Rivera renounced his position on the commission and decided to complete the journey on his own. Afterward, Rivera maintained that he had hired two Indian guides and explored by canoe the little-known waterways surrounding the Inírida River, briefly losing their way in the dense jungle. In the mythology that has subsequently developed around the genesis of the famous novel, however (some of it apparently fostered by Rivera himself), the details of the author's journey have become all but indistinguishable from those of the protagonist's.[22]

What is certain is that Rivera soon met up again with his colleague Melitón Escobar Larrazábal, who had abandoned the commission a month after Rivera, in the town of San Fernando de Atabapo. The two sent urgent messages to Bogotá and submitted an official report to

La vorágine: Dialectics of the Rubber Boom   129

Colombia's minister of foreign relations after their return to the capital. The report submitted by Rivera and Escobar prefigures key aspects of *La vorágine* in its defense of oppressed laborers, strong nationalist tone, and preoccupation with the senseless destruction of the rubber trees. Perhaps most important, the former commissioners' attitude suggests that the best way to protect Colombia's borderlands against foreign invasion is to finish the project of internal colonialism by incorporating those territories more completely into the state. For that reason, the commissioners' meeting with local tribes menaced by Venezuelan rubber traders is presented as a revisionary encounter in which the colonial practice of surveying and rationalizing the land is undertaken on behalf of its indigenous inhabitants:

> Nosotros aprovechamos las ocasiones que se presentaron para transmitirles algunas noticias sobre su nacionalidad y darles explicaciones gráficas acerca de los límites de Colombia en aquellos dominios. Muy complacidos recibían la noticia de que eran colombianos, lo que sabían por primera vez, y algunos nos dieron a conocer sus quejas y malos recuerdos acerca del tratamiento recibido de las autoridades venezolanas que han venido ejerciendo jurisdicción desde hace más de medio siglo.[23]

> [We took advantage of the occasions that presented themselves to transmit to them some information about their nationality and give them graphic illustrations of Colombia's borders in those dominions. They very gratefully received the news that they were Colombians, which they learned for the first time, and some told us about their complaints and bad memories of the treatment they received from the Venezuelan authorities that had exercised jurisdiction there for more than a half-century.]

The report continues, describing the commission's work in the area surrounding the town of San José:

> El comisionado realizó su viaje en una canoa, entrevistó a los jefes de las tribus vecinas, les enseñó su nacionalidad, les hizo explicaciones objetivas acerca de los límites entre Colombia y Venezuela y les advirtió que sólo debían obedecer las leyes y autoridades colombianas y elevar sus reclamos al Comisario Especial de San Rafael del Meta, única autoridad de nuestro país en aquellas regiones.[24]

> [The commission carried out its trip by canoe, interviewed the chiefs of neighboring tribes, taught them their nationality, gave them objective explanations of the limits between Colombia and Venezuela, and informed them that they had only to obey Colombian laws and authorities and take their complaints to the Special Commissioner of San Rafael del Meta, our nation's only authority in those regions.]

Cartography, the codification of space, brings with it the law that codifies and regulates social relations: the fixing of the limit between Colombia and Venezuela is a geographic and a political act; it is significant that Rivera was appointed to the commission specifically to serve as its lawyer. This curious official report may be read as a kind of utopian revision of first contact: the white men arrive not to displace the Indians from their land, but to establish a bond of national solidarity and offer protection from foreign intruders. The scene, complete with its grateful Indians, enacts a fantasy of recolonization, not because it did not happen as described—that we have no way of knowing—but because it presupposes the existence of a state that is both powerful enough to enforce the protection its emissaries promise and heterogeneous enough to respect the cultural and political autonomy of the Indians.

Rivera found his expectations greatly disappointed, and the expedition that inspired his greatest literary achievement was virtually the end of his career in politics. Though his revelations of the ongoing penetration of Colombia's southern borders by Arana's employees sparked a public outcry even before the publication of *La vorágine* in November 1924, Rivera found the Colombian government reprehensibly slow to respond. On May 26, *El Espectador* published an open letter from José Eustasio Rivera to the Colombian minister of foreign relations. With characteristic chutzpah, Rivera accuses the minister of failing to act on his report: "Entonces hablaba yo como ex-abogado de la comisión de límites, que había estudiado el litigio a su leal saber y entender por todas sus formas y que había observado *sobre el terreno* los resultados de la incompetencia ministerial. Nadie me creyó." [I spoke then as the former attorney for the border commission, who had studied the litigation to the best of his ability and had observed *upon the terrain* the results of ministerial incompetence. No one believed me] (17; emphasis added). Rivera, in his anger and frustration, shows himself thinking once again in terms of the relationship between the law and the land, arguing that the government's faulty administration was visible in the landscape itself.

La vorágine picks up the trope of mapping the jungle as a figure for extending national sovereignty into the troubled periphery. Inverting the analogy between the codification of space and the rationalization of social relations, the novel presents the lack of adequate maps of southern Colombia as a figure for the government's generalized neglect of the borderlands, where there was no reliable system of communication or transportation, little or no government presence, and no legitimate legal authority.[25] As in the official report, Rivera suggests that Colombia's best defense against neo-colonialism is to complete the long-unfinished project of internal colonization—but this time the figure of mapping is used in reverse. Rather than demonstrating the positive effects of establishing the nation's borders (the relief and gratitude of the Indians), Rivera shows the disastrous results of the region's chaotic state in the horrors of the rubber industry and the fate of Arturo Cova and his companions: *devorados* by the jungle. In this regard the two motifs of the latter half of *La vorágine*—the threat to the territorial integrity of the nation and the personal nightmare of disappearing in the jungle—are figured as an extended pun on the verbs *perder / perderse:* to lose / to get lost, or more literally, to lose oneself. As Balbino Jácome tells Clemente Silva, while they desperately search for a Colombian authority in Iquitos: "¡Paisano, paisanito, estamos perdidos! ¡Y el Putumayo y el Caquetá se pierden también!" [Countryman, dear countryman, we're lost! And the Putumayo and Caquetá will be lost too!] (277).

The narrative develops this figure in several different ways. Perhaps the most obvious is the barb Rivera aimed directly at the government geographers who had aroused his irritation during the 1922 expedition. In the novel's final pages, when Cova has rejoined Alicia and Griselda and had his revenge against Barrera, Clemente Silva sets off alone for Manaos, hoping to bring the Colombian consul back to rescue them and the other Colombians trapped in debt-peonage. Cova, however, pessimistically imagines the outcome of Silva's mission:

> De juro que si bajan hasta Manaos, nuestro Cónsul, al leer mi carta, replicará que su valimiento y jurisdicción no alcanzan a estas latitudes, o lo que es lo mismo, que no es colombiano sino para contados sitios del país. Tal vez, al escuchar la relación de don Clemente, extienda sobre la mesa aquel mapa costoso, aparatoso, mentiroso y deficientísimo que trazó la Oficina de Longitudes de Bogotá, y le responda tras de prolija indagación: "¡Aquí no figuran ríos de esos nombres! Quizás pertenezcan a Venezuela. Diríjase usted a Ciudad Bolívar."
>
> Y, muy campante, seguirá atrincherado en su estupidez, porque a esta pobre patria no la conocen sus propios hijos, ni siquiera sus geógrafos. (361)

> [And if they get to Manaos, our consul, on reading my letter, will most likely reply that his jurisdiction does not reach these regions—or, what amounts to the same, that he's a Colombian only for certain parts of the country. Perhaps on listening to Don Clemente's story he'll spread out that costly, ornate, lying and deficient map that the Oficina de Longitudes of Bogotá drew up, and after much searching he'll say: "There are no rivers by those names here! Perhaps they are Venezuelan. Head to Ciudad Bolívar."
>
> And, very content, he'll continue entrenched in his stupidity, because this poor country isn't known by its own sons, not even by its geographers.]

132 NATURE, NEO-COLONIALISM

As cartography becomes a figure for political legitimacy and the ability to govern, the national government's administrative neglect of southern Colombia is aptly symbolized by the official map that fails to label properly the rivers Cova and his companions have struggled to navigate during their months (and years, in Silva's case) of wandering through the jungle.

The text more subtly corrects this governmental negligence by tracing in its fevered pages a new topography to replace the old one: *La vorágine* itself verbalizes the spatial configuration of the land, capturing in its intricate structure and baroque, wandering narrative the geographic complexities of an obscure corner of the Amazon jungle. As scholars often point out, the narrative accounts of Arturo Cova and Clemente Silva's endless, often aimless trek through the jungle afforded Rivera an opportunity to interweave a dozen or more stories spanning fifteen years of the South American rubber boom.[26] What more often goes unnoticed is the topography traced by Cova and Silva: though their journeys often seem pointless and confused, the trips themselves—criss-crossing swamps and forests, staggering into El Encanto or La Chorrera, struggling to find the Río Isana or the Caquetá, doubling back when they've lost their way or changed their minds—beat out the topography of southern Colombia in extraordinary detail. For example:

> Llegamos a las márgenes del río Vichada derrotados por los zancudos. Durante la travesía los azuzó la muerte tras de nosotros y nos persiguieron día y noche, flotando en halo fatídico y quejumbroso, trémulos como una cuerda a media vibrar . . .
>
> Las que enantes fueron sabanas úberes, se habían convertido en desoladas ciénagas. (214)

> [We arrived at the banks of the Vichada River defeated by the mosquitos. During the crossing death urged them on behind us so that they pursued us day and night, floating in an ominous and querulous halo, humming like a vibrating cord . . .
>
> What was once fertile plains, had become desolate swamps.]

The result is a new, verbal map to replace the antiquated government maps of which the characters repeatedly complain. As one of Rivera's most famous admirers, Horacio Quiroga, wrote to him, "Lo que el Río Negro se llame también Guanía, es maravilloso, y para hacer gozar de tantas maravillas no se necesitan los geógrafos existiendo épico tan encumbrado como usted." [That the Río Negro is also called the Guainía is marvelous; we no longer need geographers to enjoy these wonders, since an epic as exalted as yours exists].[27]

This topographic drive is one of the strongest thematic and structural elements in *La vorágine,* and the characters' insistence upon the necessity of mapping the jungle corresponds to Rivera's own belief in the importance of protecting Colombia's outlying territories by integrating them into the nation through a process of internal colonization that would entail charting the groves, regulating the companies, and otherwise rationalizing the rubber industry. Nevertheless, a contradictory impulse that I am calling Rivera's "radical" response to informal imperialism subtly undermines this call to bring the benefits of a Western and capitalist modernity to the Colombian jungle. This response is "radical" in that rather than simply fortifying the nation's borders against foreign invaders, it seeks to subvert the ideological structures that had both facilitated and fed on the development of informal imperialism throughout the nineteenth century. As I have argued throughout this book, Britain's invisible hegemony in Latin America was ideologically based on Latin American elites' implicit sense of identification with the Christian and capitalist British Empire: this identification fostered a desire to modernize their cities with imported architecture, technology, and luxury goods—even if the increasing production that would finance those improvements meant drastically increasing hardships for workers in the agricultural and extractive industries of the interior.

Conquistadores conquistados: *Cova and Kurtz*

Rivera's radical response begins—like the work of Quiroga and Lynch—by appropriating one of the most conventional forms of British colonial literature: in this case, the jungle adventure narrative, best embodied by Joseph Conrad's *Heart of Darkness* (1899). As critics have remarked, the parallels between *La vorágine* and *Heart of Darkness* are impressive: both invoke Dante and classical myth to structure terrifying journeys into the continents' interior. Both combine Romantic subjective and emotional intensity with modernist techniques of perspectivism and psychological distortion; both mix urgent exposures of exploitation and human suffering with a surpassing commitment to literary form. Sylvia Molloy's well-known essay on *La vorágine* points to one of the most famous topographic moments in colonial literature: Marlow's explanation in the opening pages of *Heart of Darkness* of the youthful fascination with geography that inspired him to explore "the biggest, the most blank" space on the map, the central African territory that was to become the private colony of Belgium's Leopold II, the Congo Free State.[28] Molloy calls attention to this scene in order to point out that *La vorágine* and *Heart of Darkness* both begin with the protagonists' flight from the modern metropolis to seek adventure and a "singular, revelatory experience" in "a new, uncodified space—the 'blank space' Marlow dreams about as a child." While journeys into uncharted regions are commonplace in the literature of the nineteenth and early twentieth centuries, these texts will revise the standard material both stylistically and thematically. As Molloy suggests, the "blank spaces" that fascinate Rivera and Conrad include both the tropical jungles of South America and Africa and the possibility of breaking the conventions of the adventure novel genre. The heroes of colonial adventure fiction from *Robinson Crusoe* to *Doña Bárbara* are conventionally representatives of civilization who are physically and morally strong enough to withstand the challenges of the hostile wilderness and barbarous natives, and whose triumphs "prove" again and again the superiority of European or Western society over the conquered peoples.[29] In these texts, however, the standard ideological opposition between civilization and barbarism becomes blurred and confused, so that the agent of rationalism and progress becomes implicated in the anarchic savagery of the colonized jungle.

Thus far no evidence other than the strong similarities between them has turned up to suggest that Rivera was familiar with *Heart of Darkness* when he began *La vorágine* in 1922.[30] In that regard some of these affinities, such as the modernist flight from the metropolis, the Dantesque journey into the depths of hell, or the imaginative chronotope that figures the voyage into the jungle as a journey back to prehistoric times[31]—all of which may be considered derivations of the Western "ideological map" that Ordóñez astutely identifies[32]—may be considered the kind of discursive correspondences that are likely to arise when authors responding to a shared cultural tradition write on similar subjects within a relatively short time of one another. The real issue, after all, is not to determine whether Rivera read Conrad, as Quiroga read Kipling and Benito Lynch read Darwin, so much as to uncover and investigate his ambivalent relationship to the body of discourse of which Conrad was undoubtedly a part—including the parallel articulations of Latin American internal colonialism and British imperialism—and Rivera's decisive turn away from the European orientation on which this ideological map is based. Reading these texts comparatively, then, or as Edward Said would say, contrapuntally, will enable us to understand *La vorágine* as an articulation of the shifting relationship between the Latin American intelligentsia and the British Empire.[33] As we will see, *La vorágine* in many respects runs parallel to *Heart of Darkness,* but at a crucial juncture—in the encounter between Self and Other that occurs deep within the colonial jungle—Rivera's novel veers off from its identification with metropolitan discourses to formulate an oppositional identification with the exploited indigenous societies.

Perhaps the difficulty of interpreting the political vision of either of these texts may be summed up by saying that both criticize colonialism from a perspective that is self-consciously located within the economic, political, and social structures that have fostered it. Thus their first-person narrators repeat the dominant, colonialist cultural discourse so that it may be discredited by the events that unfold—but, as in a chamber of mirrors, the only narrative the reader has to interpret is the product of that very partial consciousness. Both texts show the breakdown of the rationalism and self-control of the would-be civilizing agents that occurs during the course of an intense encounter with the jungle and its indigenous inhabitants, but both also represent the white protagonists' identification with the natives as the experience or emotion that ultimately redeems them. In each case an enormous quantity of colonialist material is rehearsed and subverted in the course of this rhetorical reversal.

The jungle represented in *Heart of Darkness* draws on all of the cultural myths that constructed Africa as the "dark continent," a place of savage cannibals, poisonous plants, ferocious beasts, and a climate that spawned deadly plagues of malaria and dysentery. As Ian Watt has shown, Conrad developed Kurtz's character out of the nineteenth-century lore about colonial agents who "go native" in the African jungle, preferring the primitive and sensual customs of the natives to civilized behavior.[34] In Marlow's depiction, then, Kurtz is not only an abusive European who exploits the natives by "getting the tribe to follow [him]" in his ruthless quest for ivory: the myth of "going native" from which Kurtz is drawn combines a critique of the potentially limitless power of the colonial agent with racism and an implicit fear of miscegenation, ambivalently suggesting that he has both abused his power over the natives and betrayed the values of the civilization that educated and armed him to go among them. Marlow more than once suggests, therefore, that Kurtz has "succumbed" to the evil around him, as if "the wilderness had patted him on the head, and behold, it was like a ball—an ivory ball; it had caressed him and—lo!—and he had withered; it had taken him, loved him, embraced him, got into his veins, consumed his flesh, and sealed his soul to its own by the inconceivable ceremonies of some devilish initiation."[35]

The explicit Eurocentrism of Marlow's narrative, combined perhaps with the conservatism of Conrad's own political views, have made *Heart of Darkness* one of the most hotly polemicized texts in modern literature. One of the most famous criticisms is Chinua Achebe's essay, "An Image of Africa," in which he accuses Conrad of perpetuating all of the most virulent racist stereotypes of the "dark continent" in his representation of Africa and Africans, "which in the final consideration amounts to no more than a steady, ponderous, fake-ritualistic repetition of two sentences, one about silence and the other about frenzy."[36] Several years later the Guyanese novelist Wilson Harris took up the debate, and wrote "The Frontier on Which *Heart of Darkness* Stands."[37] In Harris's analysis, Marlow's insistence on the "impenetrability" of the bush and even the "incomprehensible" behavior of the natives bears witness to the presence of an autonomous existence and a cultural alterity that exceeds the limits of his own knowledge. Conrad's novel, writes Harris, is thus an extraordinary achievement because it signals the limits and limitations of the "homogeneous cultural logic" that legitimates imperialism. Even if Conrad does not actually cross the frontier, his work establishes a critical aperture in novelistic form that, as Harris points out, is particularly attractive for writers engaged in forming a poetics of cultural crossings, as occurs "in South America where [he] was born."[38]

One could choose from among dozens of textual examples to illustrate Harris's point. Two of the most famous describe Marlow's reactions to Africans whose appearance distinguishes them from the others. Soon after his arrival at the Outer Station, Marlow sees a young man lying under a tree, obviously dying of starvation. After giving the man one of his biscuits, Marlow observes: "He had tied a bit of white worsted round his neck—Why? Where did he get it? Was there any idea at all connected with it?" (14). Much later, near the narrative's conclusion, Marlow encounters a woman he takes to be Kurtz's African lover:

> She walked with measured steps, draped in striped and fringed cloths, treading the earth proudly, with a slight jingle and flash of barbarous ornaments. She carried her head high; her hair was done in the shape of a helmet; she had brass leggings to the knee, brass wire gauntlets to the elbow, a crimson spot on her tawny cheek, innumerable necklaces of glass beads on her neck; bizarre things, charms, gifts of witch men, that hung about her, glittered and trembled at every step. She must have had the value of several elephant tusks upon her. She was savage and superb, wild-eyed and magnificent; there was something ominous and stately in her deliberate progress . . .
>
> She came abreast of the steamer, stood still, and faced us. Her long shadow fell to the water's edge. Her face had a tragic and fierce aspect of wild sorrow and of dumb pain mingled with the fear of some struggling, half-shaped resolve. She stood looking at us without a stir, and like the wilderness itself, with an air of brooding over an inscrutable purpose. (55-56)

In contrast to Kipling, whose knowledge of Indian culture has often impressed readers of *Kim* and other works, Conrad was relatively ignorant of the colonized societies of which he wrote. Unlike Kipling's natives, however, who are often constructed so as to demonstrate their approval of the colonial administration, Conrad's Africans resist assimilation into the conceptual framework of the narrator. Communication between Marlow and the natives is extremely limited, and his attempts to penetrate their inner reality by studying outward signs like the piece of white wool generally end in an admission of defeat.

In the case of the woman, Marlow first rehearses a long series of primitivist clichés, describing her clothing, her jewelry—which he presumes to be "gifts of witch men"—and her body itself before finally attempting to step outside his own culturally conditioned worldview, which Harris more eloquently calls "the historical ego or the historical conditions of ego dignity that bind us to a particular decade or generation or century."[39] Having exhausted his supply of Victorian Africanisms in a futile attempt to assign a recognizable meaning to the "wild and gorgeous apparition of a woman," Marlow resigns himself to accepting that the woman's psychic and emotional life is rich and profound, but, like the wilderness itself, utterly beyond his scrutiny. At that point he attributes to the woman an emotional depth and authenticity that are all the more remarkable for the European company that surrounds them both—the hypocritical "pilgrims" of the Eldorado Exploring Expedition—and make her, in Watt's view, "the most affirmative image in the narrative."[40] Marlow's respect and admiration for the woman are reiterated when he juxtaposes her image, "tragic also, and bedecked with powerless charms, stretching bare brown arms over the glitter of the infernal stream, the stream of darkness" with that of Kurtz's European fiancée during the encounter that concludes the narrative (71).

Unlike Conrad's narrator Marlow or his terrible antihero Kurtz, who more closely compares to Cova, Rivera's protagonist does not leave the metropolis to seek his fortune in the southern jungles. He leaves, as Molloy points out, primarily from ennui; the scandal of his relationship with Alicia offers Cova more than anything else an excuse to escape from the tedium of his sophisticated urban existence.[41] But as he leaves Bogotá, Cova's identification with a colonial class becomes increasingly clear. As Ordóñez writes, "There can be no doubt that Arturo Cova considers himself superior in race, education, language, sex, and urban origin to all who surround him, and this is reflected particularly with regard to the indigenous. The great defender of Indians in the rubber region is at bottom a sad imitation of the European conquistador and colonizer."[42] This attitude becomes increasingly pronounced as Cova enters the geographic periphery, the plains of Casanare and the jungles of the south, regions that in the 1920s had yet to be fully colonized and incorporated into the nation. Casanare was still very much a frontier: isolated from the central plateau by a lack of roads, haphazardly governed by local strongmen, and desperately poor. Local Indian tribes were surprisingly populous and often hostile to the white cattle ranchers.[43]

As Cova and Alicia ride across the plains, he becomes increasingly drawn to the romantic, patriarchal stereotypes of Casanare that had been perpetuated in the *costumbrista* sketches of José María Samper and other nineteenth-century authors. The cultural myth of the pampa as a space of opportunity and manly challenge immediately inspires Cova. "Casanare no me aterraba con sus espeluznantes leyendas. El instinto de la aventura me impelía a desafiarlas, seguro de que saldría ileso de las pampas libérrimas y de que alguna vez, en desconocidas ciudades, sentiría la nostalgia de los pasados peligros," he comments. [Casanare did not frighten me with its lurid legends. The instinct for adventure impelled me to defy them, certain that I would emerge unscathed from the freedom-loving pampas and that one day, in unknown cities, I would feel nostalgic for past dangers] (81). Cova's confidence and ambition both inflate to parodic proportions during his sojourn at La Maporita cattle ranch. A relatively inexperienced rider, he imagines himself dazzling his friends with his horsemanship; similarly, the possibility of purchasing cattle takes flight in his fancy as an opportunity to earn a fortune that will one day impress his friends in Bogotá. Impelled by jealousy over Alicia, whom he knows he does not love, Cova dreams of murdering Barrera and jeopardizes his friendship with Fidel Franco by attempting to seduce his wife Griselda.

As they approach the jungle itself Cova begins to identify more explicitly with the conquistadors of the past: "Por aquellos intemperies atravesamos a pie desnudo, cual lo hicieron los legendarios hombres de la conquista" [We walked barefoot, exposed to the elements, like the legendary men of the conquest] (215). Once in the jungle, Cova seems to follow the familiar trajectory of the would-be civilizer (Kurtz, Quesada, Lope de Aguirre), who allows himself to become brutalized by his hostile surroundings. Like Conrad, Rivera combines a critique of the colonizers' greed and brutality with a reliance upon colonial mythologies, suggesting that the jungle itself—with its dense foliage, confusing shadows, oppressive climate, and endemic illnesses—is responsible for the corruption of the adventurers. "En estas soledades, cuando [el vegetal] nos habla, sólo entiende su idioma el presentimiento. Bajo su poder, los nervios del hombre se convierten en haz de cuerdas, distendidas hacia el asalto, hacia la traición, hacia la asechanza" [When (the vegetation) speaks to us in these solitary places only foreboding may understand its language. Under its power, the nerves of man become a bundle of cords, strung tight and aimed towards assault, towards betrayal, towards treachery] (297). Before the lengthy passage concludes Cova adds, as if in a flash of insight, "Sin embargo, es el hombre civilizado el paladín de la destrucción" [Nevertheless, civilized man is the champion of destruction] (297).

Despite Cova's insistence on the degenerative effects of the wilderness, the brutality he demonstrates as he enters the jungle is consistent with his attitudes and behavior in Casanare. There he first demonstrates his colonial attitude toward the indigenous: after an initial show of enlightened concern for their welfare (130), he quickly adopts the attitude of the "Christian" *llaneros* and enthusiastically joins in the massacre of Indian women and men that occurs near the end of the first section. The encounter with a tribe of Guahibo Indians that occurs soon after Cova enters the jungle with Franco and a small party of ranch-hands represents Cova's fantasies of colonial power and domination and follows a course not unlike Kurtz's experience among the tribes of central Africa. Encouraged by Pipa, the tribe approaches the white men's camp in the forest. The tribe, Cova notes, are half-tamed ("semidomada") and request only that the whites adhere to three conditions: allow the Indians to wear the traditional *guáyuco*, respect the indigenous women, and keep their rifles quiet (193). Of his first efforts to communicate with them Cova scornfully remarks, "inútiles fueron mis cortesías, porque aquellas tribus rudimentarias y nómadas no tienen dioses, ni héroes, ni patria, ni pretérito, ni futuro" [useless were my courtesies, because those rudimentary and nomadic tribes have no gods, no heroes, no nation, no past, no future] (207). Almost immediately afterward Cova proudly tells the story of his conquest of the tribe, which he accidentally learns to manipulate by killing a *garcero*, the white, heronlike bird he learns is the sacred totem of the chief. As the old man writhes in fear and prepares to die, Cova produces an identical living bird and "miraculously" saves him. The incident gives Cova "supernatural" power over the Indians: "Ningún aborigen se atrevía a mirarme," he remarks, "pero yo estaba presente en sus pensamientos ejerciendo influencias desconocidas sobre sus esperanzas y sus pesadumbres" [No aborigene dared to look at me, but I was present in their thoughts, exercising unknown influence over their hopes and their nightmares] (208).

Soon after, however, the narrative's tone changes sharply, replacing the clear opposition between Cova's white, "civilized" culture and the indigenous peoples of the jungle with an unexpected identification. Pipa and several other of Cova's companions decide to take part in the Guahibos' dance, a ritual that involves a powerful narcotic drink. Cova, looking on, describes the scene:

De pronto las mujeres, que permanecían silenciosas dentro del círculo, abrazaron las cinturas de sus amantes y trenzaban el mismo paso, inclinadas y entorpecidas, hasta que con súbito desahogo corearon todos los pechos ascendente alarido, que estremecía selvas y espacios como una campanada lúgubre: ¡Aaaaay . . . Ohé! . . .

   Tendido de codos sobre el arenal, aurirrijozo por las luminarias, miraba yo la singular fiesta, complacido de que mis compañeros giraran ebrios en la danza. Así olvidarían sus pesadumbres y le sonreirían a la vida otra vez siquiera. Mas, a poco, advertí que gritaban como la tribú, y que su lamento acusaba la misma pena recóndita, cual si a todos les devorara el alma un solo dolor. Su queja tenía la desesperación de las razas vencidas, y era semejante a mi sollozo, ese sollozo de mis aflicciones que suele repercutir en mi corazón aunque lo disimulen los labios: ¡Aaaaay . . . Ohé! (211)

[Suddenly the women, until then hushed within the circle, grasped the bodies of their lovers and paced along with the same step, swinging as if in a stupor; until with a slow unburdening of spirit there rose from every throat a growing lamentation that quivered through the muted jungles like the sound of a lugubrious bell: Aaaaay . . . O-ay!

Supporting myself on my elbows, I lay stretched on the sand, my skin reddened by the flames as I watched the strange celebration, pleased to see my companions spinning drunkenly in the dance. Thus they would forget their nightmares and smile on life at least once more. But I soon noticed that they were shouting like the tribe and that their lament revealed the same hidden pain, as if the same sadness devoured the souls of them all. Their lament contained the desperation of vanquished races, and it resembled my sob, that sob of my afflictions that resounds in my heart even when my lips try to hide it: Aaaaay . . . O-ay!]

Cova pauses before the spectacle of his companions joining in the ritual and "going native"—a sight that surprisingly does not disturb or offend him. Instead he seems to enjoy the scene, reclining on the sand and engaging in sensual fantasies of his own as he watches the indigenous women join their lovers in the dance. But what Cova first perceives as a pleasure-seeking indulgence in primitive customs turns into a kind of spiritual communion that reaches its height as his companions and finally Cova himself unite their voices to the Indians' lament. Significantly, it is grief and hardship that unite them, as if "the same hidden pain" and "a single grief" were shared by all. Perhaps most telling is the suggestion that "their complaint had the desperation of vanquished races," a phrase that suddenly collapses the hierarchical racial distinctions Cova has previously imposed on everyone he encounters. Despite the melodramatic tone of the final, inward turn, the passage is indicative of Cova's growing identification with the jungle's most disempowered inhabitants. At this point in the narrative his empathic response to the sorrow of the indigenous may seem hyperbolic, perhaps unwarranted; nevertheless it indicates the failure of Cova's posture as a neo-colonial adventurer and the emergence of the *conquistador conquistado,* (conquered conqueror) that will be more fully realized as his personal voice merges with Clemente Silva's in the pages ahead. Cova's impulsive vow to join Silva's struggle against the oppression of the rubber traders, which has been called an illogical breach in characterization, is prepared by these earlier instances of his identification with the oppressed laborers.[44]

The scene of the Guahibo dance cannot be regarded as a decisive turning point in Cova's transition from would-be exploiter to defender of the exploited. Indeed, one of his cruelest acts is yet to come: the terrible episode that results in the drowning of two Maipureño Indians (230–234). And yet, although Cova's "conversion" among the Guahibo is by no means permanent, it marks the emergence of a discourse of solidarity that disrupts Cova's sense of belonging to an elevated race and class. As Doris Sommer has written, Cova's self-imagining as a sovereign subject is not consistent throughout the text; but rather, it gives way gradually to "a new quasi-identification with those who are exploited by that ideal, like the laborers and perhaps women."[45] In the novel this "new quasi-identification" very significantly develops in the geographic space that is dominated by international rather than domestic economic structures—the jungle. Casanare, as Jane M. Rausch writes, at the time primarily produced beef for consumption in the cities and towns of Colombia's central highlands. Casanare also enjoyed a brief economic boom when the feathers of the native *garcero* became an expensive fashion item among the European elite.[46] However, Rivera does not introduce the dangerous practice of hunting *garcero* until Cova and his companions reach the jungle; the textual Casanare is still ruled by socioeconomic structures established during the centuries when the region was a Spanish colony, structures that will not allow the region's subordination to the European metropolis. As Roberto Crespi suggests, Rivera's representation of the plains rehearses an anachronistic celebration of the white Colombian's domination: "Rivera's ahistorical epic of Casanare, rich in *costumbrismo,* paints man against nature, conquering it (breaking wild horses, watching cockfights) and celebrating his victory with *aguardiente,* boasts, duels and praise of the triumphant masculine spirit of the descendants of the conquistadors."[47]

The jungle, on the other hand, is dominated by neo-colonial economics. Once he arrives there, Cova leads a group of Indians to a marsh infested with crocodiles and piranhas in order to hunt the valuable bird, which "a veces cuesta la vida de muchos hombres, antes de ser llevado a las lejanas ciudades a exaltar la belleza de mujeres desconocidas" [sometimes costs the lives of many men before being carried to distant cities to embellish the beauty of unknown women] (205). At the local level Cova is the Indians' exploiter, but his final words, gesturing toward the overarching economic structures, suggest that in the space of the jungle the hegemonic class is not the Colombian elite, but rather the distant and anonymous consumers of the north. The incident at the Guahibo dance builds on this earlier scene by once again suggesting that the locus of power is not in Colombia at all, but somewhere outside the three national groups represented in the scene: the capitaline intellectual, the horsemen of the plains, and the Indians of the jungle. Cova may manage to manipulate and control the Indians; as soon as he achieves that position of power, however, the text almost immediately collapses the distance between Cova as conquistador and the people he has just conquered, as if to remind us that Cova cannot be a colonial lord, cannot become the Kurtz of the Amazon, because he and the Indians belong to the same exploited and suffering people.

This moment of collapse is the crucial point in which *La vorágine* and *Heart of Darkness* diverge. Marlow's encounter with Kurtz is both the revelation of a terrifying savagery and the innermost stage in his journey; immediately afterward he sails downriver out of Africa and returns to Belgium, where he ruminates on the meaning of Kurtz's demise and ultimately confronts the bereaved "Intended" before traveling northward once again to his home in England. In contrast, Cova plunges ever further into the jungle after the moment of identification with the Guahibo; as he gives up the posture of domination, he also seems to give up his unqualified identification with Bogotá and Europe. Perhaps it is not coincidental that Rivera has Cova lie about his future plans in the early pages of the novel: soon after meeting Franco, Cova tells him that he and Alicia, like many well-to-do Latin Americans of the age, are on their way to Europe (126). But Cova does not go to Europe, or even Bogotá: instead he meets his fate in the jungles to the south.

While Cova's disappearance into the jungle may seem like a tragic conclusion and even an expression of Rivera's pessimistic suspicion that the Colombian government would fail in its duty to relieve the enslaved rubber tappers, it can also be seen more positively as a radical decentering of the nation's cultural discourse: *La vorágine*'s locus of enunciation is not the metropolitan center, as it is in *Heart of Darkness*, but the inner recesses of the jungle. Rivera pointedly stages the scene of writing in the final pages of the text: Cova describes himself setting down "las notas de mi odisea, en el libro de Caja que el Cayeno tenía sobre su escritorio como adorno inútil y polvoriento" [notes of my odyssey, in the account-book that El Cayeno kept on his desk as a useless and dusty decoration] (345). Significantly, Cova sets his own account of the rubber trade in the unused ledger of one of its most notorious criminals, demonstrating both the fraudulence of the company's business practices and Cova's own desire to fill in the missing records with a narrative of human suffering that exceeds the commodifying, capitalist language of credits and debits. But the scene is geographically important as well. Cova writes his narrative on the banks of the Guaracú, deep within the Amazon jungle; in this sense *La vorágine* goes well beyond the frontier established by *Heart of Darkness* and opens a new space of possibility in Spanish American narrative. This is the space where subsequent *novelas de la selva,* such as Rómulo Gallegos's *Canaima* and Carpentier's *Los pasos perdidos,* will begin: with the educated urbanites who decide to get lost in the jungle.

Dialectics of Nature

In analyzing the topographic drive of *La vorágine* we have seen Rivera develop the idea that the way to safeguard Colombia's southern provinces against the threat of foreign encroachment is to undertake a liberal project of internal colonization and at last incorporate those outlying territories into the central state. We subsequently saw Rivera, more radically, modify the colonial attitude behind that very gesture by subverting the traditional, hierarchical opposition between the white, urban representative of "civilization" and the oppressed peoples of the jungle and displacing cultural discourse from the nation's capital to its economic and geographic periphery. Rivera introduces yet another amendment into his initial proposal of incorporating the jungle into the nation: the modification of conventional Western discourse on nature so as to represent the jungle as a dynamic and vulnerable entity that cannot be simply brought under the domination of the state. As my summary suggests, Rivera's response to the Putumayo rubber boom is nothing short of dialectical in his insistence on repeatedly revising his own posited solutions to Colombia's problem of informal imperialism. In fact, the problem itself becomes an ever more complex set of relations among foreign consumers, capitalists, national elites, indigenous and mixed-race laborers, and the ecosystem that includes—among an almost infinite variety of plant and animal species—the rubber-producing *hevea brasilensis*.

Rivera's concentrated explorations of the shifting relationships among land, labor, and capital on the economic frontier resonate with the regionalist fictions Horacio Quiroga and Benito Lynch produced during the same period. In its degree of dialectical intensity, *La vorágine* also resembles one of the more eccentric texts from the environmental canon, Friedrich Engels's *Dialectics of Nature*.[48] Written largely between 1872 and 1882, *Dialectics of Nature* remained unfinished at the time of Engels's death in 1895, and was not published in English translation until 1940. By that time, much of the physics and chemistry supporting Engels's claims to the universal "interconnection of all processes," physical and social, had already become obsolete. Nevertheless, his comments on biology and evolutionary processes are illuminating even today. For example: having just asserted that the principal distinction between humans and animals is the human's ability to make "external nature . . . serve his ends," Engels adds a cautionary note worth quoting at length:

> Let us not, however, flatter ourselves overmuch on account of our human conquest over nature. For each such conquest takes its revenge on us. Each of them, it is true, has in the first place the consequences on which we counted, but in the second and third places it has quite different, unforeseen effects which only too often cancel out the first. The people who, in Mesopotamia, Greece, Asia Minor, and elsewhere, destroyed the forests to obtain cultivable land, never dreamed that they were laying the basis for the present devastated condition of these countries, by removing along with the forests the collecting centres and reservoirs of moisture. . . . Thus at every step we are reminded that we by no means rule over nature like a conqueror over a foreign people, like someone standing outside nature—but that we, with flesh, blood, and brain, belong to nature, and exist in its midst, and that all our mastery of it consists in the fact that we have the advantage over all other beings of being able to know and correctly apply its laws.
>
> And, in fact, with every day that passes we are learning to understand these laws more correctly, and getting to know both the more immediate and the more remote consequences of our interference with the traditional course of nature. In particular, after the mighty advances of natural science in the present century, we are more and more getting to know, and hence to control, even the more remote natural consequences at least of our more ordinary productive activities. But the more this happens, the more will men not only feel, but also know, their unity with nature, and thus the more impossible will become the senseless and anti-natural idea of a contradiction between mind and matter, man and nature, soul and body, such as arose in Europe after the decline of classic antiquity and which obtained its highest elaboration in Christianity.[49]

Engels's writing of *Dialectics of Nature* coincides almost perfectly with the emergence of ecology in western Europe; according to Lynn White, Jr., the word "ecology" itself was introduced into English in 1873.[50] Engels's ideas clearly overlap with the ecologists', contradicting the prevalent myth of Marxism's inherently antienvironmental tendencies: not only is Engels critical of Western modernity as represented by the Industrial Revolution;

he specifically recognizes and deeply regrets the new technologies' often devastating impact on the environment. "There is damned little left of 'nature' as it was in Germany at the time when the Germanic peoples immigrated into it," Engels grumbles in a note.[51] His environmentalism is unapologetically anthropocentric in its priorities, but recognizes, crucially, that the continuing fulfillment of human needs depends upon our ability to anticipate and control even the "remote" environmental consequences of the technologies we use.

Equally surprising and equally relevant to our discussion of *La vorágine* is Engels's dramatic assertion that "we, with flesh, blood, and brain, belong to nature, and exist in its midst," which he subsequently repeats by attacking "the senseless and anti-natural idea of a contradiction between mind and matter, man and nature, soul and body." Here Engels complicates his own avowed anthropocentrism by complicating the notion of what it means to be human: embedded in the environment, part and parcel of nature, rather than isolated above or against it. What is more, our increasing ability to use technology successfully—that is, with a minimum of environmental impact—will not bring "mastery" over nature, but quite the opposite: a new sense of integration that Engels refers to as "unity." (His revealing choice of analogy suggests just how far Engels was at the time from extending his imaginative powers to the issue of colonialism.) Lynn White's "The Historical Roots of Our Ecologic Crisis" traces more fully the links between western Europe's pursuit of the domination of nature through science and technology and the same cultures' Judeo-Christian heritage. In Genesis, White explains, the earth and all of its creatures were planned and created "explicitly for man's benefit and rule: no item in the physical creation had any purpose save to serve man's purposes. . . . Christianity, in absolute contrast to ancient paganisms and Asia's religions (except, perhaps, Zoroastrianism), not only established a dualism of man and nature but also insisted that it is God's will that man exploit nature for his proper ends."[52]

La vorágine similarly explores, through the troubled psychology of Arturo Cova, the links between the European and Judeo-Christian culture of Colombia's dominant class and the environmental devastation of the Putumayo. One of the last fantasies that grips the imagination of Arturo Cova on the plains of Casanare is that of living in the style of a colonial landowner, ruling over his vast property as he grows old with his wife Alicia:

> fumando en el umbral, como un patriarca primitivo de pecho suavizado por la melancolía de los paisajes, vería las puestas de sol en el horizonte remoto donde nace la noche; y libre de las vanas aspiraciones, del engaño de

los triunfos efímeros, limitaría mis anhelos a cuidar de la zona que abarcaran mis ojos, al goce de las faenas campesinas, a mi consonancia con la soledad. (161)

[smoking on the threshold, like a primitive patriarch whose chest has been softened by the melancholy of the landscape, I would see the sunsets on the remote horizon where night was born; and finally free of vain aspirations, of the illusions of ephemeral triumphs, I would limit my longings to caring for the land before my eyes, to the pleasures of rustic chores, and to my consonance with solitude.]

There are, of course, several ways to interpret this passage. One is to point out the ironic contrast between Cova's Casanare fantasy and the reality he is about to encounter in the jungle: nature, in other words, may be subject to human domination on the plains, but the jungle cannot be conquered. The jungle Cova encounters resists intrusion—let alone "mastery"—with its leech-infested, malarial swamps and armies of flesh-eating ants. It is *la cárcel verde*, (the green jail) that imprisons all those who enter it, frustrating and ridiculing their will to dominate.

One of the novel's most famous passages, the anonymous rubber tapper's lament that opens the novel's third section captures the most brutal and forbidding aspects of the jungle:

Esclavo, no te quejes de las fatigas; preso, no te duelas de tu prisión: ignoráis la tortura de vagar sueltos en una cárcel como la selva, cuyas bóvedas verdes tienen por fosos ríos inmensos. ¡No sabéis del suplicio de las penumbras, viendo al sol que ilumina la playa opuesta, adonde nunca lograremos ir! ¡La cadena que muerde vuestros tobillos es más piadosa que las sanguijuelas de estos pantanos; el carcelero que os atormenta no es tan adusto como estos árboles, que nos vigilan sin hablar! (288)

[Slave, do not complain of your labors; captive, do not bemoan your prison: you do not know the torture of wandering freely through a jail like the jungle, whose green vaults have immense rivers for moats. You don't know the torment of the shadows, seeing the sun that illuminates the opposite shore, where we will never be able to go! The chain that bites your ankles is more merciful than the leeches of these swamps; the jailer who torments you is less adept than these trees, who watch us without speaking!]

Here nature dominates men even more cruelly than men can dominate each other, confounding their efforts to succeed by rational means, and subjecting them to its most deadly creatures. In this regard, *La vorágine* substitutes one colonial mythology for another, replacing Arturo Cova's fantasy of easily aquired money and power with an equally unrealistic notion of nature—in this case the trees themselves—as a supernatural entity with an active will to harm intruders. As Taussig has written, *La vorágine*'s vision of the jungle is dominated by colonial mythologies that blur the boundaries between human and natural hazards, shifting the malicious intent of unscrupulous rubber traders onto the flora and fauna of the jungle.[53] Scholars including Monserrat Ordoñez and Sharon Magnarelli have shown that this imagined malevolence of the jungle is repeatedly feminized by *La vorágine*'s male characters, following a long-standing convention in the region still known as Amazonia.[54] For Cova and Silva, the obscure and silent jungle, space of death and constant generation, is a terrifying embodiment of a threatening and unfathomable femininity.

Rivera does not entirely put these misogynistic and antiecological mythologies to rest; nevertheless *La vorágine* begins to articulate—tentatively, intermittently—a relationship to nature that is based on a desire to understand rather than to dominate and subdue. In this regard Cova's Casanare fantasy can also be read more symbolically, as an allusion to Abraham, founder of the biblical Israel and archetypal patriarch of the Judeo-Christian tradition. Abraham is that "primitive patriarch" whom God Himself endowed with the blessings of landownership, riches, marital love, and fecundity, telling him: "'Lift up your eyes, and look from the place where you are, northward and southward and eastward and westward; for all the land which you see I will give to you and to your descendants for ever'" (Gen. 13: 14–15). Abraham is also a central figure in the cultural discourse surrounding the conquest of America and the prototype for the posture Mary Louise Pratt has called the "Seeing Man," or the "master of all I survey."[55] When Cova dreams of becoming the Abraham of the Colombian llano, lording over all the land that lies before him, he is drawing on his sense of inherited, God-given privilege as a white, European male and on a long-standing Western belief in man's "dominion" over nature. At the same time, Cova's fantasy of Abraham in the Promised Land inevitably refers back to Rivera's earlier work, *Tierra de Promisión*. The appearance of Abraham in Cova's fantasy life suggests that Rivera was quite seriously rethinking the relationship between nature and nation implicit in all of those empty spaces to which the poetic voice lays claim in *Tierra de Promisión*. If *La vorágine* is also about incorporating peripheral territories into the Colombian nation, it revises the earlier gesture of extending the sovereignty of an urban, Christian and Eurocentric state over the geographic periphery by emphasizing and exploring the autonomous existences of those territories and all they contain. In *La vorágine* the new Canaan is already densely inhabited by people, plants, and wildlife with their own complex relationships and whose incorporation into the nation implies a fundamental revision of the nation itself.

Thus *La vorágine,* while intermittently repeating the would-be conqueror's paranoid fantasies of *la cárcel verde,* also articulates discourses that resonate with Engels's *Dialectics of Nature* and anticipate some of the most radical contemporary environmental literature. We have already seen Rivera's commitment to protecting the rights of Colombia's indigenous populations in his nonliterary writings; significantly, the report he and Escobar submitted to the Colombian government after their expedition to the Venezuelan border also calls attention to the unsound environmental practices of the *caucherías:*

> Decimos que es destructor el método porque para extraer la goma derriban los árboles, y de esta manera han arrasado los gomales de estas regiones, principalmente en el Vaupés, en el Vestuario, en el Casiquiare y sus afluentes y hasta en los ríos Guaviare e Inírida. Picar los árboles de cierta manera y subir a ellos con este objeto, en vez de derribarlos [es] reglamentación que no se cumple en la mayor parte de los casos, pero que según la experiencia ha demostrado, tampoco da resultado eficaz porque la planta al fin y al cabo acaba por secarse.
> ... Se ve, pues, la necesidad que existe de tomar providencias enérgicas para evitar que se perpetúe esta destrucción sistemática e inútil de la riqueza nacional.[56]

> [We say the method is destructive because in order to extract rubber they fell the trees, and in this way have destroyed the rubber trees of these regions, especially along the Vaupés, the Vestuario, the Casiquiare and its tributaries, and even along the Guaviare and Inírida Rivers. Piercing the trees in a particular way and climbing them with the same objective, instead of felling them, is a rule that is generally not upheld, but experience has shown that this is not very efficient either, because the tree in the end dries out.
> ... Thus it is clearly necessary that energetic measures be undertaken to avoid the perpetuation of this systematic and useless destruction of our nation's wealth.]

In contrast to the often mystifying rhetoric of the novel, Rivera's nonliterary language is strikingly rational, even technical, in its explanation of the ecological hazards presented by the rubber industry. The theme of sustainable development also arises in the novel, as when Cova remarks, "Y es de verse en algunos lugares cómo sus huellas son semejantes a los aludes: los caucheros que hay en Colombia destruyen millones de árboles. En los territorios de Venezuela el balatá desapareció. De esta suerte ejercen el fraude contra las generaciones del porvenir." [And it must be seen in some places how their tracks are like an avalanche: the rubber-tappers in Colombia

La vorágine: Dialectics of the Rubber Boom   149

destroy millions of trees. In Venezuelan territories the *balatá* has disappeared. In this way they defraud the generations of the future] (298).

Much of the confusion of the latter half of *La vorágine,* as William Bull complains in his famous essay, is the vitalism that animates the textual jungle with a life and purpose of its own, dominating the narrative action and threatening to overshadow entirely the serious message of social protest.[57] Logically, what Bull calls "the anthropomorphism of nature" is the product of psychological distortion, or Rivera's decision to privilege his first-person depiction of Cova's descent into madness over a realistic representation of the exploitation suffered by the Putumayo's rubber tappers. Nevertheless, the positive, pitying images of nature offered by *La vorágine* are too consistent with views expressed in Rivera's nonliterary writings to be entirely written off. Though distanced and almost discredited, as it were, by the mediating consciousness of Arturo Cova, Rivera's extraordinary representation of the environment may also be seen as an effort to revise conventional Western discourse on nature by describing the jungle as a living organism that defies the ordering gaze of the colonial subject with what Engels calls an "endless entanglement of relations and reactions, permutations and combinations," and of which human beings are but a single element.[58]

Rivera's jungle—shifting, changing, mysterious—has a life of its own. As if to demonstrate, Cova, Silva and the others repeatedly speak to it:

> "Tú eres la catedral de la pesadumbre, donde dioses desconocidos hablan a media voz, en el idioma de los murmullos, prometiendo longevidad a los árboles imponentes, contemporáneos del paraíso, que eran ya decanos cuando las primeras tribus aparecieron y esperan impasibles el hundimiento de los siglos venturos." (189)

> [You are nightmare's cathedral, where unknown gods speak in half-tones, in the language of murmurs, promising longevity to the imposing trees, contemporaries of the first paradise, you were already decades old when the first tribes appeared and you await, impassive, the sinking of centuries to come.]

These hallucinatory passages convey a sense of vitalism and respect for nature. Not unlike contemporary environmental discourse, *La vorágine* seeks to improve on traditional Western attitudes toward nature by exchanging the will to dominate with a more modest desire to understand. Cova and his companions strain to hear the mysterious "voice" of the jungle, the sound of gods speaking in whispers, in an attitude of profound humility toward nature and its processes—which, as they recognize, have an existence completely separate from human needs. "El vegetal es un ser sensible," says Clemente Silva, "cuya psicología desconocemos." [Vegetation is a sensitive being whose psychology is unknown to us] (297).

However problematic this association may be, Rivera links the reverence for nature that eludes most of the capitalist adventurers to the indigenous. Of Cova's group, only their guide Pipa—a classic characterization of the hybrid colonial subject, slyly servile among the whites, equally at home among Indians, horrifically maimed in the end—is able to understand the "psychology" of the jungle. Under the influence of a drug the Guahibo prepare for him, Pipa tells the others that the rubber trees "[q]uejábanse de la mano que les hería, del hacha que los derribaba, siempre condenados a retoñar, a florecer, a gemir, a perpetuar, sin fecundarse, su especie formidable, incomprendida" [complained of the hand that wounded them, the axe that felled them, eternally condemned to reproduce, to flourish, to moan, to perpetuate, without flourishing, their formidable and misunderstood species] (213). In their suffering, the trees have also developed a vindictive plan to exterminate the human race, conquering cities and towns until man is eradicated from the face of the earth, "cual en los milenios de Génesis" [like in the milennia of Genesis] (213). The trees—ironically reminding the adventurers that they inhabited Eden long before the human race—acquire a living force that makes a mockery of Cova's belief in his own sovereignty and his dreams of domination.

In his recent analysis of conservationism in *Moby-Dick,* Lawrence Buell notes Melville's use of a rhetorical pattern he calls "blurring the species boundary," which Melville uses to elicit readers' sympathy for the whales and to undermine the legitimacy of hunting them.[59] The same pattern is a constant presence in *La vorágine;* at times the crossing is a playful gesture, more often it is mysterious and profound. The trees suffer pain and humiliation, plot revenge and tenderly care for their young. They are also seen as a model of solidarity, in striking contrast to the human adventurers who turn against one another in their frenzied pursuit of profit: "Tus vegetales forman sobre la tierra la poderosa familia que no se traiciona nunca. El abrazo que no pueden darse tus ramazones lo llevan las enredaderas y los bejucos, y eres solidaria hasta en el dolor de la hoja que cae." [Your vegetation forms upon the earth a powerful family that never knows betrayal. The embrace your mighty branches cannot offer one another is carried out by creepers and lianas, and your solidarity extends even to the pain of the falling leaf] (190). The beauty and strangeness of *La vorágine* cannot be overstated, and some of the novel's most extraordinary passages wrestle with the difficulty of adequately conveying the sublime mysteries of the awesome and endangered jungle. In persistently crossing the species boundary, Rivera both personifies the trees and—with apologies to Lukács—treeifies the people. Near the end of the novel Cova suffers a terrifying attack of temporary paralysis that causes him to experience quite literally Engels's words, "we, with flesh, blood, and brain, belong to nature":

> [E]ra algo postizo, horrible, estorboso, a la par ausente y presente, que me producía un fastidio único, como el que puede sentir el árbol que ve pegada en su parte viva una rama seca. Sin embargo, el cerebro cumplía admirablemente sus facultades. Reflexioné. ¿Era alguna alucinación? ¡Imposible! ¿Los síntomas de otro sueño de catalepsia? Tampoco. Hablaba, hablaba, me oía la voz y era oído, pero me sentía sembrado en el suelo, y, por mi pierna, hinchada, fofa y deforme como las raíces de ciertas palmeras, ascendía una savia caliente, petrificante. Quise moverme y la tierra no me soltaba.

> [It was something lifeless, horrible, ungainly, at once absent and present, that produced a unique discomfort, like the discomfort a tree must feel when it finds a dry branch stuck in its living trunk. Nonetheless, my brain carried out its functions admirably. I reflected. Was it a hallucination? Impossible! The symptoms of another cataleptic dream? Equally impossible. I spoke, I heard my voice and the others heard me, but I was sewn into the soil, and through my leg, swollen, spongy and deformed like the roots of certain palms, I felt the ascent of a warm and petrifying sap. I tried to move and the ground would not release me.]

As with much of the truly radical ecological discourse in *La vorágine*, the most reasonable explanation for Cova's treeification is psychological: his friends recognize the paralysis as an early symptom of beriberi, and Arturo himself accepts their diagnosis. In the context of the anthropomorphic language with which the jungle is represented, however, the passage also agitates for an extraordinary kind of interspecies identification: if the humans cannot of their own accord imagine the suffering of the rubber trees, the jungle itself—by deploying one of its endemic illnesses—will create the only conditions through which Cova, and perhaps his readers, can finally appreciate the vegetal immobility that makes them the helpless victims of capitalist exploitation. After all, unlike Melville's whales, Faulkner's Old Ben, or any of the other heroic and martyred beasts of literature, most of Rivera's readers consider rubber trees to be completely insentient.

It may be suggested that by choosing to focus on the most alien and inert of the beings who were exploited by the rubber boom, Rivera makes the trees "speak" on behalf of the region's other silent and silenced victims: not only the jungle's diverse wildlife, but its human inhabitants as well. I believe, on the other hand, that Rivera's language is ultimately dialectical rather than metonymic: as we saw earlier in Quiroga's stories about Britain's informal imperialism in the Misiones region of Argentina, Rivera also represents the conflict between nature and laborers as a relationship of mutual abuse that is created by the demands of international capitalism. The irrational relations of production in both cases may be explained in terms of Marx's theories of the expansion of capitalism; in the third volume of *Capital,* he argues that the metropolitan market's unregulated demand for primary goods cruelly distorts the established relationship between laborers and their environment on the economic periphery.[60] The anthropomorphism of nature in *La vorágine* allows Rivera to develop a nuanced—if unconventional—representation of this vicious mutual assault of labor and land, both of them acting under the unchecked pressures of metropolitan capital.

The anonymous lament that begins part 3 describes the daily labors of a rubber tapper in precisely these terms:

> Tengo trescientos troncos en mis estradas y en martirizarlos gasto nueve días. Les he limpiado los bejuqueros y hacia cada uno desbrocé un camino. Al recorrer la taimada tropa de vegetales para derribar a los que no lloran, suelo sorprender a los castradores robándose la goma ajena. Reñimos a mordiscos y a machetazos, y la leche disputada se salpica de gotas enrojecidas. ¿Mas qué importa que nuestras venas aumenten la savia del vegetal? ¡El capataz exige diez litros diarios y el foete es usurero que nunca perdona! ...
>
> ¡Así el arbol y yo, con tormento vario, somos lacrimatorios ante la muerte y nos combatiremos hasta sucumbir! (288–89)

> [I have three hundred trunks in my groves and it takes me nine days to martyrize them all. I have cleaned them of vines and opened a path to each one. On my course among the astute troop of foliage to fell the ones that do not cry, I usually surprise the castrators stealing someone else's rubber. We fight each other with bites and machete-blows, and the disputed milk is spattered with red drops. But what does it matter that our veins augment the sap of the plants? The foreman demands ten liters a day and the whip is a usurer who never forgives!
>
> Thus the tree and I, each with his own torment, are lachrymators before death and we will combat each other until we succumb!]

Passages like this one are animated and intensified by Rivera's extraordinary sensitivity to the dialectics of neo-colonialism. As the speaker suggests, the rubber tappers' day-to-day struggle for survival is played out among themselves and against the natural environment in a cycle of torment and destruction that, like the cycles of debt-peonage, ends only with death. The Christian distinction between humans and nature is explicitly collapsed: here the elaborately martyred saints are the rubber trees, while the men fight like animals, as Tennyson would say, "red in tooth and claw." Perhaps most extraordinary is the physiological intermingling of the jungle's multiple combatants. The speaker refers to rival rubber tappers as "castradores," playing on the dual meanings of the verb *castrar,* to prune and to castrate. The language of the human body—blood, tears, semen—is used to describe the fluid extracted from the trees, and the men shed blood that "augments the sap of the plants."

In its most subtle poetic practice, *La vorágine* follows Engels's call to resist "the senseless and anti-natural idea of a contradiction between mind and matter, man and nature, soul and body." Once considered simplistic and hopelessly archaic, *La vorágine* is the most complex and revolutionary text of Spanish America's regional literature. Rivera's language, particularly in the final sections, is baffling and enthralling, and its powerfully innovative combinations urge us as readers to expand our imaginative capacity in order to reinvent our relationship to nature and the material world around us. Striking tones that resonant with the most radical environmentalism of the early twenty-first century, Rivera blurs the boundary between the human and the natural in order that we may better understand our mutual vulnerability and the economic violence to which we may both be subject.

Of the authors discussed in this study, Rivera alone avoids directly indicting Britain's informal imperialism in Latin America: in *La vorágine* the Invisible Empire is almost entirely unseen. As I have argued, Rivera did not write the British out of his novel of the Putumayo scandal because he was unaware of their involvement in the abuses that took place there, but rather because writing them into the story would have meant running the risk of inadvertently mitigating his exposure of neo-colonial exploitation. He had no desire to reinscribe a notion of British civilizational superiority that for him and many others in the region had by the early 1920s become almost entirely obsolete. Instead of running that risk, Rivera chose to tell a version of the Putumayo story that sets a Colombian intellectual in the ambiguous role of exploiter and defender of the nation's laborers and natural resources. As Cova descends into the Colombian jungle, however, he crosses beyond the frontier of Western or European culture, and enters a region where the hierarchical discursive oppositions that once structured his colonial and patriarcal worldview—civilization/barbarism, creole/native, capital/periphery, male/female, human/nature—collapse almost entirely, leaving him and his readers free to reimagine a radically new, non-exploitative relationship among land, labor, and the Colombian state. Given the time and the circumstances in which Rivera was writing, he could only allow that liberating collapse to occur in a discursive space that was explicitly characterized by madness and death. But the collapse of those colonial binaries is also an act of regeneration and transformation: it severs the ties between the creole aristocracy to which Cova belongs and the British capitalists whose economic hegemony in the region ultimately depended upon their ability to perpetuate and exacerbate the internal conflicts and oppositions of Colombian society.

Afterword
Fertile Ground

THIS BOOK BEGAN WHILE I WAS still a graduate student at Rutgers University, and chanced to read *Heart of Darkness* and *La vorágine* within a few weeks of one another. The similarities between them were too striking to ignore, and I wanted to understand the reasons for their occurrence. In seeking that explanation I uncovered a vast network of economic, cultural, and literary relations that in time I began to call the Invisible Empire. Both texts, as I learned, were situated at the frontier of a worldwide process of capitalist expansion that was driven by the changing demands of British industry and the increasingly global markets it supplied. In Asia, Africa, and South America the profits to be made by meeting those demands sent scores of capitalist adventurers deep into the jungles, where they extracted their precious produce at a terrible cost to the environment and everyone in it. In the official colonies, the armed men on the front lines of empire were Europeans, and in Latin America they were often Latin Americans, but the language that describes them in British and Latin American literature is drawn—to be adapted, revised, and challenged—from a supply of colonial discourses that circulated, along with money, goods, and technology, from one part of the globe to another.

As I have argued throughout this book, the Invisible Empire took the form of a particularly pernicious kind of double colonialism: while Latin America's national economies were increasingly subordinated to the demands of metropolitan capital, local elites were driven to meet those demands by exploiting the human and natural resources of the continent's interior. Working through and beyond discursive structures that are part and parcel of that hegemonic formation, Rivera, Quiroga, and Lynch subvert the Invisible Empire by radically re-visioning first the process of internal colonialism and then (if in Rivera's case more obliquely) the overarching relationship between the local or national community and the British Empire. As we have seen, the fundamental structure of informal imperialism is not the dyad of colonizer and colonized that results in the ubiquitous and seemingly inescapable Manichean oppositions of formal colonialism, but rather a more complex and shifting triad made up of land, labor, and capital. The land is controlled by Latin American elites; the labor is provided by the exploited populations of their countries; and the capital is predominently British. At the level of economic institutions and material practices, informal imperialism may prove to be ultimately as destructive as formal colonialism; at the discursive level, however, these triangulated relationships provide the regional writers with fertile ground for radically rethinking the social and ecological practices of the class and caste with which they are ambiguously positioned.

In the seminal essay on informal imperialism cited earlier, Ronald Robinson and John Gallagher famously wrote that trying to understand colonialism based only on the evidence of the official colonies was "rather like judging the size and character of icebergs solely from the parts above the water-line."[1] This book is deeply indebted to their efforts, and to those of the many historians in Latin America, Britain, the United States, and elsewhere who have pursued the elusive subject of informal imperialism over the years. I will borrow their analogy one more time, to say that my work on Horacio Quiroga, Benito Lynch, and José Eustasio Rivera is the tip of another iceberg. In the work of these three authors the references to Britain's informal imperialism are unusually apparent. But Quiroga, Lynch, and Rivera certainly are not the only writers whose literary production is informed by the economic relationships between Britain and Latin America. Informal imperialism began during the last years of Spanish rule, and lasted in many places until well into the twentieth century. Certainly the degree and intensity of British exploitation varied widely throughout the continent and was often overshadowed—as in Mexico, for example, and much of the Caribbean—by the more overt interventions of the United States. Nevertheless, Britain's economic and, as I have argued, cultural influence was felt throughout the region, from Belmopan to Buenos Aires and Lima, where the Tudor-style homes of nineteenth-century merchants still dot the urban landscape.

Sometimes the relationship between British imperialism and Latin American state building is obvious, as in Domingo F. Sarmiento's famous *Facundo: civilización y barbarie,* which claims the necessity of "civilizing" the vast pampa by replacing its indigenous population with European settlers.[2] In other cases, uncovering the effects of British imperialism will require reading literature between the lines, or exploring the textual silences surrounding documented historical phenomena. I have discussed the strategic amnesia in Andrés Bello's rendition of Juan María Maury y Benítez's poem "La agresión británica" in detail; Ricardo Palma's *Tradiciones peruanas* perform another act of occlusion by incorporating Andean Indians, *peninsulares,* creoles, and Afro-Hispanics in a vast mosaic of Peruvian society while carefully excluding the Britons who were simultaneously transforming his city. Beatriz González-Stephan offers an inspiring example of the methodological innovations that allow us to explore and understand the Invisible Empire in her work on the so-called Universal Expositions held in London and Paris in the late nineteenth century. Along with abundant arrays of foodstuffs and other primary products—meat, coffee, lumber, and so forth—the Latin American contributions began to incorporate elaborate displays of national culture, including history, literature, and antiquities, all arranged according to the same logic of consumer capitalism.[3]

My own methodology might be considered a fusion of Marxist and environmental approaches—if the use of the term *fusion* did not create a false sense of opposition between Marxist and environmental critique. It would be more accurate to say that *Nature, Neo-Colonialism and the Spanish American Regional Writers* explores the environmental aspects of foundational texts from the Marxist canon. To scholars engaged in the developing field of literature and environment studies, Marxism offers a coherent tradition of integrated thinking, a long view of economic and social change, and a mode of analysis inherently suited to examining the dynamic interactions of complex human and non-human organisms. What could be more ecological than dialectics, or more dialectical than ecology? The similarity of these two critical models is both obvious and all too often overlooked, perhaps because Marxism's decline and environmentalism's rise have been largely contemporaneous among progressive intellectuals in the United States and Latin America. Marx and Engels are more intellectually relevant and more necessary now than ever.

This book was written in the conviction that unseen economic forces often have profound effects on the way individuals and whole societies live, and on the ways that literary writers represent the lives and the world around them. In recent years academic discourse has been dominated by the issues of colonialism and globalization, twin giants that alternately grapple for supremacy and wander the planet hand in hand. In many ways, Britain's Invisible Empire in Latin America anticipates the hegemonic style of globalization: national sovereignty is ostensibly maintained, while culture, society, and the landscape are fundamentally transformed. Globalization, like informal imperialism, brings many blessings but distributes them unevenly.

The Latin American writers of the so-called Boom generation, involved in their own struggles for emancipation in the promising and turbulent years of the 1960s and 1970s, all too often felt the need to emancipate themselves from the *novela de la tierra* as well. In the process of constructing their own political identities in opposition to authoritarian regimes, the neo-colonial United States, and what they perceived as hopelessly subservient national literatures, Fuentes, García Márquez, and many of their peers wrote the regionalists off as remote and simplistic, overlooking the anticolonial and very often anticapitalist politics in their work. The regional writers were not communists or socialists: they generally avoided the international political movements that were stirring in Europe and the Americas at the time. But when they are read alongside Marx and Engels, as I have read them here, they show a remarkably similar desire to wrestle with the ways in which the economic transformations of the period bore on and in turn transformed every aspect of life that came within the reach of the advancing capitalist economy.

By the same token, the regionalists are often environmentalists *avant la lettre*. At a time when labor collectives and First Peoples in Brazil, Mexico, and around the world are protesting the ecological and economic violence of globalization, the regional writers communicate a shared concern for issues of sustainability and environmental justice. Their sensitivity to our interdependant relationship to the rest of nature is startling and enlightening, even at a time when the academic—if not political—culture in the United States and Latin America is increasingly infused with "green" values and ideals. The resurgence (after *modernismo*) of rural landscapes in the thematics of their work is not merely a romantic "return to nature" by modern subjects seeking solace in the authentic values and lifestyles of the countryside; rather, it is an active intervention in the habits of consumption and contamination that continue to endanger rural areas and the people who live there. If they admire the aesthetic and even spiritual qualities of nature, the regional writers insistently critique the metropolitan attitudes, and the political and economic structures that put rural environments at risk. Perhaps most important, they reimagine the frontier and the people who live there as something other than resources to exploit or develop in the name of economic expansion, and create alternative paradigms of solidarity and community.

Despite the decades that divide us, then, the regional writers are very nearly our contemporaries. They wrote during a historical moment in which Latin Americans were beginning to recognize the contradictions behind the notions of "progress" and "civilization" as they had been defined throughout the nineteenth century, and to question the role of their British business "partners" in the unequal division of modernity's gains and losses. The regionalists recognize the limitations of the neo-colonial order, which they struggle to transform and transcend. While they cannot completely extricate themselves from that order or its rhetoric, they nevertheless labor in the creation of a better one, of new forms of relating to other people and the lands they collectively occupy, and new forms of language though which to express those relationships. That commitment and creative force is ultimately what makes the regional writers so astonishing and inspiring today.

Notes

Introduction: The Invisible Empire (pp. 1-38)

1. "Aquí su olivo el bético Silvano / Despoja, y Baco sus racimos de oro; / Allí cede la oveja a diestra mano / De su vellón el cándido tesoro; / Mientras purpúreo el insectillo indiano, / Ya del Sidonio múrice desdoro, / Los albos copos a teñir se apresta, / Cual púdico rubor frente modesta." Loosely translated: Here the Andalusian Sylvan throws off / His olive garland, and Bacchus his golden raiments; / There the sheep yields to dexterous hand / The innocent treasure of its wool; / While America's purple insect / By violet Sidonian already tinged, / Is prepared to dye the white tufts, Like a modest blush on a modest face. / A powder is prepared, so pure / It emulates the sapphire of the cerulean sky. Juan María Maury y Benítez, *La agresión británica*, in *Antología mayor de la literatura española*, ed., intro., and notes by Guillermo Díaz-Plaja (Barcelona: Labor, 1962), 4:607.

2. M. Menéndez y Pelayo, introduction to *Antología de poetas hispano-americanos*, 2:cxlviii–cxlvix. There is some discrepancy over the title of Bello's poem. Menéndez y Pelayo refers to it as "Silva a la agricultura en la zona tórrida," but most authorities prefer "La agricultura de la zona tórrida." The term *silva* refers to a poem of hendecasyllabic or heptasyllabic lines with a variable rhyme scheme, of which Luis de Góngora is considered the great master.

3. Andrés Bello, *La agricultura en la zona tórrida*, in *Antología de poetas hispano-americanos* (Madrid: Real Academia Española, 1926), 2:301-2.

4. Menéndez y Pelayo, introduction to *Antología*, cxlviii.

5. Quoted by Menéndez y Pelayo, ibid., cl.

6. Sarmiento was also a prolific writer and one of Latin America's most influential statesmen of the nineteenth century, serving as Argentina's president (1868–74) and providing an enduring figure for the elite project of Europeanizing Latin America's heterogeneous population as posed by the rhetorical question, "Civilization or barbarism?" I shall discuss the relationship among Sarmiento, Darwin, and Head in the chapter dedicated to Benito Lynch's *El inglés de los güesos*.

7. Iván Jaksic provides a detailed discussion of Bello's advocacy of agriculture as the basis of the independent republics' economies. See his *Andrés Bello: Scholarship and Nation-Building in Nineteenth-Century Latin America* (Cambridge: Cambridge University Press, 2001), 58–62.

8. Leslie Bethell, "Britain and Latin America in Historical Perspective," *Britain and Latin America: A Changing Relationship,* ed. Victor Bulmer-Thomas (Cambridge: Cambridge University Press, 1989), 4–12.

9. Mary Louise Pratt, *Imperial Eyes: Travel Writing and Transculturation* (New York: Routledge, 1993), 178.

10. Pratt, ibid., 172–75; Jaksic, Andrés Bello, 30–90.

11. John Gallagher and Ronald Robinson, "The Imperialism of Free Trade," *Economic History Review* 4, no. 1 (1953), 8.

12. The term "neo-colonialism" is used throughout this book to refer to the asymmetrical economic relations between Britain and Latin America from the era of Spanish-American independence to approximately 1930. Although "colonialism" and "imperialism" are today often used almost interchangeably, the primarily economic implications of "neo-colonialism" are more appropriate to the specific context of Latin America. On the other hand, when discussing neo-colonialism in regard to British policy or cultural discourse, I have adopted H. S. Ferns's coinage "informal imperialism" to signal both the consistency of purpose behind Britain's activity in Latin America and the official empire and the distinct forms that British power has taken in Latin America. H. S. Ferns, "Britain's Informal Empire in Argentina," *Past and Present* 4 (1953), 60–75.

13. A partial bibliography of economic and historical materials on the relationship between Britain and Latin America in the nineteenth and twentieth centuries would include: Tulio Halperín Donghi, *The Contemporary History of Latin America*, trans. John Charles Chasteen (Durham: Duke University Press, 1993); Gallagher and Robinson, "Imperialism of Free Trade"; D. C. M. Platt, ed. *Business Imperialism: An Inquiry into the British Experience in Latin America, 1850-1914* (Oxford: Clarendon Press, 1977); *Latin America: Economy and Society, 1870-1930,* ed. Leslie Bethell (Cambridge: Cambridge University Press, 1989), 1–57; Rory Miller, *Britain and Latin America in the Nineteenth and Twentieth Centuries* (London: Longman, 1993); Richard Graham, "Robinson and Gallagher in Latin America: The Meaning of Informal Imperialism," in *Imperialism: The Robinson and Gallagher Controversy,* ed. William Roger Louis (New York: New Viewpoints, 1976), 217–20; P. J. Cain and A. G. Hopkins, "Gentlemanly Capitalism and British Expansion Overseas II: New Imperialism, 1850–1945," *Economic History Review* 40, no. 1 (1987): 1–26. Eric Hobsbawm's *The Age of Capital: 1848-1875* [1975] (New York: Random House, 1996) explains the expansion of capitalism in Latin America as part of a global trend.

14. Doris Sommer discusses the politics of the marriage plot in all of these novels, *Sab, Amalia,* and *María,* in her study of popular novels of the nineteenth century, *Foundational Fictions: The National Romances of Latin America* (Berkeley and Los Angeles: University of California Press, 1991).

15. Here and throughout this book, there is no intended relationship between the use of the phrase "invisible empire" as referring to British informal imperialism in Latin America and the Ku Klux Klan's use of the same designation.

16. Abdul R. JanMohamed, "The Economy of Manichean Allegory: The Function of Racial Difference in Colonialist Literature," in *"Race," Writing and Difference,* ed. Henry Louis Gates, Jr. (Chicago: University of Chicago Press, 1985), 78–106. The distinction is developed more fully in the chapter dedicated to Horacio Quiroga.

17. Carlos J. Alonso, *The Spanish American Regional Novel: Modernity and Autochthony* (Cambridge: Cambridge University Press, 1990), 38.

18. González Echevarría, *The Voice of the Masters: Writing and Authority in Modern Spanish American Literature* (Cambridge: Cambridge University Press, 1985).

19. Ibid., 41.

20. Roberto Fernández Retamar, "Problems of Spanish-American Literature," in *Calibán and Other Essays,* trans. Edward Baker, foreword by Fredric Jameson (Minneapolis: University of Minnesota Press, 1989), 78.

21. Fernando Coronil, *The Magical State: Nature, Money and Modernity in Venezuela* (Chicago: University of Chicago Press, 1997).

22. Walter Benjamin, "Theses on the Philosophy of History," *Illuminations: Essays and Reflections,* ed. and intro. Hannah Arendt, trans. Harry Zohn (New York: Schocken, 1968), 259.

23. Martin Horkheimer, "The Revolt of Nature," *Green History: A Reader in Environmental Literature, Philosophy, and Politics,* ed. Derek Wall (New York: Routledge, 1994), 236.

24. See, among other publications, David Harvey, *Justice, Nature and the Geography of Difference* (Cambridge, Mass: Blackwell Publishers, 1996); Fernando Mires, *El discurso de la naturaleza: ecología y política en América Latina* (San José, Costa Rica: Editoria DEI, 1990); Richard Peet and Michael Watts, *Liberation Ecology: Environmental Development, Social Movements* (London: Routledge, 1996).

25. González Echevarria, *Voice of the Masters,* 4.

26. Raymond Williams, "Ideas of Nature," in *Problems in Materialism and Culture* (London: Verso, 1980) 81. See also Williams's *The Country and the City* (Oxford: Oxford University Press, 1973), 278–306.

27. See Pratt, *Imperial Eyes,* 178–80. Among the laudable attributes of the tropics, Bello singles out the banana tree, because "escasa industria bástale, cual puede / Hurtar a sus fatigas mano esclava: / Crece veloz, y cuando exhausto acaba, / Adulta prole en torno sucede" [a little industry is enough, slave hands / may return to their chores: / It grows quickly, and when exhausted ends, / Another mature one succeeds it] (303).

28. Gwen Kirkpatrick, "Poetic Exchange and Ethical Landscape in Nineteenth-Century Latin America," paper delivered at Rutgers University, New Brunswick, New Jersey, March 7, 2001.

29. Gregorio Gutiérrez González, *Memoria: sobre el cultivo del maíz en Antioquia, Antología de poetas hispano-americanos,* 3:120–46.

30. Williams quotes this passage from Adorno in *Marxism and Literature* (New York: Oxford University Press, 1977), 103.

31. Alonso, *Spanish American Regional Novel,* 49.

32. David Spurr provides a useful lexicon of remarkably widespread colonialist tropes in *The Rhetoric of Empire: Colonial Discourse in Journalism, Travel Writing, and Imperial Administration* (Durham: Duke University Press, 1993).

33. Edward Said, *Culture and Imperialism* (New York: Vintage, 1993), 10.

34. Martin Green, *Dreams of Adventure, Deeds of Empire* (New York: Basic Books, 1979); Patrick Brantlinger, *Rule of Darkness: British Literature and Imperialism, 1830-1914* (Ithaca: Cornell University Press, 1988); Andrea White, *Joseph Conrad and the Adventure Tradition* (Cambridge: Cambridge University Press, 1993).

35. Tulio Halperín Donghi, *The Aftermath of Revolution in Latin America*, trans. Josephine de Bunsen (New York: Harper and Row, 1973), 123-24.

36. Antonio Gramsci, *Selections from the Prison Notebooks,* ed. and trans. Quintin Hoare and Geoffrey Nowell Smith (New York: International Publishers, 1999).

37. Halperín Donghi, *Aftermath*, 82-111, and William Glade, "Economy, 1870-1914," in *Latin America: Economy and Society, 1870-1930*, ed. Leslie Bethell (Cambridge: Cambridge University Press, 1989), 1-57.

38. Karl Marx, *Capital: A Critique of Political Economy*; vol. 3, *The Process of Capitalist Production as a Whole*, ed. Frederick Engels, trans. Ernest Untermann (Chicago: Charles H. Kerr, 1909), 390.

39. Arnold Bauer, "Rural Society" in Bethell, ed., *Latin America: Economy and Society, 1870-1930*, 129.

40. Halperín Donghi, *Contemporary History*, 120, italics mine. See also Claudio Véliz, *The Centralist Tradition of Spanish America* (Princeton, N.J.: Princeton University Press, 1980), 16-28; and Victor Bulmer-Thomas, *The Economic History of Latin America Since Independence* (Cambridge: Cambridge University Press, 1994), 87-92.

41. Pierre Philippe Rey, *Las alianzas de clases* [Les alliances des classes] trans. Félix Blanco (Mexico: Siglo Veintiuno Editores, 1976).

42. Cf. Anthony Brewer, *Marxist Theories of Imperialism: A Critical Survey*, 2nd ed. (London: Routledge, 1990), 233.

43. Coronil, *The Magical State*, 37.

44. Anne McClintock, "Soft-Soaping Empire: Commodity Racism and Imperial Advertising," in *Imperial Leather: Race, Gender and Sexuality in the Colonial Contest* (New York: Routledge, 1995), 207-31.

45. Said, *Culture and Imperialism*, 10.

46. Pedro Prado, *La reina de Rapa Nui* (Santiago, Chile: Andrés Bello, 1983).

47. Though apparently uninterested in the acquisition of wealth, Prado's natives are surprisingly savvy about selling souvenirs to the tourists who from time to time visit Easter Island. When the narrator visits a local artist, for example, he inquires about the designs in his carvings: "Y estos ídolos, ¿son tus dioses?" [And those idols, are they your gods?]. To which the artist replies: "No entiendo lo que quieres decir. Hago esto porque sé hacerlo, y las gentes que vienen en los buques los piden y dan ropa por ellos." [I don't understand what you mean. I make them because I know how to, and the people who come on ships ask for them and give clothing in exchange] (55).

48. Rory Miller, 179.

49. Ibid., 179-204.

50. Angel Rama, *The Lettered City*, ed. and trans. John Charles Chasteen (Durham: Duke University Press, 1996), 93–94.

51. António Cândido, "Literature and Underdevelopment" in *Spanish America in Its Literature*, ed. César Fernández Moreno, Julio Ortega, and Ivan A. Schulman, trans. Mary G. Berg (New York: Holmes and Meier Publishers, 1980), 264, emphasis in the original. Published in Spanish as *América latina en su literatura* (Mexico City: Siglo XXI and Unesco, 1972.)

52. Ciro Alegría, "Notas sobre el personaje en la novela hispanoamericana," address delivered at the University of New Mexico, Albuquerque, New Mexico, August 1951. *Recopilación de textos sobre tres novelas ejemplares*, ed. Trinidad Pérez (Havana: Casa de las Américas, 1971), 41.

53. Rómulo Gallegos, *Doña Bárbara*, with illustrations by Alberto Betran (Mexico City: Fondo de Cultura, 1954), 10.

54. Said, *Culture and Imperialism*, 7.

55. My readings of the regionalist novels, particularly Lynch's *El inglés de los güesos*, struggle to elucidate the mutually implicated articulations of race, class, and gender as they are inscribed in the texts; nevertheless, taking this step toward a gender-inflected interpretation of regionalist literature and the cultural discourse of neo-colonialism makes all the more clear the androcentrism of the accepted regionalist canon and the need to recuperate woman-authored narratives from the same period.

56. In Britain the colonial adventure tradition was unabashedly directed toward male audiences, from its early incarnations in Captain Marryat's novels to Kipling's *Kim*. Doyle's *Lost World*, for example, contains the dedication, "I have wrought my simple plan / If I give one hour of joy / To the boy who's half a man / Or the man who's half a boy." Sir Arthur Conan Doyle, *The Lost World* (New York: TOR, 1993), unnumbered page.

57. Julie Taylor, "Accessing Narrative: The Gaucho and Europe in Argentina," *Cultural Critique* (Fall 1997), 224–25; 237, 239. Taylor provides photos of Güiraldes dressed in a variety of exotic fashions: elegant tuxedo, white pith helmet (while traveling in India), bejeweled turban, leather *chiripá*, and tweed sports jacket.

58. See Doris Sommer, *Foundational Fictions: The National Romances of Latin America* (Berkeley: University of California Press, 1991), 12–27; Fredric Jameson, *The Political Unconscious: Narrative as a Socially Symbolic Act* (Ithaca: Cornell University Press, 1981) 110–19. Jameson's work draws on Northrop Frye's discussion of the quest romance in *Anatomy of Criticism: Four Essays* (Princeton, NJ: Princeton University Press, 1957) 186–206.

59. While Borges may have been an extreme case of Anglo-Argentinean hybridization, his exposure to British culture was far from singular: the British community in Argentina numbered forty thousand by 1914, and enjoyed cricket and polo grounds, a race course, the Victoria Tea and Luncheon Room, and a Harrods department store. Leslie Bethell, "Britain and Latin America in Historical Perspective," in *Britain and Latin America: A Changing Relationship*, ed. Victor Bulmer-Thomas (Cambridge: Cambridge University Press, 1989), 11.

60. Jorge Luis Borges, *Las memorias de Borges,* published in *La Opinión* (Buenos Aires), March 17, 1974, section 2, page 3. See Daniel Balderston's study of Robert Louis Stevenson's impact on Borges in *El precursor velado: R.L. Stevenson en la obra de Borges* (Buenos Aires: Editorial Sudamericana, 1985).

61. Jorge Luis Borges in collaboration with María Esther Vázquez, *Introducción a la literatura inglesa* (Buenos Aires: Editoria Columba, 1965); published in English as *An Introduction to English Literature,* trans. and ed. L. Clark Keating and Robert O. Evans (Lexington, Ky.: University Press of Kentucky, 1974).

62. Emir Rodríguez Monegal explores this aspect of Borges' upbringing and its impact on his work in *Jorge Luis Borges: A Literary Biography* (New York: Dutton, 1978), 3–14.

63. Even after the British invasion of the Falkland Islands drew widespread accusations of neo-imperialism in the 1980s, Borges preferred not to choose between one side or the other; rather, he reconciled his divided loyalties through an aesthetic cosmopolitanism that was based on the principle of empire. As he told interviewer Roberto Alifano, "El imperio británico hizo mucho bien, y todos los imperios, en general, han hecho mucho bien. Nosotros, sin ir más lejos, somos una consecuencia del imperio romano. Y la prueba está en que hablamos un idioma que es un ilustre dialecto del latín. De manera que yo, personalmente, comprendo muy bien a Kipling" [The British Empire did a lot of good, and all empires, in general, have done a lot of good. Looking no further than ourselves, we are a product of the Roman Empire. And the proof is that we speak a language that is an illustrious dialect of Latin. So that I, personally, understand Kipling very well]. Jorge Luis Borges, interview with Roberto Alifano, in *Conversaciones con Borges* (Buenos Aires: Atlántida, 1985), 67.

Borges describes imperialism, not entirely ironically, as a powerful force of cultural dissemination that outweighs the human tragedies of conquest and colonization. As the comment above suggests, the ideology embedded in Kipling's stories coincides not only with Borges' strong identification with England, but also with the culture that descended from the Spanish Empire through his creole ancestors.

64. Julie Skurski offers a thorough consideration of the politics of *Doña Bárbara* in "The Ambiguities of Authenticity in Latin America: *Doña Bárbara* and the Construction of National Identity," *Poetics Today,* 15, no. 4 (Winter 1994): 605–42.

65. González Echevarría, *Voice of the Masters,* 49.

66. Gallegos, *Doña Bárbara,* 93.

67. I address the politics of the pastoral in both *Don Segundo Sombra* and *El inglés de los güesos* in the chapter dedicated to Lynch.

68. Coronil describes the controversy surrounding Gómez's petroleum policies in *Magical State,* 75–82.

Chapter 1. "The Freedom in the Field": Empire and Ecology in the Misiones Stories of Horacio Quiroga (pp. 39-70)

1. Emir Rodríguez Monegal, *El desterrado: Vida y obra de Horacio Quiroga* (Buenos Aires: Editorial Losada, 1968), 117.
2. William Henry Hudson's novel *The Purple Land* (1885), which Quiroga greatly admired, tells the story of the failed invasion in its epilogue. The irreverent Hudson originally subtitled the book "The England Lost." Horacio Quiroga, letter to Martínez Estrada of January 12, 1936, in his *Cartas ineditas*, ed. Arturo Sergio Visca (Montevideo: Ministerio de Instrucción Pública y Previsión Social, 1959), 91. Though long forgotten in much of the English-speaking world, the defeat of the British invaders is remembered as an outstanding moment in Argentinean history. Buenos Aires' Museo de Historia Nacional commemorates the event with an extensive display of maps, artwork, and documents, as well as the weapons and uniforms of the defenders.
3. H. S. Ferns, "Argentina: Part of an Informal Empire?" in *The Land That England Lost: Argentina and Britain, a Special Relationship*, ed. Alistair Hennessey and John King (London: British Academic Press, 1984), 49–53; Leslie Bethell, "Britain and Latin America in Historical Perspective," in *Britain and Latin America: A Changing Relationship*, ed. Victor Bulmer-Thomas (Cambridge: Cambridge University Press, 1989), 11.
4. Bethell, "Britain and Latin America," 8.
5. See John King, "The Influence of British Culture in Argentina," in *The Land That England Lost: Argentina and Britain, a Special Relationship*, ed. Alistair Hennessey and John King (London: British Academic Press, 1984), 159–72.
6. Robert C. Eidt, *Frontier Settlement in Northeast Argentina* (Madison: University of Wisconsin Press, 1971), 3–12.
7. Oliver Marshall, "Planters or Peasants? British Pioneers on Argentina's Tropical Frontier," in *The Land That England Lost: Argentina and Britain, a Special Relationship*, ed. Alistair Hennessey and John King (London: British Academic Press, 1984), 143–58. According to Marshall the last of the British pioneers did not abandon Misiones until the 1980s.
8. Rory Miller, *Britain and Latin America in the Nineteenth and Twentieth Centuries* (New York: Longman, 1993), 11. According to Miller, the severe economic restrictions imposed the British blacklists, combined with the almost immediate withdrawal of British capital, brought hardships that made many in the Río de la Plata both aware and resentful of their countries' economic subordination to Britain.
9. Rodríguez Monegal, *El desterrado*, 86.
10. Horacio Quiroga, letter to Ezequiel Martínez Estrada of April 29, 1936. *El hermano Quiroga: Cartas de Quiroga a Martínez Estrada*, ed. Ezequiel Martínez Estrada (Montevideo: ARCA, n.d.), 110.
11. Horacio Quiroga, "La insolación," in *Todos los cuentos*, edited by Napoleón Baccino Ponce de León and Jorge Lafforgue (Madrid: Colección Archivos, 1993), 57–64.

12. Dane Kennedy describes late Victorian paranoia about tropical climates and fetishism of protective garb in "The Perils of the Midday Sun: Climatic Anxieties in the Colonial Tropics," in *Imperialism and the Natural World*, ed. John M. MacKenzie (Manchester: Manchester University Press, 1990), 118–40.

13. See Martha Canfield, "Transformación del sitio: verosimilitud y sacralidad de la selva," in *Horacio Quiroga: Todos los cuentos*, ed. Jorge Lafforgue and Napoleón Baccino Ponce de Leon (Barcelona: Fondo de Cultura Económica, 1993), 1361.

14. Carlos Fuentes, *La nueva novela hispanoamericana* (Mexico City: Cuadernos Joaquín Mortiz, 1969), 24.

15. Several years earlier Julio Cortázar had also named Quiroga along with Ricardo Güiraldes and Benito Lynch as three of the most innovative writers of the Río de la Plata. Julio Cortázar, "Algunos aspectos del cuento," in *Julio Cortázar: Obra crítica*, ed. Jaime Alazraki (Madrid: Alfaguara, 1994), 2:367–85.

16. Noé Jitrik, *Horacio Quiroga: Una obra de experiencia y riesgo* (Buenos Aires: Ediciones Culturales Argentinas, 1959), 71–74, 105–7.

17. Monegal, *El desterrado*, 22–59.

18. See Alonso, "Death and Resurrections: Horacio Quiroga's Poetics of the Short Story," in *The Burden of Modernity: The Rhetoric of Cultural Discourse in Spanish America* (Oxford: Oxford University Press, 1998), 108–10.

19. H. A. Murena, "El horror," in *Aproximaciones a Horacio Quiroga*, ed. Angel Flores (Caracas: Monte Avila, 1976), 29. The Conradian tones of Murena's comment are intriguing: "the horror" of Quiroga's Misiones stories is consistent with the experience of Conrad's ignominious imperialist in *Heart of Darkness*, Mr. Kurtz, whose dying words are precisely "the horror, the horror."

20. Jitrik, *Horacio Quiroga*, 133.

21. Horacio Quiroga, "Ante el tribunal," in *Obras inéditas y desconocidas*, ed. Roberto Ibáñez and Jorge Ruffinello (Montevideo: ARCA, 1967), 7:135.

22. Horacio Quiroga, "Kipling en la pantalla," in *Todos los cuentos*, 1219.

23. In *Horacio Quiroga: Obras inéditas y desconocidas*, vol. 7, "Sobre *El ombú* de Hudson," 122–26; "La novela trunca de un espíritu," 108–10.

24. See, in *Horacio Quiroga: Obras inéditas y desconocidas*, vol. 7, "Carta abierta al señor Benito Lynch," 36–38; "Un poeta de la selva: José Eustasio Rivera," 118–22; "El cuento norteamericano," 126–28; and "El impudor literario nacional," 43–46.

25. "Un poeta del alma infantil," in *Obras inéditas y desconocidas*, 7:101–5.

26. The first rule of Quiroga's "Decálogo del perfecto cuentista," for example, is "Cree en un maestro—Poe, Maupassant, Kipling, Chejov—como en Dios mismo." In *Textos inéditos y desconocidos*, 7:86.

27. Abelardo Castillo, "Liminar: Horacio Quiroga," in *Horacio Quiroga: Todos los cuentos*, ed. Napoleón Baccino Ponce de León and Jorge Lafforgue (Madrid: Colección Archivos, 1992), xxviii.

28. Emir Rodríguez Monegal, *El desterrado: Vida y obra de Horacio Quiroga* (Buenos Aires: Losada, 1968), 186. Rodríguez Monegal also discusses Borges's reaction to Quiroga; see 222.

29. Martin Green, *Dreams of Adventure, Deeds of Empire* (New York: Basic Books, 1979), 228.
30. Joseph Conrad, *Heart of Darkness* and *The Secret Sharer*, intro. Albert Guerard (New York: Penguin, 1983), 72.
31. Horacio Quiroga, "Una bofetada," in *Todos los cuentos*, 204-12.
32. Carlos J. Alonso, The Burden of Modernity: *The Rhetoric of Cultural Discourse in Spanish America* (Oxford: Oxford University Press, 1998), 125.
33. Ibid., 19-20. See Jorge Marcone's "Del retorno a lo natural: *La serpiente de oro*, la 'novela de la selva,' y la crítica ecológica," *Hispania* 81 no. 2: (1998): 299-308; and "Cultural Criticism and Sustainable Development in Amazonia: A Reading from the Spanish American Romance of the Jungle," *Hispanic Journal* 19 no. 2 (1998): 281-84.
34. Horacio Quiroga, *Una cacería humana en Africa*, in *Obras inéditas y desconocidas*, ed. Angel Rama and Jorge Ruffinelli (Montevideo: Arca, 1967), 2:77.
35. Horacio Quiroga, letter to Ezequiel Martínez Estrada of April 11, 1936, in *Cartas inéditas de Horacio Quiroga*, ed. Arturo Sergio Visca (Montevideo: Ministerio de Instrucción Pública y Previsión Social, 1959), 94-95.
36. See Abdul R. JanMohamed, "The Economy of Manichean Allegory: The Function of Racial Difference in Colonialist Literature," in *"Race," Writing and Difference,* ed. Henry Louis Gates, Jr. (Chicago: University of Chicago Press, 1986), 78-106.
37. Ian Watt, *Conrad in the Nineteenth Century* (Berkeley and Los Angeles: University of California Press, 1979).
38. Díaz corresponds, like many of Quiroga's Misiones characters, to the emergence of what environmental historian Libby Robin has called "the sciences of settling": the study pursued, often by on-site amateurs, of the adaptations to and of the natural environment that were essential to the survival of colonists and the local populations: tropical medicine, agricultural science, forestry, soil conservation, and climatology. The problem of sleeping sickness, which killed approximately half a million people in the Congo between 1895 and 1905, was the focus of several scientific commissions sponsored by the British government in the early twentieth century.
39. See, for example, Jorge Klor de Alva, "The Postcolonization of the (Latin) American Experience: A Reconsideration of 'Colonialism,' 'Postcolonialism,' and 'Mestizaje,'" in *After Colonialism: Imperial Histories and Postcolonial Displacements,* ed. Gyan Prakash (Princeton, N.J.: Princeton University Press, 1995), 241-78; Fernando Coronil, "Can Postcoloniality Be Decolonized? Imperial Banality and Postcolonial Power," *Public Culture* 5, no. 1 (Fall 1992): 89-108.
40. Edward Said, *Culture and Imperialism* (New York: Vintage, 1994), 7.
41. See David Harvey, *Justice, Nature and the Geography of Difference* (Cambridge, Mass.: Blackwell, 1996); Fernando Coronil, *The Magical State: Nature, Money and Modernity in Venezuela* (Chicago: University of Chicago Press, 1997); Fernando Mires, *El discurso de la naturaleza: ecología y política en América Latina* (San José, Costa Rica: DEI, 1990).

42. Karl Marx, *Capital: A Critique of Political Economy*, trans. Ernest Untermann (Chicago: Charles H. Kerr, 1909), 3:954.
43. Horacio Quiroga, "Los mensú," in *Todos los cuentos*, 77–88.
44. Horacio Quiroga, "Los pescadores de vigas," in *Todos los cuentos*, 114–20.
45. Jorge Lafforgue and Napoleón Baccino Ponce de León, endnote, "Los pescadores de vigas," in *Horacio Quiroga: Todos los cuentos*, 121.
46. Juan José Beauchamp, "Subdesarrollo, ideología y visión del mundo en los relatos de ambiente de Horacio Quiroga," *Revista de Estudios Hispánicos* 6 (1979): 85–120; reference is on 97.
47. "Homenaje a Mariátegui," in *Obras inéditas y desconocidas*, 7:129–30.
48. Rodríguez Monegal, *El desterrado*, 153–54.
49. Quiroga later struck "English accountant" for "commercial accountant."
50. David Spurr, *The Rhetoric of Empire: Colonial Discourse in Journalism, Travel Writing, and Imperial Administration* (Durham and London: Duke University Press, 1993) 17.
51. Horacio Quiroga, "El hombre muerto," in *Todos los cuentos*, 653–58.
52. Eidt, *Frontier Settlement*, 174.
53. Beauchamp, "Subdesarrollo," 90.
52. Harvey, *Justice, Nature*, 137.
55. Thomas R. Dunlap, "Ecology and environmentalism in the Anglo settler colonies," *Ecology and Empire: Environmental History of Settler Societies*, ed. Tom Griffiths and Libby Robin (Seattle: University of Washington Press, 1997), 85.
56. "The Bridge Builders," *Rudyard Kipling*, ed. and intro. Daniel Karlin (Oxford: Oxford University Press, 1999).
57. Harvey, *Justice, Nature*, 138.
58. Benita Parry, "The Content and Discontents of Kipling's Imperialism," *Space & Place: Theories of Identity and Location*, ed. Erica Carter, James Donald, and Judith Squires (London: Lawrence and Wishart, 1993), 236.
59. Alonso, *Burden of Modernity*, 123.
60. Canfield, "Transformación del sitio," 1377.
61. Horacio Quiroga, "Los desterrados," in *Todos los cuentos*, 626–35.
62. Jorge Lafforgue and Napoleón Baccino Ponce de León, eds., *Horacio Quiroga: Todos los cuentos* (Barcelona: Fondo de Cultura Económica, 1992), 626.
63. Leonor Fleming, ed. *Horacio Quiroga: Cuentos* (Madrid: Cátedra, 1995) 295.
64. Horacio Quiroga, "Anaconda," in *Todos los cuentos*, 323–62; "El regreso de Anaconda," in *Todos los cuentos*, 609–25.
65. Horacio Quiroga, "El regreso de Anaconda," 613.
66. John A. McClure, *Kipling and Conrad: The Colonial Fiction* (Cambridge, Mass: Harvard University Press, 1981); James Harrison, "Kipling's Jungle Eden," in *Critical Essays on Rudyard Kipling*, ed. Harold Orel (Boston: G.K. Hall, 1989) 77–92.
67. Domingo F. Sarmiento, *Facundo: Civilización y barbarie*, in *Obras Completas*, volume 7 (Buenos Aires: Universidad Nacional de la Matanza, 2001).

Notes   169

Chapter 2. The Geography of resistance in Benito Lynch's El inglés de los güesos *(pp. 71-111)*

1. Benito Lynch, *El inglés de los güesos* (Buenos Aires: Troquel, 1960), 177. All translations are my own unless otherwise noted.

2. Manuel Gálvez's essay "Benito Lynch," included in the fourth volume of his memoir, *Recuerdos de la vida literaria* (Buenos Aires: Hachette, 1965), contains a short account of the two writers' acquaintance. He describes Lynch as "un gran tímido, y, al mismo tiempo, un huraño [timid, and at the same time, unsociable] and remarks: "Los escritores platenses que se han alabado de haber sido amigos suyos durante los últimos años, faltan la verdad o exageran" [Writers of the Rio de la Plata who claim to have been his friends in recent years lie or exaggerate] (262).

3. Quoted in *Genio y figura de Benito Lynch* by Ulises Petit de Murat (Buenos Aires: Editorial Universitaria de Buenos Aires, 1968), 52.

4. The letter concludes, "Vaya, entre tanto, mi homenaje a su talento, inequívocamente de varón, con la seguridad en mí, de que si algún día hemos de tener un gran novelista, ése va a ser usted." [Meanwhile, I send my praise of your talent, unmistakably masculine, with the conviction that if we are some day to have a great novelist, it will be you] (ibid., 271). In 1929, after the publication of *Raquela* and *El inglés de los güesos,* Quiroga confirmed his earlier opinion in a Buenos Aires newspaper: "Lo considero el único gran novelista argentino de la hora actual. Su honestidad de escritor, su probidad literaria y la seriedad de sus trabajos son la prueba de lo que afirmo." [I consider him the only great Argentinean novelist at this time. His honesty as a writer, his literary probity and the seriousness of his work are the proof]; Roberto Salama, *Benito Lynch* (Buenos Aires: La Mandrágora, 1959), 271. When *El inglés* appeared in 1924, Gálvez wrote: "Since the publication of *Los caranchos de la Florida* we have recognized him as an exceptional novelist; now we may say, a master"; quoted in "Un escritor y tres enigmas: Biografía de Benito Lynch," in *El inglés de los güesos* (Buenos Aires: Troquel, 1960), 17.

5. Salama, *Benito Lynch* (Buenos Aires: La Mandrágora, 1959), 271. Ulises Petit de Murat, *Genio y figura de Benito Lynch* (Buenos Aires: Editorial Universitaria de Buenos Aires, 1968).

6. Petit de Murat, *Genio y figura,* 61. See also Galvez, "Benito Lynch," 261–75.

7. Gálvez, "Opiniones," reprinted in 1937 edition of *El inglés de los güesos,* (original source unstated), 27.

8. Beatriz Sarlo, "Responses, Inventions, and Displacements: Urban Transformations and Rural Utopias," in *Don Segundo Sombra*, trans. Patricia Owen Steiner; critical edition coordinated by Gwen Kirkpatrick (Pittsburgh: University of Pittsburgh Press, 1995), 255. See also, in the same volume, Gwen Kirkpatrick, "Cultural Identity, Tradition, and the Legacy of *Don Segundo Sombra*" (xv-xxviii), Noé Jitrik, "*Don Segundo Sombra* and the Argentine Tradition" (209–14); and Francine Masiello, "Güiraldes and the Fiction of History" (231–44).

9. Sarlo, "Responses, Inventions," 246. If we are to believe Borges, Güiraldes' affiliation with Argentina's Europhile ruling class was part of the novel's genesis. In the famous essay "El escritor argentino y la tradición," he remarks that *Don Segundo Sombra* was inspired less by Güiraldes's experience on the pampa than by his reading of a colonial classic: "En cuanto a la fábula, a la historia, es fácil comprobar en ella el influjo del *Kim* de Kipling, cuya acción está en la India y que fue escrita, a su vez, bajo el influjo de *Huckleberry Finn* de Mark Twain, epopeya del Misisipí." [With regard to the plot, the story, it is easy to demonstrate in it the influence of Kipling's *Kim*, which in turn was influenced by *Huckleberry Finn*, the great epic of the Mississippi]; Jorge Luis Borges, "El escritor argentino y la tradición," in *Obras completas* (Buenos Aires: Emecé, 1989), 1:267–74. In fact the parallel is far from coincidental: Kipling scholars frequently point out the elaborate structures of ideological compromise Kipling constructs in support of Kim's claim to legitimacy as a native-born ruler of British India. See, for example, John McClure, *Kipling and Conrad: The Colonial Fiction* (Cambridge, Mass.: Harvard University Press, 1981), 70–81.

10. Estela Dos Santos, "Realismo tradicional: narrativa rural," in *Historia de la literatura argentina;* vol. 3, *Las primeras décadas del siglo,* directed by Susana Zanetti (Buenos Aires: Centro Editor de América Latina, 1986), 529–34.

11. Sandra Contreras, "El campo de Benito Lynch: Del realismo a la novela sentimental," in *El imperio realista,* ed. María Teresa Gramuglio (Buenos Aires: Emecé, 2002), 202–4. David Salama makes a similar point, in *Benito Lynch,* 32; as does David Viñas in "Benito Lynch: la realización del 'Facundo,'" *Contorno* (Buenos Aires, September 1955). Reprinted in Salama, *Benito Lynch,* 291–94.

12. David Rock, "Argentina in 1914: The Pampas, the Interior, Buenos Aires," in *Argentina Since Independence,* ed. Leslie Bethell (Cambridge: Cambridge University Press, 1993), 120. See also, in the same volume, Roberto Cortés Conde, "The Growth of the Argentine Economy, 1870–1930," 47–78; and Ezequiel Gallo, "Society and Politics, 1880–1916," 79–112.

13. John Foster Fraser, *The Amazing Argentine: A New Land of Enterprise* (New York: Funk and Wagnalls, 1914), 24.

14. See Mary Louise Pratt, *Imperial Eyes: Travel Writing and Transculturation* (New York, Routledge, 1991), 146–55.

15. David Viñas, "Benito Lynch: la realización del 'Facundo,'" *Contorno,* September 1955, in Salama, *Benito Lynch,* 291–94.

16. Quoted in Petit de Murat, *Genio y figura,* 48; original source unstated.

17. Jorge Luis Borges, "Nota sobre *The Purple Land,*" in *Obras completas* (Buenos Aires: Emecé, 1989) 2:114. The article was first published in the Buenos Aires newspaper *La Nación* on August 3, 1941.

18. Hudson's narrator concludes, referring to the aborted invasion of 1806: "I cannot believe that if this country had been conquered and recolonized by England, and all that is crooked in it made straight according to our notions, my intercourse with the people would have had the wild, delightful flavour I have found in it. And if that distinctive flavour cannot be had along with the material prosperity resulting from Anglo-Saxon energy, I must breathe the wish that this

land may never know such prosperity." William Henry Hudson, *The Purple Land* (New York: Random House, 1904), 364.

19. David Harvey, *Justice, Nature, and the Geography of Difference* (Cambridge, Mass.: Blackwell, 1997), 231–34

20. Karl Marx, "The Fetishism of Commodities and the Secret Thereof," *Capital*, in *The Marx-Engels Reader*, ed. Robert C. Tucker, 1:319–29 (New York: Norton, 1978), 321.

21. Ibid., 320.

22. Harvey, *Justice, Nature*, 231.

23. Benito Lynch, *Plata dorada* (Buenos Aires: M. Rodrígues Giles, 1909).

24. Quoted in *Historia argentina*, ed. Diego Abad de Santillán (Buenos Aires: Tipográfica Editora Argentina, 1965), 3:328.

25. Petit de Murat, *Genio y figura*, 32.

26. As Petit de Murat writes, Lynch's brief career as society columnist for the La Plata paper *El Día* ended with the production of a comedy entitled *El cronista social*, a thinly veiled satire of the local bourgeoisie. Though the play failed, Lynch never returned to journalism; Petit de Murat, ibid., 38.

27. The full list contains: Joseph Andrews, *Las provincias del Norte en 1825; capítulos del libro "Journey from Buenos Aires through the provinces of Cordova, Tucuman and Salta to Potosi"* (Buenos Aires: Coní, 1915); idem, *Viaje de Buenos Aires a Potosí y Arica, en los años 1825 y 1826* (Buenos Aires: Vaccaro, 1920); Alexander Gillespie, *Buenos Aires y el interior: observaciones reunidas durante una larga residencia, 1806 y 1807, con relación preliminar de la expedición desde Inglaterra hasta la rendición del Cabo de Buena Esperanza, bajo el mando conjunto de Sir David Baird* (Buenos Aires: Vaccaro, 1921); Samuel Haigh, *Bosquejos de Buenos Aires, Chile y Perú* (Buenos Aires: La Cultura Argentina, 1920); Francis Bond Head, *Las pampas y los Andes, notas de viaje*(Buenos Aires: Vaccaro, 1920); John Anthony King, *Veinticuatro años en la República Argentina; que abarcan las aventuras personales del autor, la historia civil y militar del país y una relación de sus condiciones políticas antes y durante la administración del Gobernador Rosas.* (Buenos Aires: Vaccaro, 1921); Paolo Mantegazza, *Viajes por el Río de la Plata y el interior de la Confederación Argentina* (Buenos Aires: Coni, 1916); Robert Proctor, *Narraciones del viaje por la cordillera de los Andes y residencia en Lima y otras partes del Perú en los años 1823 y 1824* (Buenos Aires: n.p., 1920); Edmund Temple. *Córdoba, Tucumán, Salta y Jujuy en 1825* (Buenos Aires: Coni, 1920); J. P. and G. P. Robertson, *La cultura argentina, La Argentina en la época de la Revolución, Cartas sobre el Paraguay, comprendiendo la relación de una residencia de cuatro años en esa República, bajo el gobierno del Dictador Francia*, trans. Carlos A. Aldao (Buenos Aires: Vaccaro, 1920); John Pullen, *Memoirs of the Maritime Affairs, etc.*, Lewis Paine, *A Short View of Spanish America, etc.*, E. E. Vidal, *Picturesque Illustrations of Buenos Aires and Montevideo, etc.*, trans. Carlos Muzio Sáenz Peña, ed. Emilio Ravignani (Buenos Aires: Casa Jacobo Peuser, 1923); Basil Hall, *El general San Martín en el Perú*, trans. Carlos A. Aldao (Buenos Aires: La Cultura Argentina, 1920); Jorge Thompson, *La guerra del Paraguay, acompañada de un bosquejo*

histórico del país y con notas sobre la Ingeniería militar de la Guerra, vol. 1, trans. Diego Lewis and Angel Estrada, ed. José Arturo Scotto (Buenos Aires: Talleres Gráficos de L.J. Rosso and Co., 1910); Jorge Federico Masterman, *Siete años de aventuras en el Paraguay,* trans. David Lewis (Buenos Aires: Ubaldo de Dovitius, 1911). See Thomas L. Welch and Myriam Figueras, *Travel Accounts and Descriptions of Latin America and the Caribbean, 1800-1920: A Selected Bibliography* (Washington, D.C.: Columbus Memorial Library, 1982) and Carlos J. Cordero's *Los relatos de los viajeros extranjeros posteriores a la Revolución de Mayo como fuentes de historia argentina: ensayo de sistematización bibliográfica* (Buenos Aires: Imprenta y Casa Editora Coni, 1936). The bibliographies also suggest that the vogue in British travel writing was a distinctly Argentinean phenomenon: in contrast to the quantity of travel narratives published in Buenos Aires, they list only a handful published in other Latin American cities.

28. See, for example, *Travel Writing and Empire: Postcolonial Theory in Transit,* ed. Steve Clark (New York: Zed Books, 1999).

29. Gillian Beer, "Traveling the Other Way: Travel Narratives and Truth Claims," in *Open Fields, Science in Cultural Encounter.* (Oxford: Clarendon Press, 1996), 59.

30. S. Samuel Trifilo, *La Argentina vista por viajeros ingleses: 1810-1860* (Buenos Aires: Ediciones Gure, 1959), 258.

31. Carlos J. Cordero, *Los relatos de los viajeros extranjeros posteriores a la Revolución de Mayo como fuentes de historia argentina: ensayo de sistematización bibliográfica* (Buenos Aires: Imprenta y Casa Editora Coni, 1936), 13.

32. Borges, "Nota sobre *The Purple Land,*" 2:114.

33. Roberto González Echevarria, *The Voice of the Masters: Writing and Authority in Spanish American Literature* (Cambridge: Cambridge University Press, 1985).

34. Charles Darwin, *Journal of Researches,* in *The Complete Works of Charles Darwin,* ed. Paul H. Barret and R. B. Freeman (London: Pickering, 1986), 37.

35. Giaconda Marún, "Darwin y la literatura argentina," in *La torre: Revista de la Universidad de Puerto Rico* 3(9) 551-77, 1998. The archaeological activity stimulated by Sarmiento's efforts is documented in "La vida científica y universitaria, 1880-1900," in *Historia argentina,* ed. Diego Abad de Santillán, 3:497-501. Grey's search for prehistoric remains on the pampa may have been inspired by the work of one of Argentina's most prominent archaeologists, a second-generation Italian-Argentinean named Florentino Ameghino, who published *La antigüedad del hombre en la Plata* in 1881.

36. Marún, "Darwin y la literatura argentina," 555.

37. Domingo F. Sarmiento, "Darwin," in *Textos fundamentales,* edited by Luis Franco and Ovidio Omar Amaya (Buenos Aires: Compañia Febril, 1959) 2:360.

38. Charles Darwin, *Voyage of the Beagle* (1839), edited and abridged by Janet Browne and Michael Neve (London: Penguin Books, 1989), 136. As Carlos Alonso has recently written, Sarmiento's writings are full of such contradictions

and misquotations of European texts, which "betray both the constant discursive peril that accompanied that commitment to modernity and his negotiating of that threat through a continual turning away from modernity's demands for a rational, rhetorically consistent discourse." Carlos J. Alonso, *The Burden of Modernity: The Rhetoric of Cultural Discourse in Spanish America* (Oxford: Oxford University Press, 1998), 62.

39. Mikhail Bakhtin, *Rabelais and His World*, trans. Hélène Iswolsky (Bloomington: Indiana University Press, 1988), 20.

40. Contreras, "El campo de Benito Lynch," 215.

41. The possibility remains that these word choices are not bad Spanish but Freudian slips. On the whole the notion of a queer James Grey is limited to the gossipy Deolindo Gómez, although it may be suggested that Lynch means to use these "accusations" to exclude the Englishman from the normative Argentinean community the text advocates.

42. More recent examples of Anglo-American sentimental primitivism might include films such as *A Walk in the Clouds, Enchanted April, Up at the Villa,* and *Stealing Beauty*.

43. The neologism "travelees" is introduced by Pratt in *Imperial Eyes*.

44. Richard Kerridge, "Ecologies of Desire: Travel Writing and Nature Writing as Travelogue," in *Travel Writing and Empire: Postcolonial Theory in Transit,* ed. Steve Clark (New York: Zed, 1999), 167.

45. Darwin, *Journal of Researches,* 2:65.

46. Francis Bond Head, *Journeys Across the Pampas and Among the Andes,* ed. C. Harvey Gardiner (Carbondale, Ill.: Southern Illinois University Press, 1967), 63–64.

47. Sander Gilman, "Black Bodies, White Bodies: Toward an Iconography of Female Sexuality in Late Nineteenth-Century Art, Medicine, and Literature," in *"Race," Writing and Difference,* ed. Henry Louis Gates, Jr. (Chicago: University of Chicago Press, 1985), 228.

48. See, for example Pratt's *Imperial Eyes,* 153; and Harvey C. Gardiner's introduction to Head's *Journeys Across the Pampas and Among the Andes,* xii.

49. Anne McClintock, *Imperial Leather: Race, Gender and Sexuality in the Colonial Contest* (London: Routledge, 1995).

50. Quoted in Petit de Murat, *Genio y figura,* 48; original source unstated.

Chapter 3. La vorágine: *Dialectics of the Rubber Boom (pp. 112-154)*

1. José Eustasio Rivera, *La vorágine,* ed. and intro. Montserrat Ordóñez. (Madrid: Cátedra, 1995), 385. All translations are my own unless otherwise indicated. In some cases Earl K. James's translation has been consulted; see José Eustasio Rivera, *The Vortex,* trans. Earl K. James (New York, 1935).

2. For more detailed histories of the Peruvian Amazon Company, see Angus Mitchell's introduction to *The Amazon Journal of Sir Roger Casement* (London: Anaconda Editions, 1997), 47–62; and Michael Taussig's *Shamanism, Colonialism,*

and the Wild Man: A Study in Terror and Healing (Chicago: University of Chicago Press, 1986), 3–73.

3. Casement traveled through the region accompanied by five "Commissioners"—Juan Tizon, Seymour Bell, H. L. Gielgud, Walter Fox and Louis Barnes—whom he perceived as corrupt colonial agents. He accused them of trying to justify and rationalize the horrific excesses of the Company (Mitchell, ed. *Amazon Journal*, 176–82). Angus Mitchell explains that "while Casement went to investigate the truth behind the atrocity reports, the other Commissioners were acting on behalf of the Peruvian Amazon Company and reporting on ways of improving the Company's commercial prospects"; second unnumbered page between 256 and 258.

4. Ibid., 183.

5. J. Hillis Miller, *Topographies* (Stanford: Stanford University Press, 1995), 46.

6. Ibid., 4.

7. Carlos Alonso, *The Spanish American Regional Novel: Modernity and Autochthony* (Cambridge: Cambridge University Press, 1990), 157–61. For Alonso, however, Rivera's overriding concern in *La vorágine* is not political but poetic; he interprets the contrast between the wild rubber trade and the plantation system as an elaborate figure for the struggle between Rivera's *Centenarista* literary generation and their more radical successors, the avant-garde.

8. Roberto Simón Crespi, "*La vorágine*: Cincuenta años después," in *La vorágine: Textos críticos,* ed. Montserrat Ordóñez (Bogotá: Alianza Editorial Colombiana, 1987), 421.

9. Ibid., 425–26.

10. Eduardo Neale Silva, "The Factual Bases of *La vorágine*," *PMLA* 54 (1939): 316–31; quotation is from 327. The publication of Neale Silva's article in 1939 established a clear link between Rivera's novel and British sources, including the Casement report; scholars since then have almost unanimously accepted the Chilean's findings as authoritative.

11. Hilda Soledad Pachón Farías, *Los intelectuales colombianos en los años veinte: el caso de José Eustasio Rivera* (Bogotá: Colcultura, 1993), 39.

12. Rivera's account of the rubber industry incorporates many of the historical figures named by Casement and others: Julio C. Arana, whom Clemente Silva encounters in La Chorrera; the French photographer Eugenio Robuchon, the humane "mosiú" murdered by Arana's henchmen; Peruvian journalist Benjamin Saldaño Roca, who courageously published accounts of Arana's crimes in his newspapers; Colonel Tomás Funes and his famous victim, Governor Roberto Pulido; see "Factual Bases," Neale Silva, 316–31. Thus the exclusion of Casement, his mission, and the existence of the Peruvian Amazon Company can only have been purposeful. As Neale Silva writes, the anonymous, ineffectual "Visitador" encountered by Silva could not have been Casement; the Visitor was more likely the Peruvian judge Rómulo Paredes, whose official report cleared the rubber traders of all but minor accusations. Nor can it be argued that Casement's visit fell outside the fifteen years of history the novel covers, 1905–20. Rivera excludes both Casement and Hardenburg, but applauds Robuchon and the Peruvian

Saldaña Roca, whose "columnas clamaban contra los crímenes que se cometían en el Putumayo y pedían justicia para nosostros" [His columns clamored against the crimes committed in the Putumayo and demanded justice for us] (268).

13. Quoted in Taussig, *Shamanism,* 17.
14. Pachón Farías, *Los intelectuales colombianos,* 58.
15. Ibid., 43–64.
16. Ibid., 47.
17. Ibid., 58.
18. Such programs are analyzed by Richard Kerridge in "Ecologies of Desire: Travel Writing and Nature Writing as Travelogue," in *Travel Writing and Empire: Postcolonial Theory in Transit,* ed. Steve Clark (New York: Zed Books, 1999), 164–82.
19. José Eustasio Rivera, *Tierra de Promisión,* 2nd ed. (Santiago de Chile: Ediciones Ercilla, 1938), poem 16, p. 34.
20. Alonso, on the other hand, has convincingly argued that the discrepancy between Rivera's only published works is more limited than commonly supposed, demonstrating that the poems are also based upon the establishment in the two quatrains of an apparent stasis that is abruptly broken in the tercets (*Spanish American Regional Novel,* 144–48).
21. On the trope of emptiness in colonial discourse, see David Spurr, "Negative Space," in *The Rhetoric of Empire: Colonial Discourse in Journalism, Travel Writing, and Imperial Administration* (Durham: Duke University Press, 1993) 92–97.
22. Neale Silva describes various possibilities in *Horizonte humano; Vida de José Eustasio Rivera* (Madison: University of Wisconsin Press, 1960), 245–50.
23. José Eustasio Rivera and Melitón Escobar, "Informe de la Comisión Colombiana de Limites con Venezuela," letter to the Minister of Foreign Relations of Colombia, July 18, 1923. Reprinted in *José Eustasio Rivera, intelectual: Textos y documentos, 1912-1928,* edited by Hilda Soledad Pachón-Farias (Bogotá: Impresa Editorial Universidad Nacional de Colombia), 44.
24. Ibid., 45.
25. Rivera's concern with the lack of infrastructure linking the southern provinces to Bogotá is evident in "Los caminos del Caquetá," an essay published in *El Nuevo Tiempo* on May 6, 1924, in which Rivera recommends a plan for building roads into the Putumayo and Caquetá regions. Reprinted in *José Eustasio Rivera: 1888-1988,* ed. Conrado Zuluaga Osorio et al. (Bogotá: Colcultura, 1988), 18–20.
26. See, for example, Crespi, "La vorágine," 422.
27. Horacio Quiroga, "La selva de José Eustasio Rivera," in *La vorágine: Textos Críticos,* ed. Ordóñez, 77–78. The narrative also counters the disastrous fate of Arturo Cova—the negation of geographic rationalism—with the positive, even redemptive figure of Clemente Silva. On Silva's role in the novel see Oscar Gerardo Ramos, "Clemente Silva, héroe de *La vorágine,*" in idem, (1987) 353–72.
28. Sylvia Molloy, "Contagio narrativo y gesticulación retórica en *La vorágine,*" in *La vorágine: Textos Críticos,* ed. Ordóñez, 492.
29. Martin Green's *Dreams of Adventure, Deeds of Empire* (New York: Basic Books, 1979); and Andrea White's *Joseph Conrad and the Adventure Tradition*

(Cambridge: Cambridge University Press, 1993) are excellent studies of the ideologies at work in the adventure tradition in European literature.

30. The possibility cannot yet be ruled out, however, that Rivera did have access to *Heart of Darkness*. Though social and cultural histories of Colombia generally downplay the importance of Britain's cultural influence in the early twentieth century (in contrast to the case in Argentina, for example), an article published in *El Tiempo* on June 12, 1913, attests to a brief period of interest in British literature that coincides with the publication of Conrad's novella in 1901. Under the title "El culto de la energía," Miguel S. Oliver writes: "Hace diez o doce años, coincidiendo con la 'literatura de desastre,' penetró en nuestro país una fuerte ráfaga de anglosajonismo. Este viento soplaba y venía, principalmente, de donde había venido la derrota material." [Ten or twelve years ago, coinciding with the "disaster literature," a strong gust of Anglo-Saxonism penetrated our country. This wind blew and came, principally, from the same direction as our material defeat]. Oliver enumerates several of the many authors who were translated into Spanish at that time: Desmolins, Emerson, Chamberlain, Roosevelt, Carnegie, Kipling (author of "la nueva epopeya zoológica" [the new zoological epic]), Whitman, and Wells. These texts, known collectively as "literatura estimulante" [stimulating literature], were intended to invigorate the Hispanic countries with "un nuevo temperamento y una nueva psicología" [a new temperament and a new psychology]. Oliver's point is that the time has come to reject the "cult of energy":

> Se creyó que una somera propaganda literaria podría fortalecer nuestra voluntad, cambiar nuestra orientación y subvenir de golpe y porrazo la índole de la sociedad española. El ejemplo anglosajón y la eficacia de estas lecturas estimulantes ha ido pasando después a un segundo término. La misma propensión imperialista de que ellas nos contaminaron, los avances del estatismo y del socialismo han contrarrestado su levadura individualista, su glorificación del esfuerzo privado y extraoficial.

> [It was believed that a superficial literary propaganda could fortify our will, change our orientation, and bolster at once the character of Spanish society. The Anglo-Saxon example and the efficacy of these stimulating readings have become secondary. The advances of statism and socialism have neutralized the imperialistic propensity with which they [the readings] contaminated us, their individualistic leavening, their glorification of private and extraofficial enterprise.]

Though the author's nationality is not specified, the reference to *El Desastre* (Spain's defeat in the War of 1898) suggests that Oliver is Spanish. The article's publication in *El Tiempo*, however, implies that it must have had some relevance for Colombian readers; what is more, the newspaper's editor seems to have found it unnecessary to provide any introductory or explanatory notes, as was often the practice with reprinted articles. Is it possible that *La vorágine* is also an implicit rejection of English literature and the Anglo-Saxon "cult of energy"? Rivera's narrative represents, however obliquely, a turning away from the imperialist and individualistic ethos toward the more inclusive, socialist politics that Oliver advocates.

31. The notion of the "chronotope" was developed by Mikhail Bakhtin, who uses it to describes the particular relationship between space and time in a given narrative. See "Forms of Time and of the Chronotope in the Novel," in *The Dialogic Imagination: Four Essays by M.M. Bakhtin,* ed. Michael Holquist, trans. Caryl Emerson and Michael Holquist (Austin: University of Texas, 1981), 84-85.

32. Ordóñez, introduction to *La vorágine,* 50.

33. Edward Said, *Culture and Imperialism* (New York: Vintage, 1994), 18 and passim.

34. Ian Watt, *Conrad in the Nineteenth Century* (Berkeley and Los Angeles: University of California Press, 1979), 144-45.

35. Joseph Conrad, *Heart of Darkness* (New York: Dover, 1990), 44.

36. Chinua Achebe, "An Image of Africa," *Research in African Literatures* 9, no. 1 (1978), 784.

37. Wilson Harris, "The Frontier on Which *Heart of Darkness* Stands," *Research in African Literatures* 12, no. 1 (1981), 86-93.

38. Ibid., 87.

39. Ibid., 86.

40. Watt, *Conrad in the Nineteenth Century,* 138.

41. Molloy, "Contagio narrativo," 493.

42. Ordóñez, introduction to *La vorágine,* 39.

43. Jane M. Rausch, *The Llanos Frontier in Colombian History: 1830-1930* (Albuquerque: University of New Mexico Press, n.d.) 297-327.

44. Crespi, "*La vorágine,*" 425.

45. Doris Sommer, Foundational Fictions: The National Romances of Latin America (Berkeley and Los Angeles: University of California Press, 1991), 477.

46. Rausch, *Llanos Frontier,* 306.

47. Crespi, "*La vorágine,*" 423.

48. Friedrich Engels, *Dialectics of Nature,* trans. and ed. Clemens Dutt, with a preface and notes by J. B. S. Haldane, F. R. S. (London: Lawrence and Wishart, 1940).

49. Ibid., 291.

50. Lynn White, Jr., "The Historical Roots of Our Ecologic Crisis," in *The Eco-Criticism Reader,* ed. Cheryll Glotfelty and Harold Fromm (Athens, GA: University of Georgia Press, 1996) 5.

51. Engels, *Dialectics of Nature,* 173.

52. White, "Historical Roots," 9-10.

53. Taussig, *Shamanism,* 77.

54. Ordóñez, introduction to *La vorágine,* 51-56; Sharon Magnarelli, "La mujer y la naturaleza en *La vorágine:* A imagen y semejanza del hombre," in *La vorágine: Textos críticos,* ed. Monserrat Ordóñez (Bogotá: Alianza Editorial, 1989).

55. Mary Louise Pratt, *Imperial Eyes: Travel Writing and Transculturation* (New York: Routledge, 1991), 7, 111-27.

56. José Eustasio Rivera and Melitón Escobar, *Informe,* 47.

57. William Bull, "Naturaleza y antropomorfismo en *La vorágine,*" *La vorágine: Textos críticos,* ed. Monserrat Ordóñez (Bogotá: Alianza Editorial, 1989), 319-34.

58. Friedrich Engels, *Socialism: Utopian and Scientific* (1892), in *Green History: A reader in environmental literature, philosophy and politics*, ed. Derek Wall (London: Routledge, 1994), 96.

59. In Buell's analysis, *Moby-Dick*'s contradictory imaging of the ocean is not unlike *La vorágine*'s treatment of the jungle: while repeating traditional and largely negative mythologies of the ocean and its creatures, Melville's novel also verges on a more contemporary conservationist message. See Buell "Global Commons As Resource and Icon," in *Writing for an Endangered World: Literature, Culture, and Environment in the U.S. and Beyond* (Cambridge, Mass.: Harvard University Press, 2001), 196–223.

60. Karl Marx, *Capital: A Critique of Political Economy*, ed. Friedrich Engels, trans. Ernest Untermann (Chicago: Charles Kerr, 1909), 3:952–56.

Afterword: The Spanish American Regional Writers: Fertile Ground (pp. 155–158)

1. John Gallagher and Ronald Robinson, "The Imperialism of Free Trade," *Economic History Review* 4, no. 1 (1953), 1.

2. Domingo F. Sarmiento, *Facundo: Civilización y barbarie*, in *Obras completas* volume 7 (Buenos Aires: Universidad Nacional de La Matanza, 2001).

3. Beatriz González-Stephan, "Showcases of Consumption: Historical Panoramas and Universal Expositions," in *Beyond Imagined Communities: Reading and Writing the Nation in Nineteenth-Century Latin America*, ed. Sara Castro-Klarén and John Charles Chasteen (Washington, D.C., and Baltimore, Md.: Woodrow Wilson Center Press and Johns Hopkins University Press, 2003), 225–38.

Bibliography

Achebe, Chinua. "An Image of Africa." *Research in African Literatures* 9, no. 1 (1978): 1-15.
Alcalde Cardoza, Javier G. *La idea de desarrollo del Tercer Mundo: La visión inglesa y norteamericana: 1900-1950*. Lima: Centro Pacífico, 1998.
Alegría, Ciro. "Notas sobre el personaje en la novela hispanoamericana." In *Recopilación de textos sobre tres novelas ejemplares*, edited by Trinidad Pérez, 34-42. Havana: Casa de las Américas, 1971.
Alonso, Carlos J. *The Burden of Modernity: The Rhetoric of Cultural Discourse in Spanish America*. Oxford: Oxford University Press, 1998.
———. *The Spanish American Regional Novel: Modernity and Autochthony*. Cambridge: Cambridge University Press, 1990.
Araujo, Simón. "Exposición del doctor Simón Araujo sobre los problemas nacionales." *El Tiempo* [Bogotá], 18 July 1915, np.
"Las atrocidades del Putumayo. Crisis de la 'Amazon Company.' Los crímenes del Putumayo." *El Tiempo* [Bogota], 9 April 1913, 2.
Bakhtin, M. M. *The Dialogic Imagination: Four Essays*. Edited by Michael Holquist. Translated by Caryl Emerson. Austin: University of Texas Press, 1981.
Balderston, Daniel. *El precursor velado: R. L. Stevenson en la obra de Borges*. Translated by Eduardo Paz Leston. Buenos Aires: Sudamericana, 1985.
"La barbárie inquisitorial del hombre blanco. Crímenes monstruosos y horrorosas atrocidades." *El Tiempo* [Bogotá], 23 November 1912, 2.
Beauchamp, Juan José. "Subdesarrollo, ideología y visión del mundo en los relatos de ambiente de Horacio Quiroga." *Revista de Estudios Hispánicos* 6 (1979): 85-120.
Beer, Gillian. *Open Fields: Science in Cultural Encounter*. Oxford: Clarendon Press, 1996.
Benjamin, Walter. *Illuminations: Essays and Reflections*. Edited and with an introduction by Hannah Arendt. Translated by Harry Zohn. (New York: Schocken, 1968.
Bethell, Leslie, ed. *Argentina Since Independence*. Cambridge: Cambridge University Press, 1993.
———. "Britain and Latin America in Historical Perspective." In *Britain and Latin America: A Changing Relationship*, edited by Victor Bulmer-Thomas, 1-24. Cambridge: Cambridge University Press, 1989.
———. *Latin America: Economy and Society, 1870-1930*. Cambridge: Cambridge University Press, 1989.

Bongie, Christopher L. *Exotic Memories: Literature and Colonialism at the Fin de Siècle*. Stanford: Stanford University Press, 1991.

———. *Islands and Exiles: The Creole Identities of Post/Colonial Literature*. Stanford: Stanford University Press, 1998.

Borges, Jorge Luis. *Conversaciones con Borges*. Buenos Aires: Atlántida, 1985.

———. *Las memorias de Borges*. Published in *La Opinión* [Buenos Aires], 17 March 1974, 1-23.

———. *Obras completas*. 3 vols. Buenos Aires: Emecé, 1989.

———, in collaboration with María Ester Vázquez. *Introducción a la literatura inglesa*. Buenos Aires: Columba, 1965. Published in English as *An Introduction to English Literature*. Translated and edited by L. Clark Keating and Robert O. Evans. Lexington: University Press of Kentucky, 1974.

Brantlinger, Patrick. *Rule of Darkness: British Literature and Imperialism, 1830-1914*. Ithaca: Cornell University Press, 1988.

Brewer, Anthony. *Marxist Theories of Imperialism: A Critical Survey*. 2nd ed. London: Routledge, 1990.

Buell, Lawrence. *Writing for an Endangered World: Literature, Culture and the Environment in the U.S. and Beyond*. Cambridge, Mass.: Harvard University Press, 2001.

Bull, William. "Naturaleza y antropomorfismo en *La vorágine*." In *La vorágine: Textos críticos*. edited by Montserrat Ordóñez, 319-34. Bogotá: Alianza, 1987.

Bulmer-Thomas, Victor, ed. *Britain and Latin America: A Changing Relationship*. Cambridge: Cambridge University Press, 1989.

———. *The Economic History of Latin America Since Independence*. Cambridge: Cambridge University Press, 1994.

Cain, P. J. and A. G. Hopkins, "Gentlemanly Capitalism and British Overseas Expansion II: New Imperialism, 1850-1945." *Economic History Review* 40, no. 1 (1987): 1-26.

Cândido, Antonio. "Literature and Underdevelopment." In *Latin America in Its Literature*, edited by César Fernández Moreno, Julio Ortega, and Ivan Schulman. Translated by Mary G. Berg. New York: Holmes and Meier, 1980, 263-82.

Canfield, Martha. "Transformación del sitio: verosimilitud y sacralidad de la selva." In *Todos los cuentos* by Horacio Quiroga, edited by Jorge Lafforgue and Napoleón Baccino Ponce de León. Barcelona: Fondo de Cultura, 1993, 1360-78.

Carpentier, Alejo. *Los pasos perdidos*. Edited by Roberto González Echevarría. Madrid: Cátedra, 1985.

Carter, Erica, James Donald, and Judith Squires, eds. *Space and Place: Theories of Identity and Location*. London: Lawrence and Wishart, 1993.

Casement, Sir Roger. *Amazon Journal*. Edited by Angus Mitchell. London: Anaconda, 1997.

Castillo, Abelardo. "Liminar: Horacio Quiroga." In *Todos los cuentos* by Horacio Quiroga, edited by Jorge Lafforgue and Napoleón Baccino Ponce de León, xxi-xxxiii. Barcelona: Fondo de Cultura, 1993.

Chatterjee, Partha. *Nationalist Thought in the Colonial World: A Derivative Discourse.* Minneapolis: University of Minnesota Press, 1986.
Clark, Steve, ed. *Travel Writing and Empire: Postcolonial Theory in Transit.* New York: Zed, 1999.
Colombia. Minister in Bolivia. *Los crímenes del Putumayo.* Circular to the Colombian Consuls in Bolivia. La Paz, 1912.
Conrad, Joseph. "Geography and Some Explorers." In his *Tales of Hearsay and Last Essays.* London: J. M. Dent, 1955, 1–21.
———. *Heart of Darkness.* 1899. New York: Dover, 1990.
———. *Nostromo: A Tale of the Seaboard.* 1904. Introduction by Martin Seymour-Smith. New York: Penguin, 1990.
Sandra Contreras, "El campo de Benito Lynch: del realismo a la novela sentimental." In *El imperio realista,* ed. María Teresa Gramuglio, 201–23. Vol. 6 of *Historia crítica de la literatura argentina.* Series directed by Noé Jitrik. Buenos Aires: Emecé, 2002.
Coronil, Fernando. "Can Postcoloniality Be Decolonized? Imperial Banality and Postcolonial Power." *Public Culture* 5, no. 1 (1992): 89–108.
———. *The Magical State: Nature, Money and Modernity in Venezuela.* Chicago: University of Chicago Press, 1997.
Cortázar, Julio. "Algunos aspectos del cuento." In *Julio Cortázar: Obra crítica,* edited by Jaime Alazraki, 2:367–85. Madrid: Alfaguara, 1994.
Crespi, Roberto Simón. "*La vorágine:* Cincuenta años después." In *La vorágine: Textos Críticos,* edited by Montserrat Ordóñez 417–30. Bogotá: Alianza, 1987.
"Las crueldades en el Putumayo." *El Tiempo* [Bogotá], 18 June 1913, n.p.
Cunninghame Graham, R. B. "Hardenburg." *El Tiempo* [Bogotá] 6 September 1913, 2.
Darwin, Charles. *Voyage of the* Beagle (1839). Edited by Janet Browne and Michael Neve. London: Penguin Books, 1989.
Doyle, Sir Arthur Conan. *The Lost World.* New York: TOR, 1993.
Dunlap, Thomas R. "Ecology and Environmentalism in the Anglo Settler Colonies." In *Ecology and Empire: Environmental History of Settler Societies,* edited by Tom Griffiths and Libby Robin, 76–86. Seattle: University of Washington Press, 1997.
Eidt, Robert C. *Frontier Settlement in Northeast Argentina.* Madison: University of Wisconsin Press, 1971.
Engels, Friedrich. *Dialectics of Nature.* Translated and edited by Clemens Dutt. With a preface and notes by J. B. S. Haldane, F.R.S. London: Lawrence and Wishart, 1940.
Fernández Retamar, Roberto. *Caliban and Other Essays.* Translated by Edward Baker. With a foreword by Fredric Jameson. Minneapolis: University of Minnesota Press, 1989.
Ferns, Henry S. "Britain's Informal Empire in Argentina." *Past and Present* 4 (1953): 60–75.
Fleming, Leonor. Introduction to *Cuentos,* by Horacio Quiroga. Madrid: Cátedra, 1995.

Fraser, John Foster. *The Amazing Argentine: A New Land of Enterprise.* New York: Funk and Wagnalls, 1914.
Frye, Northrop. *Anatomy of Criticism: Four Essays.* Princeton: Princeton University Press, 1957.
Fuentes, Carlos. *La nueva novela latinoamericana.* Mexico City: Cuadernos Joaquín Mortiz, 1969.
Gallagher, John, and Ronald Robinson. "The Imperialism of Free Trade." *Economic History Review* 6 (1953): 1–15.
Gallegos, Rómulo. *Doña Bárbara.* 1929. Illustrated by Alberto Betran. Mexico City: Fondo de Cultura, 1954.
Gilman, Sander. "Black Bodies, White Bodies: Toward an Iconography of Female Sexuality in Late Nineteenth-Century Art, Medicine, and Literature." In *"Race," Writing and Difference*, ed. Henry Louis Gates, Jr., Chicago: University of Chicago Press, 1986, 223–61.
González Echevarría, Roberto. *The Voice of the Masters: Writing and Authority in Modern Spanish American Literature.* Cambridge: Cambridge University Press, 1985.
González-Stephan, Beatriz. "Showcases of Consumption: Historical Panoramas and Universal Expositions." In *Beyond Imagined Communities: Reading and Writing the Nation in Nineteenth-Century Latin America*, edited by Sara Castro-Klarén and John Charles Chasteen, 225–38. Washington, D.C., and Baltimore, Md.: Woodrow Wilson Center Press and Johns Hopkins University Press, 2003.
Graham, Richard. "Robinson and Gallagher in Latin America: The Meaning of Informal Imperialism."In *Imperialism: The Robinson and Gallagher Controversy*, edited by William Roger Louis, 217–20. New York: New Viewpoints, 1976.
Gramsci, Antonio. *Selections from the Prison Notebooks.* Edited and translated by Quinton Hoare and Geoffrey Nowell Smith. New York: International, 1999.
Green, Martin. *Dreams of Adventure, Deeds of Empire.* New York: Basic Books, 1979.
Griffiths, Tom, and Libby Robin, eds. *Ecology and Empire: Environmental History of Settler Societies.* Seattle: University of Washington Press, 1997.
"La guerra europea y el porvenir de Colombia." *El Tiempo* [Bogotá], 12 August 1915, n.p.
Güiraldes, Ricardo. *Don Segundo Sombra.* Translated by Patricia Own Steiner. Critical edition coordinated by Gwen Kirkpatrick. Pittsburgh: University of Pittsburgh Press, 1995.
Gutiérrez, Jaime. "La República está sola." *El Tiempo* [Bogotá] 8 May 1911, n.p.
Haggard, H. Rider. *She.* 1887. Oxford: Oxford University Press, 1991.
Halperín Donghi, Tulio. *The Aftermath of Revolution in Latin America.* Translated by Josephine de Bunsen. New York: Harper and Row, 1973.
———. *The Contemporary History of Latin America.* Trans. John Charles Chasteen. Durham, N.C.: Duke University Press, 1993.

Hardt, Michael, and Antonio Negri. *Empire*. Cambridge, Mass.: Harvard University Press, 2000.
Harris, Wilson. "The Frontier on Which *Heart of Darkness* Stands." *Research in African Literatures* 12, no. 1 (1981): 86-93.
Harrison, James. "Kipling's Jungle Eden." In *Critical Essays on Rudyard Kipling*, edited by Harold Orel, 77-92. Boston: G. K. Hall, 1989.
Harvey, David. *Justice, Nature and the Geography of Difference*. Cambridge, Mass.: Blackwell, 1997.
Head, Francis Bond. *Journeys Across the Pampas and Among the Andes*. Edited by C. Harvey Gardiner. Carbondale, Ill.: Southern Illinois University Press, 1967.
Hennessey, Alistair, and John King. *The Land That England Lost: Argentina and Britain, a Special Relationship*. London: British Academic Press, 1984.
Hobsbawm, Eric. *The Age of Capital: 1848-1875*. 1975. New York: Random House, 1996.
Horkheimer, Martin. "The Revolt of Nature." In *Green History: A Reader in Environmental Literature, Philosophy and Politics*, edited by Derek Wall, New York: Routledge, 1994, 235-37.
Hudson, William Henry. *Green Mansions: A Romance of the Tropical Forest*. 1904. New York: Dover, 1989.
———. *The Purple Land*. New York: Random House, 1904.
"El imperialismo y los pueblos débiles." *El Tiempo* [Bogotá] 8 August 1913, n.p.
"Inglaterra contra nosotros." *El Tiempo* [Bogotá] 18 November 1915, 2.
James, Earl K. *The Vortex*. By José Eustasio Rivera. New York, 1935.
Jameson, Fredric. *The Political Unconscious: Narrative as a Socially Symbolic Act*. Ithaca: Cornell University Press, 1981.
JanMohamed, Abdul R. "The Economy of Manichean Allegory: The Function of Racial Difference in Colonialist Literature." In *"Race," Writing and Difference*, edited by Henry Louis Gates, Jr., 78-106. Chicago: University of Chicago Press, 1986.
Kerridge, Richard. "Ecologies of Desire: Travel Writing and Nature Writing Travelogue." In *Travel Writing and Empire: Postcolonial Theory in Transit*, edited by Steve Clark, 164-82. New York: Zed, 1999.
Kipling, Rudyard. *The Portable Kipling*. Edited by Irving Howe. New York: Penguin, 1982.
———. *Rudyard Kipling*. Edited and with an introduction by Daniel Karlin. Oxford: Oxford University Press, 1999.
Klor de Alva, Jorge. "The Postcolonization of the (Latin) American Experience: A Reconsideration of 'Colonialism,' 'Postcolonialism,' and 'Mestizaje,'" In *After Colonialism: Imperial Histories and Postcolonial Displacements*, edited by Gyan Prakash, 241-78. Princeton, N.J.: Princeton University Press, 1995.
El libro rojo del Putumayo. Bogotá: Arboleda y Valencia, 1913.
"Liquidación de la Peruvian Amazon Company." *El Tiempo* [Bogotá] 2 November 1911, 3.
Lukács, Georg. *History and Class Consciousness: Studies in Marxist Dialectics*. Translated by Rodney Livingstone. Cambridge, Mass.: MIT Press, 1971.

Lynch, Benito. *El inglés de los güesos*. Buenos Aires: Troquel, 1960.
MacKenzie, John M, ed. *Imperialism and the Natural World*. Manchester: Manchester University Press, 1990.
Marcone, Jorge. "Cultural Criticism and Sustainable Development in Amazonia: A Reading from the Spanish American Romance of the Jungle." *Hispanic Journal* 19, no. 2 (1998): 281–84.
———. "De retorno a lo natural: *La serpiente de oro*, la 'novela de la selva,' y la crítica ecológica." *Hispania* 81 no. 2 (1998): 299–308.
———. "*Historia secreta de una novela* de Vargas Llosa o *La casa verde* y el viaje de 'retorno a lo natural' en la 'novela de la selva' hispanoamericana." *Monographic Review / Revista monográfica* 12 (1996): 392–97.
———. "Jungle Fever: Primitivism in Environmentalism, Rómulo Gallegos' *Canaima*, and the Romance of the Jungle." *Primitivism and Identity in Latin America: Essays on Art, Literature, and Culture,* edited by Erik Camayd-Freixas and José Eduardo González, 157–72. Tucson: University of Arizona Press, 2000.
———. "'Nuevos descubrimientos del gran río de las Amazonas': La 'novela de la selva' y la crítica al imaginario de la Amazonía." *Estudios: Revista de investigaciones literarias y culturales* 16. (2000): 129–40.
Marshall, Oliver. "Peasants or Planters? British Pioneers on Argentina's Tropical Frontier." In *The Land That England Lost,* edited by Alistair Hennessey and John King. London: British Academic Press, 1984.
Marx, Karl. *Capital: A Critique of Political Economy*. 3 vols. Translated by Ernest Untermann. Edited by Friedrich Engels. Chicago: Charles H. Kerr, 1909.
Marx, Karl, and Friedrich Engels. *The Marx-Engels Reader*. Edited by Robert C. Tucker. New York: Norton, 1978.
Maury y Benítez, Juan María. *La agresión británica*. In *Antología mayor de la literatura española*, edited and with an introduction and notes by Guillermo Díaz-Plaja, 7:607–10. Barcelona: Labor, 1962.
McClintock, Anne. *Imperial Leather: Race, Gender and Sexuality in the Colonial Contest*. London: Routledge, 1995.
McClure, John. *Kipling and Conrad: The Colonial Fiction*. Cambridge, Mass.: Harvard University Press, 1981.
———. *Late Imperial Romance*. London: Verso, 1994.
Menéndez y Pelayo, Marcelino. Introduction to *Antología de poetas hispanoamericanos*, 2:i–clxxxviii. Madrid: Revista de archivos, 1927–28.
Miller, J. Hillis. *Topographies*. Stanford: Stanford University Press, 1995.
Miller, Rory. *Britain and Latin America in the Nineteenth and Twentieth Centuries*. New York: Longman, 1993.
Mires, Fernando. *El discurso de la naturaleza: ecología y política en América Latina*. San José, Costa Rica: DEI, 1990.
Molloy, Sylvia. "Contagio narrativo y gesticulación retórica en *La vorágine*." In *La vorágine: Textos críticos,* edited by Montserrat Ordóñez, 489–516. Bogotá: Alianza, 1987.
Navarro, Felipe. "La pampa omnipresente (Notas a propósito de Benito Lynch y *El inglés de los güesos*)." *Río de la Plata* 4–6 (1987): 303–7.

Neale Silva, Eduardo. "The Factual Bases of *La vorágine*." PMLA (1939): 316-31.
———. *Horizonte humano: Vida de José Eustasio Rivera*. Madison: University of Wisconsin Press, 1960.
Oliver, Miguel S. "El culto de la energía." *El Tiempo* [Bogotá] 12 June 1913, 2.
Ordóñez, Montserrat. Introduction to *La vorágine*, by José Eustasio Rivera. Madrid: Cátedra, 1995.
———, ed. *La vorágine: Textos críticos*. Bogotá: Alianza, 1987.
Orgambide, Pedro. *Horacio Quiroga: Una bibliografía*. Buenos Aires: Planeta, 1994.
Pachón Farias, Hilda Soledad. *Los intelectuales colombianos de los años veinte: El case de José Eustasio Rivera*. Bogotá: Cocultura, 1993.
Peet, Richard, and Michael Watts. *Liberation Ecology: Environmental Development, Social Movements*. London: Routledge, 1996.
Petit de Murat, Ulises. *Genio y figura de Benito Lynch*. Buenos Aires: Editorial Universitaria de Buenos Aires, 1968.
Platt, D.C.M., ed. *Business Imperialism: An Inquiry into the British Experience in Latin America, 1850-1914*. Oxford: Clarendon, 1977.
Prado, Pedro. *La reina de Rapa Nui*. Santiago, Chile: Andrés Bello, 1983.
Prakash, Gyan, ed. *After Colonialism: Imperial Histories and Postcolonial Displacements*. Princeton, N.J.: Princeton University Press, 1995.
Pratt, Mary Louise. *Imperial Eyes: Travel Writing and Transculturation*. New York: Routledge, 1991.
Quiroga, Horacio. *Cartas inéditas*. Edited by Arturo Sergio Visca. Montevideo: Ministerio de Instrucción Pública y Previsión Social, 1959.
———. *Obras inéditas y escondidas*. Under the direction of Angel Rama. 7 vols. Montevideo: ARCA, 1967.
———. *Todos los cuentos*. Edited by Jorge Lafforgue and Napoleón Baccino Ponce de León. Barcelona: Fondo de Cultura, 1993.
Rama, Angel. *The Lettered City*. Edited and translated by John Charles Chasteen. Durham, N.C. Duke University Press, 1996.
———. *Transculturación narrativa en América Latina*. Mexico City: Siglo Veintiuno, 1982.
Ramos, Oscar Gerardo. "Clemente Silva, héroe de *La vorágine*." In *La vorágine: Textos criticos*, edited by Montserrat Ordóñez, 353-73. Bogotá: Alianza, 1987.
Rausch, Jane M. *The Llanos Frontier in Colombian History: 1830-1930*. Albuquerque: University of New Mexico Press, 1993.
Real Academia Española. *Antología de poetas hispano-americanos*. 4 vols. Madrid, 1927.
Rey, Pierre Philippe. *Las alianzas de clases* [Les alliances des classes]. Translated by Félix Blanco. Mexico City: Siglo Veintiuno, 1976.
Rivera, José Eustasio. "Los caminos del Caquetá." *El Nuevo Tiempo* [Bogotá] 6 May 1924, n.p.
———. *Tierra de Promisión*. 1922. Santiago, Chile: Ercilla, 1938.
———. *La vorágine*. 9th edition. New York: Editorial Andes, 1929.

———. *La vorágine*. 1924. Edited and with an introduction by Montserrat Ordóñez. Madrid: Cátedra, 1995.
Rodríguez Monegal, Emir. *El desterrado: Vida y obra de Horacio Quiroga*. Buenos Aires: Losada, 1968.
———. *Jorge Luis Borges: A Literary Biography*. New York: Dutton, 1978.
Said, Edward. *Culture and Imperialism*. New York: Vintage, 1994.
———. *Orientalism*. New York: Vintage, 1978.
Salama, Roberto. *Benito Lynch*. Buenos Aires: La Mandrágora, 1959.
Sarlo, Beatriz. "Horacio Quiroga y la hipótesis técnico-científica." In *Todos los cuentos*, by Horacio Quiroga, edited by Jorge Lafforgue and Napoleón Baccino Ponce de León, 1274–1292. Barcelona: Fondo de Cultura, 1993.
Skurski, Julie. "The Ambiguities of Authenticity in Latin America: *Doña Bárbara* and the Construction on National Identity." *Poetics Today* 15, no. 4 (1994): 605–42.
Smith, Adam. *The Wealth of Nations*. 1776. Introduction by D. D. Raphael. New York: Knopf, 1991.
Sommer, Doris. *Foundational Fictions: The National Romances of Latin America*. Berkeley and Los Angeles: University of California Press, 1991.
———. "El género deconstruido: Cómo releer el canon a partir de *La vorágine*." In *La vorágine: Textos críticos*, edited by Montserrat Ordóñez 465–88. Bogotá: Alianza, 1987.
Spurr, David. *The Rhetoric of Empire: Colonial Discourse in Journalism, Travel Writing, and Imperial Administration*. Durham, N.C.: Duke University Press, 1993.
T.R.V. "'Los Boy Scouts.'" *El Tiempo* [Bogotá], 17 June 1913, n.p.
Taylor, Julie. "Accessing Narrative: The Gaucho and Europe in Argentina." *Cultural Critique* (1997): 215–43.
Trifilo, S. Samuel. *La Argentina vista por viajeros ingleses: 1810-1860*. Buenos Aires: Ediciones Gure, 1959.
Uribe Celis, Carlos. *Los años veinte en Colombia: Ideología y cultura*. Bogotá: Aurora, 1985.
Véliz, Claudio. *The Centralist Tradition of Spanish America*. Princeton, N.J.: Princeton University Press, 1980.
Wall, Derek, ed. *Green History: A Reader in Environmental Literature, Philosophy and Politics*. New York: Routledge, 1994.
Watt, Ian. *Conrad in the Nineteenth Century*. Berkeley and Los Angeles: University of California Press, 1979.
Welch, Thomas L., and Myriam Figueras. *Travel Accounts and Descriptions of Latin America and the Caribbean, 1800-1920: A Selected Bibliography*. Washington, D.C.: Colombus Memorial Library, 1982.
White, Andrea. *Joseph Conrad and the Adventure Tradition*. Cambridge: Cambridge University Press, 1993.
White, Lynn, Jr. "The Historical Roots of Our Ecological Crisis," In *The Ecocriticism Reader: Landmarks in Literary Ecology*, edited by Cheryll Glotfelty and Harold Fromm, 3–14. Athens, Ga.: University of Georgia Press, 1996.

Williams, Raymond. *The Country and the City*. Oxford: Oxford University Press, 1973.
———. "Ideas of Nature." In his *Problems in Materialism and Culture: Selected Essays*. London: NLB, 1980.
———. *Marxism and Literature*. Oxford: Oxford University Press, 1977.
Woolf, Virginia. *The Voyage Out*. 1915. Introduction by Phyllis Rose. New York: Bantam, 1991.
Zanetti, Susan, director. *Historia de la literatura argentina*. vol. 3. Buenos Aires: Centro Editor de América Latina, 1986.
Zuluaga Osorio, Conrado. *José Eustasio Rivera: 1888-1988*. Bogotá: Cocultura, 1988.

Index

Achebe, Chinua, 135
Adorno, Theodor, 12, 60.
Adventure fiction, 31–34. *See also* British literature; Colonial literature
Alberdi, Juan Bautista, 76
Alegría, Ciro, 28, 29
Alifano, Roberto, 164n63
Alonso, Carlos, 8–10, 16, 49–50, 63, 118, 172–73n38, 174n7, 175n20
Amazon jungle, 19, 21, 22, 37, 122–25
Ameghino, Florentino, 172n35
American Renaissance, 15
Anthropomorphism of nature, 152
Arabian Nights, 32, 33
Arana, Julio C., 112–13, 118, 174–75n12
Argentina, 22, 30, 36–37, 38–40, 75–77; city of La Plata, 81–85; Conquista del Desierto, 75; modernization of, 39–40, 49–52, 75–77, 81–82, 110–11; pampa, 39–40, 75–77
Ascasubi, Hilario, 75

Baccino Ponce de León, Napoleón, 57, 64
Bakhtin, Mikhail, 95–96, 177n31
Bauer, Arnold, 20–21
Beauchamp, Juan José, 52, 57, 60
Beef trade, 22, 39, 75–76, 83, 90
Beer, Gillian, 91
Belize, 156
Bello, Andrés, 2–6, 7, 13, 28, 53, 122, 123, 156, 159n2, 161n27
Benjamin, Walter, 10
Bernardin de St. Pierre, J. H., 1, 13, 31
Bible, 66, 145, 147
Blanco, Rufino, 16
Bolívar, Simón, 5

Bolivia, 21
"Boom" in Latin American literature, 8, 15, 44, 157–58
Borges, Jorge Luis, 31–33, 39, 47, 74, 78, 92, 164n63, 170n9; "El sur" (The south), 33
Boshell, Guillermo, 121
Brantlinger, Patrick, 17
Brazil, 18, 22, 128
British literature, 17, 23–24, 30–37, 38, 39, 44–48, 78, 133–37, 163n56, 176n30. *See also* Adventure fiction; Colonial literature; Conrad, Joseph; Hudson, William Henry; Kipling, Rudyard; Travel writing
Buell, Lawrence, 150, 178n59
Bull, William, 149
Byron, George Gordon, Lord, 13

Cambaceres, Eugenio, 75
Cândido, Antonio, 28
Cané, Miguel, 75
Canfield, Martha, 63
Canning, Lord George, 4–5, 6
Cárcel verde (Green jail), 146, 148
Carpentier, Alejo, 44, 143
Cartography, 129–33. *See also* Maps, Topography/toponymy
Casement, Sir Roger, 37, 113–16, 119–20, 123–24, 174n3, 174n10, 174–75n12
Castillo, Abelardo, 47
Cather, Willa, 15
Cervantes, Miguel de, 95
Chateaubriand, François-René, Vicomte de, 13, 31
Chile, 23–25, 156
Christianity, 147, 152–53

Index

Colombia, 21, 22, 37, 112–54; Caquetá, 121; Casanare, 125, 141, 145–46; geographic periphery of, 124–25; 137; Huila, 125; Putumayo, 112–25; Thousand Days' War, 125; vulnerability to neo-colonialism, 124–25
Colonial literature, 25–37, 38, 45–48, 49, 54, 122, 133–43, 163n56. *See also* Adventure fiction; British literature
Colonization, 38–40, 45–46, 52, 54
Commodity fetishism, 80–81
Congo, 22, 113–14, 167n38; fictions about, 50–52, 53, 133–37
Conrad, Joseph, 8, 38, 46–51, 70, 176n30; *Heart of Darkness*, 23–25, 33, 34, 37, 46, 48–52, 53, 133–37, 166n19; *La vorágine* (compared to *Heart of Darkness*), 137–43; *Nostromo*, 31; *A Personal Record*, 47
Contreras, Sandra, 75, 96
Cooper, James Fenimore, 15
Cordero, Carlos, 91–92
Coronil, Fernando, 10–11, 23, 55, 154n68
Cortázar, Julio, 44, 166n15
Costumbrismo (Spanish American literary movement), 28, 44, 73, 138, 141
Cotton industry, 40
Coward, Noel, 42
Crespi, Roberto Simón, 118–19, 141
Cunninghame Graham, Robert Bontine, 120, 122

Dante, 133
Darwin, Charles, 3, 92, 93–94, 101
Death, 63, 69
Deleuze, Gilles, 56
Dialectics, 10–12, 55, 143–45, 152–53, 157. *See also* Marxism
Díaz, Porfirio, 26
Díaz de Guzmán, Ruy, 51
Doctrine of Dominion, 36, 66, 67
Doyle, Arthur Conan, 24–25, 30, 31, 163n56
Dunlap, Thomas R., 60–61

Easter Island (Rapa Nui), 23–25
Ecology, 60–61, 144–45

Economic structures, in Latin America, 15–23, 26, 39–40, 75–77; reflected in literature, 10–15, 38, 71–72, 75, 81–85, 90, 141–42, 152, 155–58
Eidt, Robert, 40, 59
Elites, Latin American, 17–19, 21, 22, 53–54, 81–85, 88–90, 104–6, 125, 133, 155
Emerson, Ralph Waldo, 15
Engels, Friedrich, 12, 143–45, 148, 149, 151, 153, 157, 158
Environment. *See* Ecology; Environmental literary criticism; Nature
Environmental literary criticism, 12–14, 43–44, 61–70, 79–80, 110–11, 143–53, 157, 158
Escobar Larrazábal, Melitón, 128–29
Espectador, El (Bogotá newspaper), 130

Faulkner, William, 15, 151
Ferns, H. S., 160n12
First Peoples. *See* Indigenous peoples
Fleming, Leonor, 64
Foster, E. M., 100
France, 30, 124; cultural influence in Latin America, 39
Fraser, John Foster, 76
French literature, adapted by Latin American writers, 30–31
Frontier, 29, 40, 63–64, 136, 143
Frye, Northrop, 163n58
Fuentes, Carlos, 44, 157–58
Funes, Tomás, 174–75n12

Gallagher, John, 15, 17, 18, 156
Gallegos, Rómulo, 27, 28–29; *Canaima*, 27, 44, 143; *Doña Bárbara*, 27, 28–29, 34–36, 64, 104, 134
Gálvez, Manuel, 72, 73, 74, 169n2
Garavito, Justino, 128
García Márquez, Gabriel, 57, 157–58
Garzón Nieto, Julio, 128
Gauchesque literature (*literatura gauchesca*), 37, 71, 72. *See also* Lynch, Benito; Güiraldes, Ricardo
Gender and sexuality in regional literature, 101–7, 147, 163n55. *See also* Homophobia

Germany, 26, 145
Gillespie, Alexander, 90
Gilman, Sander, 102
Globalization, 157
Gómez, Juan Vicente, 34
Gómez de Avellaneda, Gertrudis, 6, 30–31
González Echeverría, Roberto, 9–10, 12, 34–35, 92–93
González-Stephan, Beatriz, 156–57
Gramsci, Antonio, 17
Great Britain, 1–2, 4–8, 16–19, 38–40, 75–78, 86, 112–14, 118; cultural influence in Latin America, 23, 30–34, 163n59. *See also* Hegemony; Informal imperialism; Neo-colonialism
Green, Martin, 17, 47–48
Grey, Sir Edward, 120
Guatemala, 21
Guattari, Felix, 56
Güiraldes, Ricardo, 30, 44, 163n57; *Don Segundo Sombra*, 31, 74–75, 104, 170n9
Gutiérrez, Eduardo, 75
Gutiérrez, Jaime, 120–21
Gutiérrez González, Gregorio, 14, 28

Haggard, H. Rider, 30, 34
Halperín Donghi, Tulio, 17, 21
Hardenburg, W. E., 113, 122, 124, 174–75n12
Harris, Wilson, 136–37
Harvey, David, 12, 55, 60, 80–81, 86
Haya de la Torre, Víctor Raúl, 27
Head, Francis Bond, 3, 31, 90, 93, 101–3, 108
Hegemony, 157; Britain's hegemony in Latin America, 22–24; defined, 17–18; Marxist theories of, 18–22. *See also* Informal imperialism; Neo-colonialism
Hemingway, Ernest, 45
Heredia, José María, 2–3
Hernández, José, 75
Hidalgo, Bartolomé, 75
Holmberg, Eduardo L., 93
Homophobia, 98, 107, 173n41
Horkheimer, Max, 12, 60

Hudson, William Henry, 8, 38, 46, 78, 92, 165n2, 170–71n18
Humboldt, Alexander von, 1, 3, 92

Immigration to Latin America, 38–40, 74, 76, 81–83
Import/export houses. *See* Merchant houses
Independence Wars, Spanish American, 4, 18, 39
India, 16, 17, 51, 62
Indigenous peoples, 21, 112; genocide of, 39, 75, 112, 116; Rivera's contact with, 129–30; writing about, 43, 139–40, 141
Industrial Revolution, 12, 144–45
Informal imperialism, 38–39, 41, 123–25, 160n12, accusations in Colombian press, 119–22. *See also* Neo-colonialism
Invasion of Buenos Aires and Montevideo, British, 4–5, 39, 165n2, 170–71n18
Investment in Latin America: British, 27, 39–40, 75–76, 112–25; U.S., 27
Invisible Empire, 15–25, 112–18, 122–24, 153, 155, 160n15. *See also* Hegemony; Informal imperialism; Neo-colonialism
Isaacs, Jorge, 7, 30–31, 44

Jaksic, Iván, 159n7
Jameson, Fredric, 31, 33, 163n58
JanMohamed, Abdul R., 7, 53
Jitrik, Noé, 44–46, 58
Judeo-Christian tradition, 145, 147
Jungle, writing about, 134–35, 143–54. *See also* Conrad, Joseph (*Heart of Darkness*); *Novela de la selva*; Rivera, José Eustasio (*La vorágine*)

Kafka, Franz, 45
Kennedy, Dane, 166n12
Kerridge, Richard, 101, 175n18
Kingsley, Charles, 31
Kipling, Rudyard, 8, 30, 36, 38, 45–48, 50, 66, 67, 70, 71, 136–37, 164n63, 170n9, 176n30; "The Bridge Builders," 61–62
Kirkpatrick, Gwen, 14

Index

Labor, history of, 20–21, 26, 27, 76; represented in regional literature, 40, 65, 102–5, 112–16, 119–22, 146, 152–53
Laclau, Ernesto, 21
Lafforgue, Jorge, 57, 64
Lawrence, D. H., 100
León de Mera, Juan, 44
Libro rojo del Putumayo (Putumayo red book, anonymous), 114–16, 119
Logging industry, 59
López Méndez, Luis, 5
Lugones, Leopoldo, 40, 45
Luxemberg, Rosa, 20
Lynch, Benito, 8, 30, 44, 46, 71–111, 122, 143, 155, 156, 169n2, 171n26; early life, 82–83; *El cronista social*, 88; *El inglés de los güesos*, 36–37, 40, 71–72, 77–80, 85, 86–91, 94–111; *El romance de un gaucho*, 72; *Los caranchos de La Florida*, 72–73, 85; satire of Argentinean elites, 88–90; treatment of "race," 83–85, 107–9; treatment of sexuality, 83–85, 101–7; use of differential geography, 80–90; use of failed pastoral, 78–80, 87, 110–11; use of ground level perspective, 111; *Raquela*, 72, 85

Magnarelli, Sharon, 147
Maps, 115, 117. *See also* Cartography, Topography/toponomy
Marcone, Jorge, 50, 167n33
Mariátegui, José Carlos, 27, 57
Mármol, José, 6
Marshall, Oliver, 40
Martí, José, 16, 83
Martínez Estrada, Ezequiel, 41, 52, 74
Marún, Giaconda, 93–94
Marx, Karl, 12, 19–20, 55, 59, 80–81, 152, 157, 158
Marxism, 10–23, 55, 57, 60, 80–81, 118, 143–45, 157
Maupassant, Guy de, 45, 50
Maury y Benítez, Juan María, 1–4, 7, 122, 151
McClintock, Anne, 23, 103
Melville, Herman, 150, 151, 178n59
Menéndez y Pelayo, Marcelino, 2

Merchant houses, 17, 18, 23, 120
Mexico, 21, 26, 30, 156; Mexican Revolution, 26
Miller, J. Hillis, 116
Miller, Rory, 40
Mining, 19
Mires, Fernando, 12, 55
Mitchell, Angus, 173n2, 174n3
Mitre, Bartolomé, 39
Modernismo (Spanish-American literary movement), 8, 30, 127–28, 158
Modernization, 17, 18, 19, 39–40, 49–52, 75–77, 82–84, 110, 144–45
Molloy, Sylvia, 133–34, 137
Morel, Edmund, 123
Murena, H. A., 45

Napoleonic Wars, 1
Nation, 147. *See also* Nationalism; Argentina; Colombia; Uruguay; Venezuela; *and other specific countries*
Nationalism, 26, 74, 121–22, 124–26, 147, 153
Nature, 12–15; effects of neo-colonialism on, 54–55, 60; discourse of, 1–9, 12–15; writing about, 54–60, 78–80, 80–81, 110–11, 126–28, 138–39, 143–54. *See also* Ecology; Environment; Rubber (trees)
Neale Silva, Eduardo, 119, 174n10, 174–75n12
Nelson, Admiral Horatio, 2
Neo-colonialism, 10–15, 16–23, 38–40, 44, 53–54, 75–78, 86, 112–16, 122–25, 133, 155–56; defined, 6, 160n2. *See also* Beef trade; Investment in Latin America; Logging industry; Rubber (industry); *and specific industries and trades*
Newspapers, Bogotá, see *El Espectador, El Nuevo Tiempo, El Tiempo*
Novela de la selva (Spanish American novel of the jungle), 44, 133–34. *See also* Carpentier, Alejo; Isaacs, Jorge; León de Mera, Juan; Quiroga, Horacio; Regionalism, Spanish American; Rivera, José Eustasio; Vargas Llosa, Mario

Novela de la tierra (Spanish American telluric novel), 8, 29, 157. *See also* Gallegos, Rómulo; Güiraldes, Ricardo; Lynch, Benito; Regionalism, Spanish American

Ocampo, Victoria, 39
Oil industry, 35–36, 125–26
Oliver, Miguel S, 176n30
Ordóñez, Montserrat, 134, 137, 147
Ordóñez y Batlle, José, 26

Pachón Farias, Hilda Soledad, 125–26
Palma, Ricardo, 156
Panama, 16, 125–26
Pankhurst, Emmeline, 120
Paraguay, 38
Paredes, Rómulo, 174–75n12
Parliament, investigation of Putumayo atrocities, 113, 120
Parra, Teresa de la, 30
Pastoral, 74–75, 78–80, 87, 106, 110–11
Peet, Richard, 12
Peru, 21, 26, 112, 113, 118, 156
Peruvian Amazon Company, 112–25, 174–75n12
Petit de Murat, Ulises, 73, 171n26
Poe, Edgar Allan, 45, 50
Popham, Home Riggs, 4, 18, 39
Prado, Pedro, *La reina de Rapa Nui* (The Queen of Rapa Nui), 23–25, 33, 162n47
Pratt, Mary Louise, 5, 6, 76, 90–91, 147, 173n43
Pulido, Roberto, 174–75n12
Putumayo Blue Book (Parliamentary blue book on Putumayo atrocities), 119
Putumayo caucho y sangre (anonymous book), 119
Putumayo scandal, 112–16, 119–22, 153

Quest romance, 31–34
Quiroga, Horacio, 8, 27, 37, 38–70, 74, 122, 132, 143, 155, 156, 165n26, 169n4; pioneering activities of, 40–42; reading interests of, 44–48; use of ground-level perspective, 43–44, 58–59, 111; "Ante el tribunal" (Before the Tribunal), 46; "Una bofetada" (A Blow), 48–49, 55; "El Hombre muerto" (The Dead Man), 59, 63; "Una cacería humana en Africa" (A Man-Hunt in Africa), 49–52, 53; "A la deriva" (Adrift), 60; "El desierto" (The Wilderness), 60 "La insolación" (Sunstroke), 38, 42–44; *Los desterrados* (The Exiles), 36, 61–70; "Los mensú," 56; "La miel silvestre" (Wild Honey), 45; "El monte negro" (Black Mountain), 59–63; "Los pescadores de vigas" (The Log-Fishers), 56–59, 168n49; "En la noche" (In the Night), 60; "El pique," 59; "La vitalidad de las víboras" (The Vitality of Snakes), 59

"Race," 40–41, 53, 83–85, 101–3, 107–9, 133–43
Railroads, 39, 75, 120
Rama, Angel, 27
Rausch, Jane M., 141
Regionalism, Spanish American, 25–37, 155–58; treatment of gender and sexuality, 104, 163n55. *See also* Gallegos, Rómulo; Güiraldes, Ricardo; Lynch, Benito; Quiroga, Horacio; Rivera, José Eustasio
Retamar, Roberto F., 10–11
Rey, Pierre Philippe, 20, 21–22
Reyes, General Rafael, 125
Rhodes, Cecil, 40
Rivadavia, Bernardino, 76
Rivera, José Eustasio, 46, 112–54, 155, 156; early life, 125; expedition to Casanare, 128; government work, 124, 148; *La vorágine* (The Vortex), 27, 28, 30, 36, 37, 44, 104, 112–54; letter to *El Espectador,* 130; letter to *El Nuevo Tiempo,* 175n25; "liberal" response to informal imperialism, 125–33; "radical" response to informal imperialism, 133–54; "Tierra de Promisión," 122; *Tierra de Promisión* (The Promised Land); 124, 126–28, 147, 175n20; Venezuelan border expedition, 128–30, 148–49

Robin, Libby, 167n38
Robinson, Ronald, 15, 17, 18, 156
Robuchon, Eugenio, 124, 174–75n12
Rodó, José Enrique, 16, 83
Rodríguez Monegal, Emir, 38, 40–41, 42, 47, 57
Rosas, Juan Manuel de, 18, 39, 94
Rubber: industry, 22, 26, 112–25, 128–30, 148–53, 174–75n12; tappers, exploitation of, 112–16, 119–22, 146, 152–53; trees, 143, 148–54

Said, Edward, 17, 23, 29, 54, 65, 70, 134
Salama, Roberto, 73
Saldaño Roca, Benjamín, 174–75n12
Samper, José María, 138
Sand, George, 31
Sarlo, Beatriz, 74–75
Sarmiento, Domingo F., 39, 93–94, 96, 159n6, 172n35, 172–73n38; *Facundo*, 3, 34, 70, 76, 92–93, 156
Schwelm, Adolf J., 49
Scott, Robert Hilton, 38
Shelley, Percy Bysshe, 13
Skurski, Julie, 163n64
Social realism, 78–80, 87
Socialism, 65, 176n30
Sommer, Doris, 30–31, 34, 160n14
Spain, 1, 5. *See also* Spanish colonialism
Spanish-American War (War of 1898), 16, 17, 176n30
Spanish colonialism, 22, 23, 53, 114, 138, 156
"Species boundary," 150–51
Spurr, David, 161n32
Stanley, Henry Morton, 24–25
Steinbeck, John, 15

Taussig, Michael, 147, 173–74n2
Taylor, Julie, 163n57
Tennyson, Lord Alfred, 153
Thoreau, Henry David, 15

Tiempo, El (Bogotá newspaper), 119–24, 176n30
Topography/toponomy, 116–18. *See also* Cartography, Maps
Travel literature, British, 71, 77–78, 90–94, 171–72n27; critiqued by Lynch, 95–101
Trifilo, Samuel, 91
Tropical diseases, 51, 56, 58–59, 146–47, 150–51
Twain, Mark, 170n9

Ugarte, Manuel, 16
Uruguay, 26, 39
U.S. imperialism in Latin America, 16, 35, 122–23, 125–28

Vanguardia (Spanish American avant-garde), 8, 74
Vargas Llosa, Mario, 44
Vasconcelos, José, 16, 83
Venezuela, 26, 34–36, 128–30
Verne, Jules, 46
Victorian ideology, critiqued by Lynch, 97–100
Viñas, David, 170n11
Virgil, 1, 3

Watt, Ian, 135, 137
Watts, Michael, 12
Weber, Max, 31, 99
White, Andrea, 17
White, Lynn, Jr., 144–45
Whitman, Walt, 15, 176n30
Williams, Raymond, 13
Woolf, Virginia, 31, 100
World War I, 26, 120–22, 165n8
Wyeth, Andrew, 97

Yerba mate, 40